ECHOES
OF MASKS
AND SHADOWS

Calliope Blair

MILTON & HUGO L.L.C.
4407 Park Ave., Suite 5
Union City, NJ 07087, USA

Website: *www. miltonandhugo.com*
Hotline: *1- 888-778-0033*
Email: *info@miltonandhugo.com*

Ordering Information:
Quantity sales. Special discounts are granted to corporations, associations, and other organizations. For more information on these discounts, please reach out to the publisher using the contact information provided above.

Library of Congress Control Number:		2025900012	
ISBN-13:	979-8-89285-237-1	[Paperback Edition]
	979-8-89285-238-8	[Hardback Edition]
	979-8-89285-239-5	[Digital Edition]

Rev. date: 02/20/2025

To Maximus and Harriet —
I would be nowhere without you.

For those who have been changed by pain —
I hear you.

CONTENT WARNINGS !

This book contains content that some readers might find troubling. Topics such as, but not limited to, are as follows:

Blood
CNC
Self-harm
Bondage
Death by illness
Death by accident
Familial trauma
Sexual aggression

Please be mindful of these triggers! Your mental health matters to me and it should not suffer because of my insane imagination.

This is a work of fiction, and all characters are above the age of 18.

If you dare...enjoy!

AUTHOR'S NOTE

You flipped the page! Hello! My name is Calliope Blair, and I just wanted to thank you so much for picking up my book!

Unless we are related. In which case, for the love of good God... put this book down. We have to see each other.

Anyways...

It has been an absolute joy writing this. Cold hard truth? I didn't even know I was writing a book until I was fifty pages deep, LOL. I just picked up my iPad and the next thing I knew... I had hundreds of pages telling a story of Harriet and Maximus.

Echoes of Masks and Shadows is just the beginning. I intend on finishing their story, so don't worry! More is coming!

Thank you to everyone who has been involved in this process: my publishing team, my marketing team, and most of all, Harriet and Maximus. Another cold hard truth? I didn't tell a single soul I was doing this... so if you're reading this... this was my secret project! I hope you fall in love with Harriet and Maximus as much as I did. Thank you again and enjoy reading!

Love always, love forever,

CB, Calliope Blair

P.S., If we are related, and you're about to ignore my warning...I'm sorry, I love you, and whatever you do...do not tell Grandma.

I thought I knew what love was.

It was stolen kisses at red lights, playful slaps on the ass while opening doors, and kissing in the rain. It was summer drives down winding roads, blasting music and shouting out the lyrics, no matter how awful. It was curling up for movies, trying to catch popcorn in each other's mouths. It was long walks on the beach, comfortable in the silence. Wanting their kiss even with morning breath or when they were sick. Sharing gum, ignoring the marks left by each other's chew. It was the warmth of waking up next to them and falling asleep in their arms. It was stealing their fries even when you had your own. It was licking ice cream off their nose and gawking at their beauty. It was pure connection, euphoric and soulful.

Love was meant to be inspiring, passionate, and impenetrable.

I was wrong.

Love has no rules, no walls. Love is a puzzle. Love is at times painful. Love is sacrifice, making you question everything you think you know about yourself. It makes you want to rip your hair out. It sneaks up when you least expect it, often with someone you never imagined.

Without love, there is no pain, but without pain, love would not exist. It's a pain no doctor can cure, a love that suffocates you with every breath.

A love so poetically agonizing it transforms you from who you were to who you never thought you'd be.

Love is peeling off your skin because they asked for your bones.

Is it worth it?

The simple answer, no. The complicated answer, yes.

CHAPTER

1

Harriet

In the beginning, it felt like an echo. Never to be listened, but always to be heard. If I could give it a feeling, it was a yellow warm. If I could give it a colour, it was a muted wine. If I could give it a sound, it was a broken heart. If I could give it a purpose, it was bound freedom.

Less than three months after my high school graduation, I was unpacking my dorm at Greenlake University. My parents told us they were getting a divorce that summer. So what best way to avoid that? Running away to a university two hours from my hometown.

My entire family had come to set up my room. It was fun, my fairy lights, my strings of faux leaves across the top of the cemented brick walls. Hanging pictures of the friends I left behind, and my art. I made it as comfortable as I could, less than stripping the bricks from the wall. Other students had put up tapestries and posters to block out the hardness.

My building had an upstairs and downstairs, my room was on the middle floor. *Thank god. Sunlight.* When you walked in, the common area was right at the front, accompanied by vending machines and a pathetic excuse for a half-kitchen with a microwave and kettle. Sprawling off the sides were hallways lined with single and double rooms, each one filled with new students beaming with excitement. Although one girl looked like she was going to throw up. I guess not everyone was excited to move away from home, but I leaped at the opportunity to get away from my helicopter mother and distant father; happily avoiding their constant fighting.

———————◆◆◆———————

After a few long hours of decorating and unpacking, my family finally left. I introduced myself to Olivia, who I later would become frequently annoyed with, and went to the common area to meet everyone else on the floor. Liam, Jane, Mia, Charlotte, Bella. All friendly faces and eager to make new friends. Even the girl who actually threw up in her new garbage can, for the pale green hue hadn't left her face.

The dons talked about their experiences and what expectations we should have now that we're in university. The conversation of safe sex and consent was brought up quick and rather thoroughly. *Fair.* It was awkward at first, listening to the dons explain dental dams and how unreliable the pull-out method was, but after awhile it became normal.

I'd seen the amount of emergency posts laid evenly about the campus, so it was nice to know student safety was a priority. The campus was split into two sides with the Arlow River in the middle. A beautiful bridge, though slippery in winter, bridged both sides of the campus. Arr Bank and Low Bank. There was always a friendly feud between the two sides of the river, though both sides were basically equal. I had no idea what I was picking when I chose Low Bank, other than it having all the bars and clubs. Typical university behavior.

———————◆◆◆———————

Classes started in a week. Until then, frosh week was well underway. Parties, activities, introductions, everything you could think of filled the campus. A lot of people already made their friends or came with them, whereas I was here with no friends, no expectations, and a thick shell. I often wondered how my home friends were doing at their new schools, with people they knew from high school.

Olivia and I weaved through the crowds of students on Low Bank, meeting new people and going to bonfires at night before taking the bus back to our dorm. I quickly learned that the best parties were at the dorms on campus so if I was going to meet new people, that was where I had to be.

Universities operated much different from high school. If you heard of a party, you were allowed to just walk in, I wasn't accustomed to that. It took me three months to go to one because I had finally gotten an invite from Charlotte who met some party animals during frosh week.

The dorm was basic. A small living room, kitchen at the back, rooms banked off to the sides, one washroom. I had no idea where anyone got their alcohol from, I thought most of us were still eighteen. Charlotte handed me an unopened drink, and I chugged it. I needed something to calm my nerves.

"Well, you're definitely seasoned." She laughed, watching as I guzzled the entire thing.

"I'm Irish." I laughed, knowing that had nothing to do with it. I wiped the remaining drips from my chin with an awkward smile. I needed some liquid courage if I was going to talk to anyone other than Charlotte and Mia.

By the fourth drink, the courage was in full flow. I shamelessly danced to the beat of the music filling the room in the middle of those around me. I fell into the blissful buzz until the ride home. No length of time could stop the spinning in my head. I swayed in the middle of the bus, calmly reveling about the peace and quiet I was going home to.

It's already been months, but the quiet never got old.

———— ·❦· ————

The next weekend came around, and yet another party invite. This time it was just Mia, Jane, and me. We took a taxi and linked arms all the way to the front door of the same dorm, but this time the party was an absolute disaster. There were spilled drinks everywhere, people swallowing each other's faces on the couches, and girls sitting in the shower. The only thing that seemed normal was the kitchen table had a round of beer pong going.

One team of two were on either side of the long table. Two boys, two girls. The boys were clearly winning since the goal of the game was to throw the ping-pong balls into the cups across the way, and the girls kept missing.

"That's Ben. He's so hot." Mia shouted at me over the music. She angled her head toward the short, brown-haired guy. Her olive skin was glowing with sweat and her brown eyes were lustful.

"And his teammate?" I took one look at his teammate and immediately knew he was the most frat boy a frat boy could get. They had chlamydia written all over their sex-crazed faces, staring at the pair of hot blondes across the table.

"That's Maximus," Jane shouted. "They're the best pong players yet!"

I nodded, not thinking anything of it as we continued to drink ourselves into oblivion and dance until our lungs gave out. By the time we headed to leave, there were people compiling. We stumbled through the crowd arm in arm as I caught a glimpse between a quick separation of people.

It was Maximus. And some curly brown-haired boy. They were fighting. By the looks of it, Maximus was winning. I couldn't care over what, but in a split second between movements, he caught my eye as someone pulled him off the guy on the ground.

We taxied home with three familiar faces from our dorm house. Mia ended up vomiting out the window. No doubt an extra charge for that. Ten minutes later, we were back in the parking lot of our residence, trying to climb out of the taxi as carefully as possible. Mia fell out. Students across the parking lot rushed over as I hurried out to try to catch her. Liam did most of the lifting when he saw how drunk we were. I tried my hardest not to laugh, I really did.

He carried Mia into her room and left a garbage can beside her bed with some water and Advil for the morning. She'd need it.

I made sure to tell Jane, her roommate, the events of this evening just in case she woke up with a concussion. Or didn't wake up at all.

Once I flopped on my bed, I let the spins take over. My entire room was swirling like a drunken lollipop. I had to convince myself not to throw up, but it was a very close call.

Eventually, I drifted off to sleep, begging my head not to wake me up before noon.

CHAPTER

2

Harriet

First year was the same thing over and over again. Parties on the weekend, smoking weed during the week and going to classes. I skipped more than I cared to admit but I made up for it by studying the lectures posted online afterward.

One of my home friends, Theo, came to visit me which I appreciated. I enjoyed his company, and he allowed me a taste of home. I introduced him to my friends, smoked joints and played games while he caught me up on what was going on back home. To my annoyance, nothing unusual was happening. Not that Winston County had much going for it, but I thought at least one person would reveal a pregnancy or a wedding after graduation. Guess people from Winston County weren't as exciting as I thought they were once I got out.

Everyone thought Theo and I were fucking, but I kept telling them no. We weren't, but they didn't need to know the complicated history between the two of us, and his girlfriend back home.

Other than Theo, no one else had come to visit. I was okay with that. I liked being far away, I could be my own person, live how I want, speak how I want, enjoy what I want. Plus, mentally and physically putting distance between my parents and older sisters was a thrilling idea.

I felt myself changing day by day. Course by course. Following my own interests. Becoming more curious.

Originally, I came to Greenlake because I thought I wanted to be an entrepreneur.

I didn't. What I actually wanted to do, I was judged for. It was only when I realized I was by myself did I finally work up the courage to enroll in my program.

I switched into Mortuary Science that summer, thanking the high heavens for allowing me to be true to myself. After years of watching crime shows and documentaries, I realized it was the coroners and morticians I wanted to learn from.

Pathetic way to choose a career, I knew that. But deep down, I'd always known I was intrigued by death. What it looks like, what it smells like, what it feels like, the reactions that happen—or don't happen—after the body stops functioning. Even what happens after the after. I'd never know until I was dead, but I liked to think maybe we lived continuous lives. Recycling our souls in different forms. I'd want to come back as a butterfly. Or a black panther.

I was annoyed when we had to move back home after exams, but I couldn't help but be thankful for my own space again. Although first year was fun and I made friends, it drained me. University was a lot different than high school, and it took some adjusting, so sitting at home for a while was rejuvenating. Until I got antsy. Mia Zidan and Jane Romano lived close to my hometown, so I would often spend weekends with them. Eventually, we got close enough to sign a lease together in the coming school year.

The three of us, and my best friend Kimberly who was coming to Greenlake after taking a leap year, found a house close to the university. Finally. No more dorm stench and no more listening to Olivia fuck Liam.

My own room. My own space.

CHAPTER

3

Second year

Harriet

Thirteen Shore Court. The address to our brand new house in Greenlake. The house was huge. Ten-foot ceilings, white walls, cream carpet in our rooms, and light brown hardwood throughout. The main floor was open concept aside from the slim wall in the middle that held our microwave. Our stairs banking immediately to the left and the balcony off the back door. The basement had been marked off so our landlord could have more tenants downstairs.

Upstairs, Kim and I grabbed the bedrooms adjacent to the Jack-and-Jill bathroom because we wanted to be close together. Jane in the master down the hall past the bathroom, and Mia in the room at the top of the stairs.

The entire month of September was immaculate. The four of us hotboxed every room in the house, lighting candles and opening windows after. We studied, we laughed, we partied, we had family dinners, our friends came to visit. Everything was good. No more listening to people having sex, and no more paying off legal-age town folks. We were all nineteen by our second year. Thank fuck for that.

—◈◈◈—

October was just as pleasant. We had a Halloween party, Mason, Theo's best friend and the third in our trio, came up to visit this time and we drank and danced and played games. It was a classic house party. Although I didn't recognize many of the people, it was still fun. There were people making out, taking body shots on the balcony, and daring each other to eat inhumane substances. *Gross.* Jane and Mia did most of the inviting since I was still slowly coming out of my shell. One crack at a time.

Just a week after Halloween, I had gone through my usual "Hot or Not" on Tinder, feeling lonely since Theo had practically vanished, making up every excuse not to come see me. I swiped while I was on the toilet, between study breaks, basically whenever I could.

I was lonely, and I was bored out of my mind. One particular afternoon of my incessant swiping, someone popped up.

Maximus White. Close proximity, I suppose. I hadn't seen him since the last party I went to with Mia and Jane two weeks before our final exams in April. I hadn't thought of him the whole summer, but the moment I saw his face on my screen, it was like he never left my mind.

I swiped right.

So did he.

Nothing came from it. I was just playing my game so it didn't bother me.

It wasn't until me, Liam, Charlotte, and a friend of Liam's went to dinner at the college bar downtown that it bothered me. Liam ran with the same crowd as Maximus in first year, so when he saw Liam, he came over to the table. My whole body tensed, and I cringed at myself.

"Hey Liam. Hey Charlotte..." He lingered, eyeing the fresh-faced girl next to me.

"I'm Vic." The girl spoke. She was Liam's lab partner last year, and they had become good friends. Sometimes I wondered how good. I guess that thing with Olivia was over.

He wandered over her face for a while. "Nice to meet you."

It was the first time I had paid any attention to the sound of his voice. It was deep, mischievous. Almost wicked.

I sat up straight. Wondering if he was going to remember me. He took one long look, eyed me up and down, smirked, and walked away.

Guess not. *Prick.*

It bugged me. For a short while. I got over it after about thirty minutes of catching each other's stares from across the bar. The usual leaning-against- the-bar-because-I-think-I'm-cool position. *You're being stupid, Harriet,* I told myself. *Boys don't matter.* I didn't need to think about this right now. I'm with my friends having a nice dinner.

"His name is Maximus," Liam shouted across the music. "He's single, too." A smirk. He must've caught me glaring at him.

"I know." I sneered. His name, not that he was single. I could figure as much, he eyed Vic like she was candy.

CHAPTER

4

Harriet

They say we accept the love we think we deserve but I think Maximus was the love I needed but didn't see coming. I needed him in more ways than one, and I can confidently say that went both ways.

When I met him, he was your classic playboy. Standing six-foot-four, blue eyes with brown hair, lanky but lean, a man who loved his women and all that they came with. One after another to fill the cheating void his last girlfriend left him with. Until he found comfort and solace in me, and I him.

We had no idea the years ahead of us after we spent our first night together.

———⬦❖⬦———

The party boomed so loud I thought our neighbors were going to smack us clean across the face. People lured in, one after another. People I didn't think cared enough to show up. I was wrong. Beer pong and flip cup were fully underway, and body shots were being taken on the balcony again.

Laughter and music filled the house, enveloping my brain in a sweet bliss. If only my sixteen-year-old self could see this. She'd never believe me. Cringing at the sight of my now roommates, Mia, Jane and Kim were funneling beer into their mouths with a long tube. They looked so carefree; laughing, dancing, flirting with cute boys. I, however, was a growing bundle of nerves.

As people were piling in, a group of guys stepped through the front door. A short brunette with a bottle of rum under his arm, a fluffy blonde with striking blue eyes, and among them, a very tall, lean guy with blue eyes and a bright smile. Right off the bat, I knew who they were. Everyone did. They were the popular kids here. Ben Allister, the classic frat boy. Alec Haybank, mainly known as Banks, the wild animal. And Maximus White, the bulldog who loved to fight and drink his problems away.

They wandered about, talking to the friends they met here. I didn't know their names, but they stopped at two guys. One with dark brunette hair and a beer in his hand, and a strawberry blonde with what looked like a piña colada, but it couldn't have been.

I guess we were throwing a good party since they bothered to show up. They mingled for a few minutes until finally, the three of them came across me. One of the three remaining hosts. Kim tapped out. Mostly likely passed out on her bed drooling. Ben and Banks didn't really care and continued on to talk their way through my house. Maximus on the other hand, came to a full stop.

"You must be Maximus. I'm Harriet." I spoke first with a smile, looking up at the most stunning man I had ever seen. I suppose I had to break my shell one way or another.

"That would be me. Max." He bowed, flexing his jaw and staring into my eyes. "Nice to meet you, Harriet. Quite the turnout." He smiled back, his blue eyes sparkling.

"Thank you. Have fun, Maximus!" I grinned, turning to walk away and silently cringe at myself. Completely setting aside the Tinder or the bar mishaps. *Have fun? What is this, a ball pit?*

Jane, Mia, and I lingered around the party, here and there talking to people and sharing glances. But more people kept piling in the house, scaring me about the fine for after-hours noise, and the police in general. It felt like the door was revolving. My roommates were just realizing the same thing when the police showed up around midnight. *Fuck.*

I didn't know until people were already running. They were yelling *police* while I was outside on my balcony talking to our downstairs tenants who we met last week. Tori, Lori, and Cade. Maximus was standing on the other side of the balcony talking to some brunette. I didn't mean to keep one eye on him.

When a guy came rushing through the balcony door to scream *police*, Maximus took one look at me and threw himself over the ledge. Bee lining it for the forest that backed our university house, leaving the brunette scoffing and completely unsatisfied.

I laughed so hard I thought I was going to pass out. How he landed that jump, I had no idea. But I remember wondering if we'd ever cross paths again. Under different circumstances.

I don't have an authority issue, but police officers send me over the rail due to an unpleasant night in my childhood. I crouched around the corner with my hands over my face while Jane handled them. We didn't get a fine, just a warning that everyone should be heading home. She thanked the officer and started shouting for everyone to leave. I don't know when, but I had started crying in my corner of the house.

I didn't look up until I felt big, warm hands on mine. "They're gone." He whispered. I looked up, and it was him.

He came back.

"Thank god. I'm sorry, I haven't had the best experiences with the police." I awkwardly laughed through my tears. *At least I'm not sobbing.*

"Me too. You're okay." He smiled softly. I thought he was just trying to comfort me, to which I indulged.

"Do you want to stay?" I asked out of nowhere, wiping my tears and smudging my make-up in the process. Shocking myself at my own words. *What was I gonna do with him? Feed him?*

"I'd love to." His smile instantly calmed something in me. He must've noticed my shock because his eyebrows pinched, but he didn't say anything.

Everyone had gone home, and my roommates retreated to their rooms. Still shaken from the fact the police showed up at our doorstep. Relief was distant, but it was there. No ticket.

He followed me up the stairs and sat on my bed while I took off the rest of my make-up in our bathroom. He poked his head in, taking in that one of my roommates' bedrooms was through the door on the other side. "Has she ever walked in on you shitting?" He laughed. "Plenty." I laughed back, wiping the last of my eyeliner and remembering the few times Kim walked in on me. He laughed again, sitting back on my bed to wait for me.

I started getting nervous. I'd never had a one-night stand before, but I hadn't had sex in an embarrassing amount of time. I didn't know what to expect so I lingered in the bathroom as long as I could before going back to my room. Brushed my teeth, my hair, wiped the sink. Anything I could think of that wasn't suspicious while staring at myself in the mirror in an attempt to calm myself down. My blonde hair wasn't as curled as it was before the party, and my plain gray-blue eyes were wide with angst.

He was perched on my bed, knees spread as I stood a few feet in front of him, leaning against my mirror on the wall. Trying to cover the "You're Good Enough" written in black sharpie in the top corner. We stared at each other for longer than I expected, as if wondering what was going to happen or who was going to make the first move. His eyes narrowed and he gave me a smirk that rolled my stomach. I caved.

"Fuck it." I whispered.

And straddled myself in his lap.

CHAPTER

5

Harriet

It was hot, and it was rough. My knees were bent at his sides and his hands were in my pockets grabbing whatever he could, to no avail. I could feel him hardening under his pants, pressing against me. Leaning us back on the bed, he ran his hands through my hair, biting my bottom lip and twirling his tongue over mine. He tugged my hair back so he could reach my neck and planted tiny hard bites along the hollow of my throat. His brown hair was soft on my fingers and his grin was devil incarnate on my skin.

Far cry from ignoring me at the bar. I grinned on his lips.

I pulled back. Happily staring at the face that was keeping me from my drunken sleep. "Shall we?" He purred in my neck.

I mumbled, out of breath. "We shall." The devilish tone came from nowhere.

That's when I noticed it the first time. As soon as he got my consent, everything changed, everything sped up. His eyes went dark and his grin went wicked.

He stood up, looping me around his waist as he rammed us into the wall of my bathroom. I heard the beams of my house shake under his strength. One hand under me, one hand on the wall to stabilize himself.

He kissed me hard, and fast. His tongue was so deep in my throat, I prepared myself to choke on it. I giggled against his mouth as he turned to put me on my back. *Sorry, Kim.*

My shirt was basically a bandana that just fit over my breasts. I untied it from the back and tossed it off the side of my bed while he was unbuttoning my skinny jeans. Terrible pants to wear. *If only I knew.* He noticed my chest bounce as he tugged on my jeans, and gave himself a grin, knowing he was about to palm them until they turned blue and purple. His eyes beamed for my shirt on the floor as he chucked my pants behind his head.

I questioned it but didn't say anything. He picked up my shirt and straddled himself atop of me. Pulling my hands above my head, he tied them together with the fabric.

"Much better." He mumbled against the skin just below my navel. His breath was warm and daring, he glanced up at me and my insides stirred. *Oh. My. God.*

He pulled himself back to my face and continued to kiss me, never wavering in depth, never faltering as we moved in unison. He tasted like whiskey and toothpaste, an addictive combination of flavors. He pulled my bottom lip between his teeth while holding down my arms, slowly trickling his other down my stomach and in between my thighs. I winced at the ticklish spot in the space of my groin. I let out a gasp, and he smiled on my mouth, slowly inserting a finger inside me. He kissed me one last time before lowering to my neck. Palming one breast, biting and licking the other. Then my stomach, then inside of my left thigh. The right.

He gave me a sly smile and slid his fingers out. Licking them, one by one, tasting me, before planting his mouth on the sweet spot between my thighs. "Oh, fuck...me..."

He let out a low chuckle. "As you wish."

I tried to cover my face but my hands were still tied together atop my head. I looked down, his eyes met mine and continued blissfully doing what seemed like his party trick. He pulled up to my face and smiled, "No peeking." As he bent my arms so he could pull the fabric over my eyes.

As soon as my sight had vanished, everything heightened. Something he surely knew would happen. The sweet spot between my thighs started to grind against him, a slight beg for more. He lifted my hips, throwing my legs over his shoulder and quickened his pace. Second after second, until my first quivering release.

"Good girl." He purred wickedly when he felt my muscles squeeze against his tongue. Pulling the fabric from my eyes, hands still bound.

He leaned over the side of the bed into the pocket of his pants to pull out his wallet. A wallet condom. *Classic.*

He ripped open the package with his teeth. *Dear god.* The entire length of him so hard, I thought it might burst. *He's done this many times*, I silently thought. He rolled the condom on himself while I just laid there, vibrating in a puddle of my own doing. I made eye contact between his legs and smiled. *That would do the trick.*

One hand beside me, one on himself to hold him in place. He slowly entered the space between my thighs and I let out such a gasp he smacked a hand over my mouth with a smile across his face. He looked me in the eye and gave me a nod. I nodded back.

"One." He pushed, kissing a different inch of my body between his words. "Two."

"Three." His breath was hot and heavy, I could feel the smile on my skin.

"Four." He breathed.

"Five." I was starting to thrash against my shirt, the anticipation killing me. I wanted him to hurry up, but deep down there was something there. Something I couldn't explain.

"Six." He was getting thicker now. Inch by inch.

"Seven." I could feel him stretching me, it was glorious, I had never felt anything like it. He could see the tiny pinch of pain on my face as he smiled over me.

In one punch, he pounded his last inches into me, hitting my hilt so hard I moaned out in erotic pain. The hand over my mouth sunk its fingers into my cheeks.

"Eight." He growled.

Maximus pulled in and out, soft. As if to tease me before going so hard my bed shook my room. I groaned into his hand, arching my back to swallow every last inch of him. Every last inch of the nine.

He pulled out, no less than to stop himself from his own climax, not wanting it to end as quickly as his body demanded. I thrashed against the fabric bounding my hands in the quick pause.

To our surprise, I got free of them and pushed him. I straddled his legs and lowered myself onto him. I rose, up and down. Slow and fast. Pulling his hair back and licking the hollow of his throat before biting hard enough to leave a mark. He let out a grunted breath and slammed his lips onto mine in frustration. I felt a dark laugh roll through the folds in my brain.

He tilted his head, no doubt curiosity. "Did not see that coming." He purred against my mouth. I guess I wasn't what he was expecting. I wasn't even sure if I was what I expected anymore.

I could tell he was a dominant, and didn't like his power being taken away, but what did I care?

His frustration loomed in a cloud over his head until he had enough of his power being taken away. He grabbed my hips and in less than a second, I was flipped over on my hands and knees like I weighed nothing more than a dime. Taking it one step further.

The Maximus from the party had vanished, this was someone else entirely.

He made a tsking sound with his mouth, spanking me hard enough to leave a mark. As if to teach me a lesson.

A lesson I had no interest in learning.

His voice dripped with venom as I opened my mouth to speak but he forced his fingers down my throat, causing me to gag. "Shut up and take it."

He spread my legs with his knee and planted himself in me once more, pulling my hair so hard my neck cracked. I felt my ass fit perfectly in his hand as he leaned forward, ready to palm me. Letting go of my hair, he crushed my breast and squeezed the back of my neck, while dragging his tongue up and down my spine.

"Good girl...fuck, you feel so good." He purred behind me and I couldn't help but smile. I arched my back, taking in everything he had to offer.

He sped up, I felt him flex, and then pour himself into me. Even in the heat of the moment, I could feel his warmth. Panting, he slid out with one last gasp. His lips touched the low of my back just before he flopped down beside me.

With a smile that could end world war three.

In that simple kiss, the Maximus everyone knew came back. There's more to him than what meets the eye.

CHAPTER

6

Harriet

We knew nothing about one another other than the pure lust we felt from our simple appearances. I was a petite blonde with large, pierced breasts, blue eyes and bright smile going through her parents' divorce and he was a typical find-peace-in-the-chaos guy who had a knack for flirtatious looks and loud kinks.

That first night changed something in us. It boomed with orgasms and unforgettable sex traits but that's what pulled us in so much and so fast. As he suggested various tricks and kinks, he realized I wasn't as plain as I looked. In blatant terms, I was down for anything as long as I got a sip.

I got every last drop. So did he.

And we relished in our chaos.

I knew he had done this before from the way he tore the condom packaging with his teeth and swiftly pulled it over on himself. It didn't bother me, I gleamed with the opportunity to be devoured by such a man. After all, this was just one night. It had to be on my list of experiences at least once, right?

Thrown this way and that, our bodies collided in a kink of passion, without a care in the world. However, the time spent afterward was what caught me off guard.

As someone who went into this with shallow thoughts about a quick fix, him releasing his entire life story to me was not what I expected.

His dad, Andrew. His mom, Laura. His sister, Lily. Even that time he got arrested. By sunrise, I had known everything from his favorite color to his aspirations in life. It was weird and amazing all in one. After he spilled all he could, he asked me to do the same. It was odd, a hook up asking me to tell him about myself.

Nevertheless, I took him up on it, and even though he fell asleep halfway through, I relieved my life story as well.

I left out certain details, he'd have to prove himself before I revealed those parts. I kept it superficial. Assuming he did too.

We slept through most of the morning. Around eleven a.m., I woke up to his arm flung around me. No one can control what they do in their sleep, so I let it slide. I texted my roommates that he stayed the night and that it was riveting. Also apologizing if they heard anything.

"Good morning," he groaned. His morning voice was even better. A scratchy rasp. *Delicious.* "What time is it?"

"Good morning," I whispered back. "It's around eleven. I can drive you home."

We got dressed, scavenging for our clothes that got dramatically thrown during last night's festivities. I chuckled.

"What?" He laughed, buttoning up his pants.

"Nothing. I just—nothing." I lowered my voice.

"Tell me."

Fuck it. "You're, um, my first one-night stand." I actually laughed out loud.

"I'm honored." He smirked. The wicked grin made its comeback. "Although, if you wish for my services again, you'll have to make an appointment. I'm booked this weekend, but afterward I'm widely available."

"Appointment?! Jesus." I laughed in utter shock. "Let me brush my teeth and I'll drive you home." Disregarding he basically offered himself up like a roasted turkey. I shrugged.

Pig. At least he didn't ask me if "I liked it," or "if it was good for me,".

We headed downstairs, my roommates gawking at us as I was looking for my keys. The house was littered with cans, bottles, clothes, decorations. Cups were half drank and spilled over the floor and tables. We had a lot of cleaning up to do today.

Remembering I put them in my shoes in the upstairs hallway, I went up. But my shoes were empty.

"Jane, do you know where my keys went? I need to drive him home!"

"Last I saw they were in your shoes!" She yelled from downstairs.

"Hmmm... they aren't here. Odd," I muttered to myself.

My heart sank.

I rushed down the stairs, fearing the worst, and when I opened the door, the worst appeared. Or disappeared.

"Someone stole my car!" I yelled from outside. Jane and Maximus rushed out and saw the same fate I did.

"Oh... my... god..." Maximus gasped.

"You." I turned to Maximus, angry at this point. "Do you have friends who would do this?" Because apparently I associated people who like to get into fights with people who like to steal cars. I was right.

"Well..." he hesitated. "...yes, but they wouldn't take yours. Not while they saw I was interested in you. Too hot." *Too hot? What kind of fucking language?*

"Call them. Call everyone. Right fucking now." I growled.

We called everyone, to no avail. No one would fess up anyway. My car, Veronica the Volkswagen Beetle, was gone. My fingers were twinging with adrenaline. My father. *Oh my god, he's going to kill me.*

I had to call him. At least we had a couple hours to clean up before he would be here to meet the police.

Jane ended up driving Maximus home, and we exchanged numbers so he could update me if he heard anything. I called him throughout the day, feeling bad that his most recent one-night stand would not leave him alone. However, he showed no annoyance and was rather kind over the phone.

"This is really fucked up. I'm so sorry. No one should ever do that."

I bet you have. Prick.

He continued, "I'm just playing games and catching up on my lectures, so call me whenever you need to. I'm so sorry, again." He hung up.

I was itching for answers but I knew I would never get any. I slouched on the couch, my face buried in my hands. I wanted to crawl under a rock and die from the embarrassment I brought this house, and my family back home.

Even as they reassured me everything was going to be fine, we all slept with one eye open for that week. Because *that* would do anything to help forget the obscenity of this situation.

I reminded myself I had an assignment due by Monday so I headed upstairs to settle down at my desk and to start—and finish—my assignment. I threw on my dad's old Led Zeppelin t-shirt and a pair of granny panties when I went to check out my lack-of-an-ass in the mirror. *God, I need to work on that.*

Written in the same black sharpie, "More than Enough."

——◈◈◈◈——

A week later, Veronica was found not even fifteen minutes away from my house. After the reckoning my father unleashed on my roommates and I, he was thrilled. Nothing had been taken, including my favorite purse I got for my eighteenth birthday and my wallet. They just wanted a joy ride and to scare us, my father had said. Sounding like maybe he participated in one of these *joy rides* back in his day.

With Veronica back in my custody, my father's rage subdued, and an itch for a pick-me-up, I sent a risky text:

HQ: Hello. Is this Maximus Services? I'm inquiring about an appointment for Saturday around 9pm.

CHAPTER

7

Harriet

You could tell this was an all-boy house. The most run-down furniture, beer cans everywhere, dishes stacked so high things were starting to grow on them. I nearly vomited.

"This..." I stumbled over their shoes, "...is disgusting." I said, unapologetically.

"I know. Guys aren't exactly the most cleanly. My apologies Miss..." he trailed.

"Quinn. I'm here for my appointment." I smirked.

"Right this way, milady." He twisted so I could walk through the long grimy hallway that led to the living room, off to the side was his bedroom. I could have sworn I stepped over day-old boxers and a half-eaten bagel. *What the fuck has my life come to?*

His wood-paneled room was neater than I expected, aside from the clothes piled on the floor. Perhaps cleaned for my company. It was decently sized. His L-shaped desk at the door with his two monitors and his bed beside it with the classic university mini fridge in between. It was in reach no matter where he sat. TV across the bed, next to his double door closet. *Game of Thrones* posters on the wall and a periodic table of alcohol recipes. I chuckled at the sight of it. *That's genius.*

"Is it just you on the main floor?"

"Yeah. Everyone else is upstairs. It's nice. I get the bathroom down here, and it's quieter during the day. It sucks at night though when I have…" he stretched.

"Got it." I cringed. *His appointments. Why on earth am I doing this?*

I sat on his bed, noting how soft it was, and he sat in his desk chair.

"What do you play?"

Please don't say League of Legends.

"*League of Legends* and *Minecraft* mostly."

Jesus fucking Christ, Harriet. I laughed anyway.

"So you're a gamer nerd. Of course." I looked down at my hands in my lap, contemplating all my life choices. Especially the one sitting in that chair.

"Yeah…it…keeps my head straight. Escape through the rough patches." He looked down, his voice quieted.

There was something that trailed off in his voice that told me something like gaming had saved his life one time or another. There was more to his story. I felt bad for calling him a nerd and laughing. I, too, had my escape. I painted, smoked too much weed, read fantasy books, and watched crime shows to keep the reality of my life at bay. To allow a few moments of distracted silence.

Watching him throw fists in first year at that party flashed through my mind. Maybe he was broken. Like me. Maybe he had demons so bad, he ached for physical pain to drown out the emotional ones. I sympathized, related even. For a brief moment, I allowed my heart to thaw as I ran my fingers over my forearms.

"Sorry." I choked out.

"Everyone's got their thing, right?" He shrugged, with a warm smile as if to ease my guilt. "I go to school, game, drink and hang out with my friends, and…" he trailed off again.

"Sex." I laughed. *Sex-crazed chlamydia faces.*

"…yeah." He flushed, *on that note.*

I stood up, walking over to him to offer some sort of support. I hate hugs, but he seemed like he needed one. He was still perched in his chair so he got a face full of breasts. Purposefully accidental.

"I know we don't know each other well... but I'm—" I quieted. He slowly rose from his chair, already hardening at the seam of his pants as the whole front of his body brushed mine.

"—good at listening..." I was still as death as he towered over me. I don't think I blinked. His chest muscles were twitching, intimidating me as my heart started to hammer.

When I looked up, he was already staring at me. "Deal." The wicked smile returned. The heat in my stomach was beginning to spread to the tips of my fingers. *God, he's even hot when I'm sober,* I thought.

With no hesitation and no strain, he picked me up and straddled me around his waist.

"I can't have any unfulfilled, or unsatisfied customers." He grinned.

I had enough of this *appointment* bullshit. "Would you just shut up and—" I laughed as he grabbed my face to kiss me. He was devilishly warm and unbearably welcoming. Our tongues swirled, immediately gnawing at each other in desperation.

He took one step and threw me flat on the bed, I could tell it had been broken by the creaking sound. *From someone else,* I shoved out the thought. *Ew...*

I knew Maximus was of a different breed when it came to sex, but when he pulled the Velcro straps from the four corners, it excited me more than I cared to admit. That unexplained feeling came back. Something new. He looked at me, asking for permission. I gave a curious nod. *I have nothing to lose.*

He strapped me in. An arm. A leg.

I had no idea what I was expecting but being fucked like that wasn't even top five. I was harnessed in a star position, unable to move an inch. It was positively terrifying. He had total control over my body. It scared me, but I was intrigued by the fear. Walking the edge, blurring the lines. It wasn't until the blindfold where the terror started to kick in, the increase in my heartbeat, the sweat dotting my forehead. It was exhilarating, wondering where he would go next. How deep his experience went.

"We—you need a safe word. At any point if it gets too much, I will stop immediately. I promise on my mother's life, I will never hurt you." He said it so firmly it sent chills down my spine.

So filthy, yet so kind. I could tell he knew I hadn't done anything like this before. Being handcuffed was one thing, but giving up all control of your body to the will of someone else in such an intimate way was far beyond my experience.

I giggled at the word I came up with. The exact opposite of our newly developing friendship. Something we could have as an inside joke, to hold in our own little fuck bubble.

"Vanilla." I chuckled. He roared a laugh, toppling over me. He breathed hard, clutching his chest.

"Deal." He breathed out, forcing himself back into his mask. Kissing my lips softly before spreading my knees to fit inside me.

Except he didn't.

He lowered his face in between my thighs. I could feel his breath on me. My heart started beating faster and faster, if not for the blindfold I would've been convinced I could see it protruding through my chest.

But all he did was kiss me. My inner thighs, the top of my knees, my calves, and then the bottom of my bare feet. *Interesting.*

Then he licked. From the bottom of my feet, over my knee and inner thigh. Repeating on my other leg. It was sensational. My breath quickened at my heightened senses as I stirred against the restraints.

They say when one sense is extinguished, the rest heighten themselves to make up for the fact one was lost. I could feel everything. The tastebuds on his tongue, the gentle touch of his fingertips, the sound of his hands running up my thighs, the pressure of his grip. My body did not let me down, and I silently thanked the human brain for its wisdom.

At last, he pressed his tongue against me. His hands gripped my hips, pulling me closer to his mouth. I got lost in the feeling of his tongue and drifted into my own little pocket of time. Not caring what anyone would think about my position right now. Only that he was here to please me. And by pleasing me, he pleased himself.

He was soft at first, gentle and painfully slow before I grunted and arched my back into him, now thrashing at the restraints. He knew he was teasing me for what was yet to come, but I was slowly starting to lose what little control I had left.

He smiled against my pussy and huffed a deep chuckle, he was taunting me. And he loved it. Loved every second of my body begging for him. Begging to hurry, begging to let me fill his mouth. When desperate tears started to brim my eyes, he finally quickened his pace, enough for a euphoric orgasm to blossom out of me.

It may have been less of a gentle blossom and more of a volcanic eruption. My squirt filled his mouth, so much so that part of me was dripping out of his mouth. My cheeks heated as my panic set in, trying to push away my embarrassment. I knew some girls could, I also knew other girls couldn't. But men liking it was hit or miss.

I could feel my cheeks flaming under the blindfold. Not knowing his reaction tormented me. Did he like that? *Did I just ruin this?* I couldn't help but worry about how he was feeling. If he was about to show me the door and let it hit my ass on the way out.

He raised himself to my face, squeezed my jaw so tight it had no choice but to open, and poured part of me back in my mouth. He swallowed the rest.

"Taste yourself." He whispered on my lips.

I did as I was told, swallowing myself, feeling it soothe my own throat with its sweetened flavour. He lifted the blindfold to find me staring at him with wide eyes, heaving deep breaths.

His mask dropped. "Harriet?"

"I'm sorry—" I muttered. Not thinking about him spitting myself in my mouth, but if he was comfortable. If he was pleased.

His face lightened again. "I love how you taste." As he undid the straps around my ankles. I sighed in relief.

"I do too." My smile was sinister as I ran my tongue over my teeth, the remnants still lingering between the buds of my tongue.

I was relieved at his comfort. A genuine belief. Someone this fucking kinky has got to be okay with a little juice, right? There's no way he can expect his conquests to be treated like this and not pour themselves into his mouth. It was impossible.

My heart calmed at the convincing thought, and he kissed me.

He jumped off the bed to grab a condom, I could see his cock bouncing as he moved and it only made me throb more. I couldn't help but make eye contact with it again, he was long and well groomed. He rolled it on himself before kneeling back on the bed.

"Raise your hips." He demanded as he placed a hand in the middle of my stomach and another underneath me on the small of my back.

I obeyed. As soon as my hips lifted off the bed, he flipped me over. Forcing me into an arched position due to the tightness around my wrists.

I was up on my knees and my face was buried in his pillow, my crossed arms still tied to the corners of his bed. Everything was bared to him. He strapped my ankles back in, leaving them loose enough to keep me on my knees. He kissed up from my lower back to the spike in my shoulder blades, until lowering his face to mine to plant another smiling kiss. Grasping my chest as he did so.

He retreated to his knees, using one to spread my legs farther apart, opening myself up to him from behind. He bent over to kiss my ass and slid a finger into me. I could hear him suck on the finger as he guided himself into me. The throbbing between my legs was becoming unbearable.

He pumped himself in me tirelessly, starting slow but quickening faster than before. He was desperate for release after being hard for so long. He must've been aching by now.

His hands gripped my hips and he thrust so hard I yelped into the pillow. He slowed, waiting for a response from me, but he didn't get one. He continued. I could feel his head ramming into my cervix at each pummel. It was painful, but I couldn't say that. I wasn't at my breaking point. I wasn't in need of Vanilla. I wasn't sure if I would ever be.

There was a dark part of me liking the pain. It felt good. Distracted silence. It was inching me toward another release.

The knot in my stomach released, my toes curled as I squirted around him, leaving a pool around my knees.

"Holy fuck," He moaned in surprise, his come filling me once again. He kissed my back and squeezed my breast before tearing my limbs from his trap. "You did it again!" He panted, stepping off the bed to cheer with his arms up as if he was proud of himself.

————⋅◈⋅————

He stopped cheering. I immediately turned around.

"Are you okay?" I said, getting up on my knees to meet his flushed face. I knew this was extracurricular but panting that hard didn't seem warranted.

"Absolutely glorious, darling." He panted in a British accent.

I huffed a laugh and sat back down, crossing my legs and placing my hands in between them. I was still soaked. I could feel myself dripping on his bed.

"The question is, are you okay?!" He said, taking a seat between me and the wall of his room, legs stretched out.

"Absolutely glorious, darling!" I laughed in a foolish tone.

"Phew. Don't ever stop yourself from squirting for me. It's fucking incredible. You're incredible. Promise?" He sighed with a corny smile, plummeting his head into my neck and wrapping his arms around me.

He couldn't see, but my eyes widened in surprise. I guess he was into it. "Fine. I promise," I smiled above his head, glancing at ceiling.

"You're quite ravishing yourself. I see why you need appointments." I whispered in his hair, then kissing the top of his head. It wasn't a secret that he had girls lined up around the block. He leaned up, taking my face in his hands. "I don't do this shit with other girls."

I pinched my eyebrows together and he cocked his head at me, like he was studying my face. *Why me?*

I wasn't sure I was ready or wanted the answer to that so I kept my mouth shut, changing the topic with a convincing smile.

"What now?" I said sarcastically, shrugging at the same time. *What more could I possibly give you right now?* I thought, leaning my forehead against his. His sweat beads transferring to mine, but I didn't care. After all, he did do all the work. *Pillow Princess*, I muttered to myself in my head.

"Again." His grin was wicked as it was deadly. As sweet as he may be, his mask was serious.

Round two was just as euphoric. As was round five.

CHAPTER

8

Harriet

Leaving his house the next morning was painful. My legs were on fire and my anatomy was throbbing beyond belief. I had to give myself a few minutes before bracing myself to stand up and walk out without looking like an idiot. I needed to compose myself like I was used to this frequency.

I failed.

I stood up from his bed and groaned. "Oh... fuck me." I muttered under my breath.

"I believe I did. Plenty." His morning voice was back and my stomach curled. What is it about hot men's morning voices that's so compelling? I rolled my eyes away from him and attempted to stand. My legs were nothing short of pure Jell-O, but I was determined to convince him otherwise.

I failed again.

"Sore?" His pride was overflowing so much I thought it was going to pour out of his eyes and ears.

"No." A lie.

"Liar. You're walking like you have a pickle up that gorgeous ass." He snarked, leaning forward to slap my cheek before laughing to himself.

"Mind your fucking business!" I couldn't help but laugh and shake my head. My legs were obviously in pain and it wouldn't do my muscles any good to ignore them.

He rolled up behind me, folding his arms around my waist. He whispered into my naked side, "I might be able to apply some relief." Kissing my side, my back, and finally biting my bare ass against his chest. He slid his hand around my lower abdomen and palmed me. Saying no to this man had proven difficult, but I had to at least try to fight for my dignity. Before I could no longer drive myself home.

His room smelled like hot sex and I wanted—needed—to shower. His room wasn't the only thing that smelled like devouring lust. I pictured my shower back at my house and it gave me the motivation to get dressed. *Don't get attached. Leave,* I thought.

God, I need to brush my teeth.

"As tempting as that may be... this girl"—I angled my hands toward my body— "needs a shower. Stat." I laughed, struggling to pull up my pants.

"Don't forget to rate your appointment five stars, milady." He smiled, standing up and getting dressed himself.

"Meh. Maybe like a three point five." I shrugged. Hauling my t-shirt over my head, and shoving my bra into my purse. I was trying so hard to ignore the shaking in my legs. Or the feeling like a bowling ball got shoved up my fucking vagina. I turned around to see him staring at me with a blank face.

"Is that a challenge?" He raised a dark eyebrow at me.

"Perhaps." Perhaps you need to be fucking humbled, sir. Not really, but to hell with fawning over a man I just met.

He took a step toward me, and then another. Until my back was pressed against his door and his chest was mere inches from mine. His hands were against the wall at my sides and he leaned down to my face.

He ran a finger over my bottom lip and lifted my chin to force me to look at him. It took everything in me not to let my knees buckle.

"I accept that challenge." He said daringly deep, grabbing my throat in a single palm of his hand and brushing his lips over mine.

I giggled against his mouth and ran my hands through his hair.

"You'll have to book an appointment with Harriet Services."

CHAPTER

9

Harriet

In the weeks coming, we spent every day together. Our appointments never wavered, only escalated. Six to eleven times a day. We never tired.

I had only met this man a mere two months ago, but somehow he was creeping in on me. My curiosity about him took over, and I succumbed to his dues and practically every appointment I got. I wasn't sure if I cared it came off desperate or if it looked like I was addicted to him. Either way, he was craving my taste simultaneously, although he would never admit it.

Being in university, I was around his roommates all day long and they were some of the coolest people I had ever met. Banks, Maximus's best friend, was amazing. So full of life and had impeccable taste in music. Dylan Jones, the dark brunette who single handily kept beer and cigarettes in business, formed a friendship with me in the kindest of ways. Chase Bennett, the strawberry blonde who constantly smoked weed and cracked dad jokes, also seemed to like me.

All I had was a few friends back home and my roommates. What was one hook up, left me with three new friends and experiences I could never repay. It got to the point that I would wake up at his house and go into the living room to hang out with his mates, who wouldn't even bat an eye. It began to feel like a home.

We started trading off houses, he became acquainted with my roommates as much as I did his. Bringing mine coffee and donuts after class and watching movies with us. And I would bring marijuana and a pack of beer to his.

He became one of the girls as much as I became one of the guys.

I had never met anyone like him, much less a man like him.

He made me laugh, he made me throb, he made me nervous. It was incredible. The excitement I would get driving to his house would fill my ears with the sound of my heartbeat.

Here I was, this young university student with a dream to work in a morgue, but all I could think about was one beating heart.

He was a hardcore gamer, so I would walk into his house with a drink from Starbucks and sit with him while he played.

"Hello, Miss Harriet." He said to me over the microphone in his headset as I walked into his room. I handed him his drink and kissed the top of his head before sitting down to study for exams.

December had come in full force. Snow was brushed over everything and I was at my happiest. Winter had always been one of those things that comforted me. Even nature had to have its dark and cold moments before opening up flowers and fields.

Mother Nature was capable of vulnerability, and harsh brutalities.

I've always been a nighttime person, there was an allure about the stars. Being so far away from big cities, our university town was blanketed by them. I loved stargazing, even though I never admitted it to anyone.

A few hours after the sun set, I set my books down and took off my glasses. My eyes were stinging from staring at a screen for the last four hours. I needed a break. I had finished my drink. Now it was my stomach growling. I glanced over at Maximus playing his game, shouting at his friends through the other side of his headset.

Realizing what I was hungry for.

In two strides, I was behind his chair. I lowered my face to the side of his headset with the microphone. Knowing it was on, I slid the right side off his ear.

"Play with me." I purred in his ear, biting his earlobe.

His cheeks curled into a smile and he turned to me, lowering the chord that held his microphone to his mouth.

"I would absolutely love to, but can you wait until I finish this game first? We're winning." He geeked out. He continued to explain to me about Druids and fighting masters, showing me how they were winning. Truth, I didn't care. There were so many flashing colors and vast movements of characters I couldn't follow. But sure as hell pretended I was understanding every word he was saying. His smile was too precious to crack so I allowed him to finish geeking all over me.

I let out a low chuckle and ran my fingers through his hair as he turned back toward his monitors. "Absolutely I can," I replied. *But I'm not going to.* I smirked to myself.

I got down on my knees and crawled under his desk to sit in front of him. He followed my movements, moving his microphone once again.

"What are you doing?" He asked. His eyes were beaming like the stars blanketing the sky.

I tried my best to hold back a smirk, but ultimately I failed. I was too excited. I leaned up to put his microphone back in front of his mouth and started bustling at his belt.

He traced my fingers with his eyes. "Hmmm…" His throat hummed, raising an eyebrow at me.

"Play your game." I demanded, never breaking eye contact. "And leave your microphone on."

He lifted his hips as his fingers were slamming against the keyboard above me. He was talking and laughing with his friends by the time I got his boxers down to his ankles.

I had only been told by one person that I was good at giving head. So this was going to be nerve racking and tricky, especially because he has a fucking horse cock, but I was itching and would do anything for a scratch. I propped myself up on my knees and took his length in my hand.

Looking up at him, I kissed his tip and swirled my tongue over it. I'd never felt anything so soft. He looked down at me and smiled. "You're acting dangerously, Miss Harriet."

"What was that, White?" I could hear coming from his headphones.

"The girl I told you about is under my desk." He said under his breath with that wicked grin.

"Told you about" echoed in my head. He told his friends about me? All we do is fuck, what was there to say? My bra size? How tight I was? How wet I would get just by catching his glance from across the room? *Tell yourself he told them you were kind, smart, and funny. That'll help.*

I shoved out my thoughts and added my other hand to him with a grin. I spat on his cock and thrusted it in my mouth, still eyeing his face.

I rose and ebbed over him. He looked down at me, face serious as ever as he began to adjust his hips and flex in my mouth. His eyes went black as he tilted his head, gripping the armrests of his chair until his fingers left imprints.

"White!" Came barrelling through his headphones.

His head jolted. "Shit, sorry guys." He apologized, repositioning his character in the game.

"Maybe I am. Maybe I'm not," He said into the headphones. "What can I say? Might have to keep this one if she keeps acting this way."

I paused my duty and glanced back up at him. His pearly whites were shining at me, almost as much as his eyes were. He was loving this.

"What?" I mouthed, not wanting them to hear me. "They know what you're doing." His grin widened.

I rolled my eyes. There was nothing I could do about it now. Even though I purposefully wanted the adrenaline, knowing they were aware I was sucking his dick under his desk felt differently. I'm coming off as a slut.

Or am I? A kinky slut, I smiled around his cock in my mouth. *His kinky slut.*

I bobbed, I spat, I choked. I thrusted his length as far down my throat as I possibly could when he started yelling from above me.

"YEAH!" He yelled. "Let's fucking go, boys!" He concluded. "Good job, guys. Play later? I have a lesson to teach."

He laughed into his headset, "Yes, Cole."

Uh oh. Perhaps I teetered on dangerous grounds. I knew by now not to mix his gaming with my actions but I wasn't waiting and now he knew I wouldn't. He took his headset off and looked down at my mouth still around him. He pulled my hair back with one hand and squeezed my throat with the other. Forcing me to rise from beneath the desk and stand, my body was bent over his chair as he locked my head in front of his face.

"What the hell are you doing to me?" He whispered, tilting his head at me. Questioning himself more than expecting a response. My mouth was jarred from his pinching fist and spit seeped from my mouth onto his bare stomach. I just stared at him, there was nothing else I could do. I was locked in. My eyes darkened with a smirk, and he released my throat, clamping my jaw instead. He tilted my head up and repeated himself fiercely. Demanding an answer from me now.

"What are you doing to me?" A firm tone. I could see the mask flickering as his fingers tightened under my jawline. Should I be turned on? Cuz this just got dangerously provocative.

He brushed his lips against mine, as I went for the kiss he backed away and his wicked grin beamed at me. He pushed my hair over my shoulder, exposing my neck to allow him a bite. I gasped.

"Did I do something wrong, sir?" I taunted. He clenched his jaw and swiveled his head on his shoulders, cracking every bone in his neck. No response. Just his death stare and a huff of breath. His eyes were still beaming so I knew he was enjoying this. I was borderline terrified I was going to get choked to death, but dying mid-fuck didn't sound like the worst way to go.

I was at his submission. "Do your worst, Maximus." I whispered at him, biting the air between us.

CHAPTER

10

Harriet

We were cuddling by the time midnight rolled around. His curtains were drawn but I could still see the night sky from my position. I was sitting at an angle and he was between my thighs, head comfortably on my stomach. His hair and hands were softly slipping through my fingers as we watched his bedtime tv show.

My cheeks were on fire from the spanking I received earlier for teasing and pulling his focus from the game. They won anyway, but I had fun making him fight his urges.

"Remember the safe word." He reminded me just before forcefully bending me over his bed and sliding his fingers inside me.

I nodded. The anticipation was killing me. I had never done this before. I didn't even get spanked as a child, other than a spoon that one time. I was excited.

In and out his fingers went, complimenting the lashes from his dominant hand. My eyes watered. It was a different feeling, like running something sharp over a hangnail. There was pain, but it was a pain you kept putting yourself through because the rush was worth it.

"Behave." He growled when my body instinctively pulled away. He spun me around like a gust of wind, to be greeted by watery eyes and a wide grin. He gave himself a laugh while he brushed my jaw with the tips of his fingers. He pinched his eyebrows together when I didn't flinch, like he was expecting me to become afraid.

His phone buzzed, and he raised his head. Completely turning himself around to hug my middle and look at his phone.

"They want me to play another game," He said in a questioning tone.

"Go. I'll be right here." I smiled.

"Keep that ass planted in this bed. I want to win. Deal?" He said, kissing my bare tummy and burying his face in it.

"I promise. You liked it, though," I grinned.

"More than you'll ever know. I've never really gotten head." He admitted, shrugging like he didn't care.

I raised a brow at my disbelief, "What? Why?"

"I think they're scared of it." He motioned below his belt line with a crooked smile on his face. I let out a total laugh, his head jolted from my stomach.

"Sorry, sorry, it's just that—" I hesitated. "You got some serious inches, and that is scary. I was terrified, but I just wanted your attention." I admitted lightly. Enough to make him realize they have a right to be timid, but not enough to deny him.

"And maybe to pay you back for all that you do to me." I admitted again, avoiding eye contact.

His tone went flat as he palmed my face. I flinched this time, he caught me off guard. "Never assume I expect anything in return. You are the best thing I have ever tasted." He was genuine. He kissed both my cheeks and my forehead before getting up.

He played his game, and I sat on his bed, blushing beyond belief while changing the tv show immediately after he sat down in his chair. This show was awful, but it was his house, his room. I was a guest, so he could put on whatever he wanted. Until he got up. Then I switched it without a second thought.

———⋅◈⋅———

"One more, and then I'm coming to bed. I promise." It's been forty-five minutes since he started the first. I could feel the itch building again.

Whatever, his house, his time. I let out a laugh and offered a proposition. "Okay, but only if you tell me a secret after." I responded, not taking my eyes off the screen.

He smiled with relief. "Okay!" He gleamed.

No less than ten minutes later, I decided his promise wasn't good enough. I scanned myself, comparing my size to his chair. I was convinced I was small enough to cradle his lap and put my legs through his arm rests. So, I stood up, grabbed a shirt, and pulled his chair back from his desk, catching his questioning glance.

"Just wait. You'll see." As I climbed onto him and slid my legs through the openings in his chair.

As soon as he understood, he unwrapped his headset chord so it wouldn't choke me and placed them back on his head. "Hi."

"Hi." I kissed his shoulder. He pushed back my hair and kissed my neck. His hands were electrifying on my skin, sending a shiver up my spine and into the base of my neck as he traced my entire back.

I returned the gesture, simultaneously watching the tv from his desk. I knew he understood when he rested his head against me and started playing with my hair.

I ended up falling asleep with his arms around me at his keyboard, every now and then running a hand through my hair, or kissing my shoulder under his chin. My body was beginning to trust him. It started relaxing at his touch, getting excited when he walks in a room, even shake with pleasure when I watch him tear his clothes off.

Why was it so easy with him? I often thought to myself it was because we had no obligations to each other, no labels, no expectations, just pure fun. Freedom. But maybe it was because whatever problems we had disappeared the moment we were together.

No more divorced parents.

No more... okay well I don't really know what his problems are but that's besides the point.

Either way, he was rocking my world physically while I rocked his emotionally.

"LET'S GO!" He yelled in my ear. I jolted awake and sat up gasping immediately.

"I'm so sorry. Were you asleep? I didn't know." He held my face and his eyes softened. He genuinely looked hurt he woke me, I felt bad for him.

I gave him a sleepy smile. "I underestimated how comfy that would be." Wiping the drool from my mouth. "Sorry." I looked down and curled my head into his shoulders once more.

His chest rumbled. "Yeah, she was sleeping there. I feel bad I woke her up." He said into his headphones.

"Tell your friends I say hi, and to get a life." It was two thirty in the morning and they were still high-energy playing games. Don't they have school or work or some shit? Knowing deep down it had nothing to do with them.

I heard a laugh through the headset telling me to turn around. So I did. Maximus's camera was on and I was staring at myself through his computer monitor. Jesus, I'm glad I'm wearing a shirt. *Did they watch him rub my back and kiss me? Did they know more about how he felt about me than I did?*

I was beginning to think the answer to those questions were yes.

"I'm done. Let's go to bed." He was careful not to hurt my legs as he picked both of us up and laid me out flat. He took off his boxers and my shirt and got in next to me.

"Not before you tell me a secret." I gave him a soft smile, poking his chest. The sleep slowing creeping back in, I could feel my eyelids weighing.

"Your wish is my command. I'll even tell you two."

But then he hesitated. He could've told me a lie, or even something mindless.

"I never sleep with my hook ups," He admitted, playing with my hair.

"What? Wait... what?" I was baffled. Why? I was awake again. I waited for his response.

"I never sleep—slept—with them." He repeated. Smiling at my disbelief.

I was shocked. "Like, you just fucked them, and then sent them packing?" I tilted my head and my voice raised in question. *That's rude.*

"Yep. Never."

"Why?"

"Didn't want attachments or to be attached." He looked down.

"What changed for you?" I softened my voice. There was a reason, but I wasn't sure I was going to get the truth. "You kissed me the first night we met."

He looked me dead in the eye. "You never chased me. Those parties in first year, on Tinder, and then again at the bar. Then that night, something told me to stop running to that forest and turn around. That's when I found you crouched in the corner, upset about the police," he said and laughed, rubbing the back of his neck. "But overall, you made me come to you. I usually let everyone come to me, it was easier that way." He sighed a breath and looked down again.

He continued, "Except you. I don't know what it was, I just felt this pull." His eyebrows pinched together like he still didn't understand.

I was speechless. I didn't know what to say, so I just laid a hand on his face and looked at him. I felt him soften under my touch and it clicked.

It felt like he started to morph. I wasn't sure if he was going to admit that or not, so I decided against bringing that up. I had come to learn that boys and men alike have a hard time voicing their feelings. Although it foolish, I knew society expected a different role from them. They needed to come off strong and independent—impenetrable.

As many a woman would agree, when a man opens up to you, it offers a concrete sense of security. It volunteers his comfortability with our presence to bare himself. It means he trusts you with his words, and your confidentiality. Maximus could trust I wouldn't judge, make fun, or exploit.

That's all I wanted from him, from any man really. Just pure honesty. It's the main component a woman needs in order for success in a relationship, even a non-labelled, lighthearted one such as ours.

Neither of us were striving for an actual romantic relationship, only a strict fuck-buddy system that guaranteed both of our safety and satisfaction.

Physically: avoiding sexually transmitted diseases.

Emotionally: a friend.

Him saying all that was already a step in the right direction, although it didn't say much about how he felt about me currently. I didn't want to pry, I assumed he would tell me eventually.

So I made a lighthearted joke. "So, you wanted to conquer me just to say that you could and then…"

We laughed and spoke at the same time. "…and then you realized you actually liked me."

We both caved in laughter. Probably waking the whole house but I didn't care. His smile came back from whatever place in his mind it was hiding.

"And the second?"

He rolled his eyes and pressed his lips into a thin line. "My favourite flowers are poppies, but don't tell anyone that."

I smiled softly, raising a brow. "You like flowers?"

"Nope." He popped the p sharply, like that was going to convince me.

"Right."

He softly hummed as he pulled me into his chest and kissed the top of my head before wrapping his body around me.

He joked, "Don't think too hard about it. I just like fucking you."

Right.

CHAPTER

11

Harriet

Exams were finished and Christmas was just around the corner. Winston County was blanketed in just as much snow as Greenlake, despite the driving distance. The last few winters were nothing but muggy winds and brown slush. Having a green Christmas just wasn't the same as having a white one. So when I got home and saw our backyard was covered to the point you no longer could see the pool, it warmed my chest.

As soon as I walked in the door, the smell of my favorite chocolate chip cookies filled my nose. My mother was standing in the kitchen pulling out a fresh batch. If there was anything to know about Leanne, she was always in the kitchen.

She gasped when she saw me. "You're home!" She squealed. Her hair was in her famous claw clip. Her roots were graying, soon to be covered up by her famous blonde highlights, and her smile lines were beaming behind her thin black glasses. She was beautiful. And since now being separated from my father, happy.

Fighting was one thing, every couple fights, but I never noticed she shut down. I never noticed how miserable she was until we got the news that day. She had completely changed, and I hadn't yet decided whether I was okay with that or not.

She immediately came to hug me, putting her head on my shoulder as she wrapped herself around me and kissed my cheek. "I missed you. How was exams?" she asked.

Yes, exams. The entire drive here I was thinking about how I was going to tell my mother about Maximus, or if I was even going to. She was just beginning her sixties and was about as "up to date" with my generation's lingo as my dog was. Bless her little beagle heart.

How was I supposed to explain him to my mother? *How did you guys meet? We slept together at a party. What's he like? A light switch. What do you guys do together? Fuck.* I could imagine the whole conversation and her sinking facial expressions when she learned her daughter wasn't even dating the man she offered her body to like a human sacrifice.

Hell, how could I look my own mother in her eye and tell her he has no label, he isn't anyone specific, just someone I was starting to feel alone without? We weren't even in a "talking" phase, so I couldn't explain that to her. Definitely weren't dating. God no. And we sure as hell weren't *just* friends. He was my in between and all of the above.

"Exams were good. I'll find out if I've passed them all sometime before Christmas break is over. I've missed you and your cooking." I smiled, taking a hot cookie off the rack on the counter.

My house wasn't the biggest, but it was home. When I walked in my front door, the stairs were immediately in front of me, holding up the wall next to the living room that no one ever goes in. That room has horrible memories, so I make my best efforts never to go back in there.

To the right of the stairs was my dad's study, now filled with my mom's crafting supplies since he moved out—the month after I moved into my dormitory at school. It was sad looking. His computers and mug collection used to sit across his desk. He sat there every Saturday and Sunday before watching whatever sports were on that weekend. Now it was just scraps of colored paper, gems, and photo albums.

I shoved the memory out of my mind, grabbing another cookie from the rack. Beside the study was a blue painted bathroom. I have lots of memories in there, yet I will not tell the loving woman in the kitchen.

My kitchen was the biggest and best part of my house. The speckled marble island covered the entire room before leading down one step to the family room with our famous couches and television. The stone floors were scraped from the chairs being pulled out by family and friends. My height markings on the wall, a constant reminder of the life I've lived. The cupboards surrounding the top half of the entire room were mahogany brown which complimented the light beige walls and white crown molding on the ceiling.

I stood in the doorway to the kitchen, staring at the double doors that led to our backyard then glanced over to my right to see my mom pulling out yet another rack of baking. This time, banana bread.

"Oh, give me some of that!" I chirped as soon as I saw the pan.

She smacked my hand away, "It's too hot, and it's for Christmas," she said sharply.

"Fine, I'll wait." A lie. I *will* be eating that after she goes to bed.

I sat down on the bench closest to the doorway and watched her pile cookies and banana bread into take-out containers. She raised an eyebrow.

"What's new?" she questioned.

"Nothing really," I lied. She could tell from the sound of my voice that something was new.

"I like to think I know my daughter—" she began. I cut her off before she could finish that sentence. She was famous for thinking she knew me. I didn't even know me. Like I devastatingly did not know her.

The divorce was surprising and hurtful but seeing her acting this way now was even more jarring. I didn't know whether to take it with a grain of salt or to be grateful she no longer yells at me for no reason.

The memories of her yelling at me for laughing at my phone or telling me I couldn't go hang out with my friends because I did yesterday were burning in my brain, raising my blood temperature.

"I made a new friend." Shaking my head and smiling at my hands in my lap.

"A friend you say?" she said sarcastically. "Does this friend have a name?"

God, he does, and it sounds so hot rolling off my lips.

"Maximus." I said quickly, reeling back the wetness starting to form between my legs.

"Tell me about him. How did you guys meet?" she said lightly. Not knowing I was never going to give her the full story.

"At a party, no less." I rolled my eyes. That sounded so cliché, but we were becoming everything but cliché these days.

I continued, "He's tall—"

"Of course he is. That I already knew. Tell me something I couldn't guess." Signaling at my type of men in the past.

I ignored that comment. "He's really smart, he likes to play games"—an understatement— "he—" *likes to fuck you until your brain melts to mush?*

I coughed, "He's kind. He's different. Annoyingly captivating, actually." I awkwardly laughed.

She waved her fingers in my face and my focus went back to her. I hadn't realized I zoned out thinking about him.

She placed her hands on the counter and looked at me with that motherly eye-twitching grin. "You are passing school right? What you're over there to do?"

She knew. She could see it written all over my face.

"Yes, Mom. I'm passing all my classes and I felt really good about these exams. Now can we eat? I'm starving."

She rolled her eyes and got me a plate.

⸙

I snuggled into my bed that night, alone. It'd been so long since I had been back in this bed. I missed Thanksgiving because of midterms so it was nice being able to sink into familiar sheets and old stuffed animals. Booga was curled next to me. A big stuffed dog-bear thing my older sister's ex-boyfriend had gotten me when I was sick. I've kept him for years against her will. She still asks me if she can burn it every time she makes her way home. The answer is always the same: No.

I drifted to sleep that night with ease, and surprisingly not thinking of Maximus. My house was flooding me with memories that I had wished to forget, especially that stark white room below me. I did my best to ignore the feelings they stirred.

Every corner I turned, every chair I sat, they all had a memory. I never realized growing up would make me reflect on my younger years so vividly. This must be one part of growing up that's dreadful.

Maximus was the last thing I dreamed of that night. I wish it was filled with his touch, but instead I was jarred awake in the middle of the night, gasping for air.

The white room filled my nightmare. They had sat all of us down in that room to tell us they were divorcing. My sister, Anna, who just turned thirty-three looked like she already knew, and my oldest sister of thirty-five started crying. I sat on the floor next to Roxanne and tried to speak, but my dreamworld wouldn't let me cry out or plead for my parents to try again. I thrashed at my throat to let it speak, but nothing came out.

That's when they all turned to me, blank stares, unblinking and laughing at me.

I jolted awake. Clutching my throat at its mercy to let me breathe again. Tears rolled down my face as I reached for my phone. *No, Harriet. You're fine. You're fine. You're fine.*

After a few short minutes, I was fine. I swear. Only thinking about how everything in my nightmare was an unfortunate reality.

It took me about an hour, but eventually I faded into the dreamworld of Maximus's bed, eagerly waiting for the Christmas festivities in the next two weeks.

CHAPTER

12

Maximus

In the beginning, it felt like a shadow. Never to be seen, but always to be felt. If I could give it a shape, it was a waning crescent. If I could give it a smell, it was a budding rose. If I could give it a colour, it was a lonely black.

It wasn't until November I realized if I could give it a face, it was hers.

"I'm home!" I yelled to no one in particular. My mother sitting on the couch reading like always and my dad preparing dinner, like always.

"Hey, son! Welcome back." He smiled with a kitchen towel over his shoulder.

"Hi, Max." My mother didn't bother looking up from her book. Nothing out of the ordinary, wherever my mother is, so is a book.

I walked in our back door so I could easily run up the stairs to the left. "Hey, wait!" I heard her call after me.

My sister was only two years younger than me but she was almost my height. I'm not sure where the height came from, considering my mother was five-foot-five and my father was five-foot-nine. Lily and I grew past them by the time we were sixteen.

"I haven't seen you in a while." She smiled, walking toward me with her arms stretched out.

I dropped my bags, wrapping my arms around her and squeezing tightly. "Missed you too, Li." Rummaging through her brown hair before going upstairs to unpack my things.

I collapsed on my bed as soon as I entered my room, hand on my chest. My angled wall above covered in more *Game of Thrones* posters. How I have missed this bed. I had so many good nights in this bed, also sleepless ones.

I haven't been back here since the beginning of the semester since I missed Thanksgiving due to my exams. Being pre-medical wasn't exactly the easiest on a student, but it would be worth it in the end. Understanding why we are the way we are. Why I am the way I am.

I opened my duffle bag and started unpacking my clothes. Filling my closet with shirts, pants, socks, underwear. Until I found that one sweater Harriet had left at my house. I brought it home with me. I wasn't going to admit that to her, but she never asked about it so I assumed she wasn't missing the sweater.

It was plain black with specks of dried paint, and it smelled like her. I pulled it to my face, inhaling the sweet scent of vanilla and lavender.

The decision to text her was lingering in the tips of my fingers, but we have been spending a lot of time together recently. Individually speaking, we should take this time with our families and friends. *Or I could use the sweater as an excuse.*

I opened my desk drawer to put away my laptop, freezing in my spot as soon as it opened. The moment I saw them, I felt every bone, muscle, and atom in my body begin to weigh me down.

Ignoring the rattling pill bottles, I slammed the drawer, leaving my laptop on the bed.

———◈———

"So! Tell me about school. How are your grades?" My dad, Andrew, asked, guiding mashed potatoes in his mouth.

"They're good, all above seventy-five so far." I responded, eating my own mashed potatoes and avoiding eye contact.

"That's great to hear, son." Andrew nodded in approval. Everyone knew I was smarter than what I applied but after my last year in high school, no one questioned me anymore.

"Have you been—" My dad started before my mom interrupted.

"Andrew, not now. We're eating dinner." Laura said.

Three simple words. That's all it took to send a course of tension through the once-decent air. I knew what he was about to ask and I was thankful for my mother's interruption.

I did not want to lie to him.

The first year after I was diagnosed, my family walked on eggshells around me. Thinking I would crack every time I got angry or anxious. They even refused to let me go for walks or to the gym in case I would collapse from the strain. It enraged me; them thinking I was this fragile boy when I had proven myself over and over again I was not.

I can do everything a regular person can. I can run, I can dance, I can swim, I can jump, I can fight. I can definitely fuck. Sometimes the latter at the same time.

But for whatever absurd reason, my family thinks I'm made of glass. Like after two minutes of laughing, I'd corrode myself into nothing.

So I hide. In plain fucking sight.

Unfortunately, that ruined our night. We made small, awkward talk for the rest of dinner before Lily and I excused ourselves.

———⬥⬦⬥———

"Who's sweater is that?" Lily asked from behind me. She was standing in my doorway with her favorite monkey pajamas on. Her long brown hair in a messy bun with a toothbrush in her mouth. She was legally an adult but if anyone saw what she wore to bed, there would be a debate.

"What?" I asked, I hadn't heard her the first time. I moved my headphones off my ears.

Over her toothbrush she asked, "I said whose sweater is that?"

I didn't want to tell her. If I told her, there would be a million questions, none of which I had the knowledge to answer. Truth be told, I had no idea whose sweater that was.

Harriet wasn't in any category. It'd been a couple months of constantly seeing each other, and I still had no idea what she was. We definitely weren't dating, nor would we. She wasn't exactly my friend. You usually don't know what the inside of your friends feel like, or how they taste. So I just lied, as usual.

"No one. Get out," I muttered, putting my headphones back over my ear to continue playing my game. I thought she left for good, but she came back.

She came from behind me and shoved off my headphones, grabbing my chair and spinning it toward her. Her toothbrush was gone and her hair was down her shoulders.

"Whose sweater is that?" She lifted an eyebrow, giving me an I-know-you're-lying expression with her green eyes.

"No one," I emphasized. "Do you mind?" Spinning my chair back toward my monitor and putting my headphones on.

"Testy, testy, testy." Clicking her teeth. I heard my door close behind her and I turned in my chair to stare at the folded piece of Harriet sitting on my bed.

"What the fuck am I going to do with you?" I said to the sweater.

Offensively, I got no response.

CHAPTER

13

Maximus

"Breakfast!" I heard my dad yell from the kitchen.

"Ugh..." I pulled my blankets over my head. It was Christmas Eve. I should get up, be a good son, but I had no energy. Sitting up in my bed, I caught a glimpse of my hair in the mirror on the back of my closet door. *Yikes*, I thought to myself.

"Max, breakfast. Let's go." My dad said on the other side of the door. "I'm coming..." I groaned back.

It felt like I slept like a baby but I knew that was a lie. As soon as I stood up, my head went light and my chest went heavy. I could feel every inch of my body trying to ground me.

I buckled to my knees with a crack on the hardwood floor. "Ah, fuck." I exhaled, clutching my chest.

Immediately my parents were busting through my door. They heard my knees on the floor and came rushing to check on me.

"Max!" My mom gasped, sliding to the floor.

"Where are your meds?" My dad asked, scanning my room for the pill bottles I had hidden away. Lily rushed into my room from hers.

"What's going on?!" She sounded worried, watching me rise to my feet.

"Nothing, nothing. I'm fine. Let's go eat." I exhaled, trying to catch my breath. My father had found my meds in my drawer.

"You're not taking them?!" He yelled at me. "Max, you heard the doctor, you—"

"I said I'm fine!" I yelled back the best I could. I didn't want to hear this right now. It was Christmas Eve. *I am fine*, I repeated in my head.

Andrew opened one of the bottles and shoved the pills in my hand, handing me the bottle of water from my nightstand. In that firm voice everyone hated, he glared at me and said, "Now."

If you were to do anything, it shouldn't be crossing my father. He had a rough upbringing and often fended for himself while his mother was passed out drunk on their couch. He never met his father, so he was determined to work his ass off to provide for us in the way he never got. It was admirable. But right in that exact moment, I hated his intentions.

"No, I'm okay. Really. I just got up too quick." I said, trying to walk past him to put a shirt on. But that didn't help. He grabbed my hand the pills were in and starting pulling it to my mouth.

"Take them, son. I will not lose another one of you." His voice hardened even more as I tried to pull away. No one ever mentions our older brother, Sam. He died when I was twelve and Lily was ten. It was years ago for us, but it was yesterday for my parents.

I stared at him in defeat. I raised my hand to my mouth and dry swallowed the pills. Bringing up Sam was no easy thing, but it often became my father's choice of weapon during emotional seasons. This was going to be one hell of a day for me.

Merry fucking Christmas.

———⋅◈⋅———

To my annoyance, my chest did feel better. I had no pain. Anywhere. Everything had gone numb and I was just floating in space on our couch. I was supposed to take my medication every day, but I'd gotten lost in the numbness before and it worked against me.

Getting in fights, drinking around the clock, fucking anything that breathed. Anything to make me feel. These meds just made me a zombie. I felt hollow with them in my system, like I was surviving, not living. I didn't want that anymore, regardless of putting myself at risk.

After Eve, I didn't mind the numb combination my meds and lifestyle gave me, but when first year ended and I had felt good for a few months straight, I stopped taking them. Now I was addicted to how it felt to be off them. I had actual joy. I made great friends, and I had more energy for my studies and fun extracurriculars.

Not that my parents would ever understand that. Lily never said much about it, something I appreciated her for. She never questioned me. Sure, she gave me lectures about not taking them, but never forcefully shoved them down my throat like my father. "They're scared to lose another child." She would tell me. I understood that, but I thought I had my own choices when it came to my body, my illness. Being twenty and living away from home had its perks.

"Dinner's ready." My dad announced, setting out pancakes, hash browns, eggs and bacon on the table. Our family tradition was to eat breakfast at every meal on Christmas Eve. Sam loved it so it was solidified when he died.

I hadn't realized what time it was. *These fucking pills.* I groaned as I stood from the couch, feeling like I had to haul a thousand tonnes with every step.

As soon as I sat down, my phone buzzed on the table. I immediately grabbed for it to look at the message.

"Is that the owner of the sweater?" My sister smiled and made kissing faces at me.

"Shut up," I snapped. It wasn't Harriet, I hadn't heard from her in days. Not that it bothered me. She was probably with her family too.

"Who? What sweater?" Laura looked at me, pouring syrup all over her stack of pancakes. I chucked my phone behind my head and it landed on the couch.

"Max has a mysterious sweater in his room and he won't tell anyone whose it is." She raised an eyebrow at me as I scolded her for opening her fat mouth.

"Can we just eat and pretend like we're one big happy family, please?"

"I want to know too!" My mom smiled with a pancake in her mouth. Until my dad chimed in.

"Does this mysterious sweater know?" His eyes lowered, sucking the fun right out of the room.

"No one does." I snapped. All of their eyes staring at me. My dad went to say something but my mom stopped him with a hand on his arm, letting me finish.

"Everyone treats me different when they find out, like I'm fragile or, for whatever dumb reason, I can't have fun. Please leave it alone." My blood was starting to boil with these questions.

"You haven't told any of your friends at school." It wasn't a question. My mom's voice saddened, speaking to the half eaten pancakes on her plate. This was the first time she realized I dealt with my health alone. Out of sight. I hated everything about it. I hated the awkward sympathies, the special treatment, the vulnerability. Especially the look in their eye when they see me as weak.

I shot up. My voice went shaky and I coughed for breath. My head was going light again and by the time I looked up, Laura was already looking for the spare oxygen tank we got from my last hospital visit. She put it to my face and I breathed deeply. Andrew shoved more pills in my hand and I didn't hesitate. As much as I hated them, they did soothe this part.

I pushed away the oxygen mask. "I'm fine, I'm fine." I breathed. Feeling as normal as I possibly could. Their constant hovering made me feel weaker than I was. Lily sighed in relief, resting a hand on her chest as if to check she was still breathing herself.

"Breathe," she demanded, putting the mask back on my face.

"I said I'm fine. Again." I tilted my head and smiled. I knew they didn't see the irony in this, but sometimes all I could do was just laugh at what my life had become.

I also knew it was my job to make this easier for them. My parents had already lost a child, my sister a sibling. So letting them see how I actually felt in this moment was not an option. I couldn't do that to them.

No matter how many times I wanted to scream in pain, cry in panic, or punch them in their hovering throats, I wouldn't show them. I'd stay that way for as long as I could. *Mind over matter, Max,* I told myself. Over and over again.

I effortlessly gave a practiced smile and watched my family's faces light up with relief.

They saw what they wanted to see. They wanted me to be okay, so I was.

They spent the rest of Christmas Eve dancing on eggshells around me, and I pretended not to notice for their sake.

CHAPTER

14

Maximus

"Merry Christmas!" My mother sang as she barged into my room, again.

"Merry Christmas, Mom." I grumbled under my blankets, still sleeping.

Christmas had always been a tough day of the year for my family. The four of us felt guilty for enjoying time together when one of us was missing. Sam had eighteen Christmases, but his absence was grave. We didn't know how to be happy again without feeling sorry for it. Other than Lily. Although she understands our pain, you can tell she wishes for different traditions.

Laura always hangs his stocking on our mantle, making sure to fill it like it would make a difference. My father tried to convince her to not put it up since my diagnosis, a constant threat to what one day will be two filled stockings, buried in ash.

But she refused every year.

Ear buds, toothbrush, hair combs, gum, candy. All the necessities were in the stockings, and all the fun stuff was under the tree. "To Samson, Love Mom and Dad XO" was marked on one of the presents.

The same present.

The Christmas before he died, my mother had accidentally misplaced one. It was tucked in so far behind the tree it was forgotten about until the following weeks when the tree was taken down. My mother and Sam laughed about it, how there were so many that we lost one.

"Leave it for next Christmas. It could be fun to open it then." He laughed his happiest laugh, my mom agreed.

He never made it to the next Christmas.

The present remains unopened, untouched. Forever frozen in time. My mother couldn't let go of it, so every year she fills his stocking and brings out his present. She won't tell anyone what it is, not even my father. She kept that secret to herself, and I think that's what she needed.

A secret passage between her and her first dead son.

———◈◈———

"Would you guys mind if I invited someone to dinner?" I blurted out in the middle of lunch. It was unexpected, given the faces of each of my family members. My dad nearly choked on his sandwich, my mom stopped dead in her tracks, and Lily just gave me a grin, she knew who I was about to say.

"Anyone in particular? Or just..." My dad trailed off, dancing lightly around the topic of Harriet.

"The owner of that sweater." Lily interrupted before I could get a word out.

I shot her a look before clearing my throat. "Yes."

"I would love to meet the owner of this mysterious sweater, who is clearly important enough to get an invite to Christmas." My mom smirked.

"Is she your girlfriend or—"

"She's just a person." I stiffened. I wasn't sure if they would like her, with all my health issues and her being utterly blind to the fact I'm sick. I was nervous they would judge her for not noticing my fluctuating weight or my sunken eye sockets. Though, they had gotten a lot worse since Christmas break started, I prayed she wouldn't notice, let alone ask about it.

"I'd like it more if she knew." My dad said firmly.

I just stared at all of them, waiting for them to shut up about it and tell me yes or no so I can pace back and forth for an hour about how to word this message to her. We hadn't talked all week and now she was about to get an invite to my family Christmas dinner.

Before I could talk myself out of it, my mom responded.

"Absolutely she can come. The more the merrier," she said with a smile.

The moment I realized what I had done, I regretted my very being. I didn't want her to meet my family, to see the sorrows in their faces, the pain in their eyes. I didn't want her to see the toll the death of my brother took. I didn't want her to find out about my health.

Most importantly, I didn't want her opinion of me to change. But I was craving that feeling she gave me.

She was pure ecstasy, an addictive chaos I couldn't quit because I've never gotten enough.

She didn't pity me or see me as weak or incapable. She saw me as a human being. Someone who could plan a future because they had one. Feel anything but fear because they had hope.

Her ignorance was my bliss.

CHAPTER

15

Maximus

The knock at the door shook my whole body. My fingers and toes set ablaze as I threw on my basic black button up and black jeans. I didn't want to look over dressed, just the right amount for Christmas. As compared to the red and green pajamas my family all wore this morning while we opened our gifts and emptied our stockings, leaving Sam's alone.

"I think your flavor of the month is here." Lily teased in the doorway of my room.

"If I ever hear you say that again, I will beat the shit out of you." I said. I knew she was joking but the threat was true. In reality, I would do much worse to her if she slandered Harriet in that way.

"Geesh, I was just joking." She shrugged, before making her way downstairs to where the rest of my family awaits Harriet's arrival.

My father stood in his basic t-shirt and khakis, my mom in her comfiest dress possible, and my sister in her basic work out uniform. I was clearly the best dressed, but it wasn't too obvious. I'm sure Harriet wouldn't notice anyway, she'll probably be focused on the fact that I haven't reached out.

She responded within minutes. Reaching out to her in the midst of the most sensitive time of the year, my emotions were running too high. I'll do whatever I can to keep her from knowing the truth. Including avoidance, deceit.

Most of all, I was afraid. She would run away, leave me to die in retribution from the lies I've spun her. *Or worse, she'd stay.*

I took a deep breath, lingering on the door knob. As soon as the lock clicked, my heart sank to my stomach. My hands were quivering and my anxiety sky rocketed. *This should not be happening, I cannot let her in these doors. She will see. She will see everything that I have tried to hide.*

I opened the door and all that anxiety, all that fear, disappeared. Her tight black jeans made my mouth water, and her off-the-shoulder top was loose but I could still see the outline of her tits through them. They were bouncing in my memories. Her hair was curled, a simple weakness of mine she doesn't yet know. Her eyes were cautious and wary. She's not happy about my obvious absence, but her attention to the care and detail of her appearance betray her. She wants to be here. She wants to see me. She wants to know why I haven't spoken. *I'm sorry, Harriet.*

"Hi, Harriet." I smiled, moving aside to let her pass. She cocked her head at me and gave me a curious smile.

"Merry Christmas."

Hers was forced too. The question awkwardly hung in the air like a noose. You could slice through the tension with a knife and my family was about to notice.

"Hello!" My mom smiled over her glasses. She was setting out dinner plates for dinner. "I'm Laura, Maximus's mom." Harriet finally tore her glance from my face and turned toward my family.

Where my mother was kind, my father was not. He didn't acknowledge Harriet for the first few minutes, heavily focused on carving the ham for the table. My sister on the other hand, couldn't wait to embrace her. Probably a tactic to get under my skin since she thought she knew something.

"Hey! I'm Lily." Wrapping her arms around Harriet's shoulders. Harriet's shock was undeniable, I'd never known her to be a hugger but she didn't defer my sister, instead she laid her hands on my sister's side. Just enough to convey the idea of returning a hug.

Before letting Harriet get a word out, my sister's words were filling the air. "Take off your shoes! What's your drink of choice?"

"Hello," she said awkwardly. Poor thing. I don't think this is what she was expecting.

"Gin and tonic usually. I brought some red wine for you guys. Thank you for inviting me." That smile wasn't forced. Her shoulders relaxed after Lily let go of her.

"Hope you like ham." My father mumbled without looking up from the counter top.

"I'm sure she does, Dad." I bit, stepping to her side.

"I love ham. Thank you." She interrupted, nudging an elbow into my ribs. She looked at my father and her smile frowned. I could tell she was noticing his lack of effort.

"Here you go, have a seat." My sister handed Harriet her drink and motioned toward the table in the middle of my house. She took one look at me and I knew she wanted to know where everyone sat first, not wanting to step on any more of my father's toes. She walked slowly so I could lead.

Taking my seat to the left of my father at the head of the table, she took my left, my sister sat in front of her and my mother to my father's right. The table was decorated with red napkins with golden holders, our best white and gold ceramic plates, and finest cutlery our money could buy. She sipped her drink calmly at first. The second was far more plentiful. I laid my hand on her shaking knee, softening at my touch but didn't acknowledge it.

She turned to me. Her gaze wandered over my face, hovering on my sunken eyes before scanning my entire body. Her eyebrows creased as she squeezed my hand under the table. Making eye contact with me, she broke the silence first.

"How are you?" Nothing more than a whisper only I could hear. *You have no idea.*

"I've missed you." Completely avoiding the question, hoping she would hang on my words. Instead she just smiled and squeezed my hand again.

But she followed through with what I feared.

"How are you?" she repeated.

I close my eyes every night not knowing if that day was my last. My father forces pills down my throat. My mother panics every time I stand up too quickly. My sister stirs at night praying I wake up. My brother's death looms over my family like an alarm clock.

I am your favorite lie.

"I'm good. Glad you're here. How was your Christmas morning?"

Her eyes lowered and her face sunk. I've seen enough pained looks to be able to smell them. Something about this Christmas was off. Something wasn't the same and it was weighing on her. I didn't think she was going to answer, but she did the same as me.

"I missed you too." Her smile was soft but I understood all the same. Whatever it was, she didn't want to talk about it. For a quick moment, we were the same. Hiding underlying, unspoken problems that didn't want to surface.

Across the way my sister gawked at us, seeing what we couldn't. The uncomfortably comfortable tether between us. She rolled her eyes and chuckled but before I could scowl a question, my father interrupted.

"Incoming!" My dad yelled, walking over to the table with slices of steaming ham. My mother laid down green beans, potatoes, and salad.

"This looks delicious! Thank you so much again for allowing me to join you guys." Breaking our eye contact and turning her focus to my family, now seated.

"We're happy to have you...?" My mother's question hung in the air. Harriet's presence had me so on edge, I completely forgot to introduce them.

"Oh sorry. This is... um... this is..." I stuttered.

"Harriet," she smiled. "I go to school with Maximus."

"What program are you in?" My father finally taking interest in the girl I had not so easily brought home.

"Mortuary Science." Harriet turned toward him. "Runs in the family so I've taken—"

"Ah, so you're family has a medical background?" His interest officially peaked.

"Yes, sir. My sisters and aunts are nurses, a couple of my cousins are doctors. You can imagine the dinner conversations growing up." She awkwardly laughed, trying to make conversation.

But the whole table went silent. *Nurses. Doctors. People to notice. People to educate her on my deterioration.* Everyone was thinking it. My mother's face had dropped and my sister had practically choked on her potatoes.

"Would you like to be a mortician some day?" My father continued.

"I would be happy as a mortician, but the dream would be a coroner. I've always been interested in human anatomy. Why we work the way we work, even how we work after... expiry." She hesitated. I knew she didn't want to make my family uncomfortable but the passion in her words betrayed her yet again. *Death. She wants to study death.*

Little did she know I was a poster child for it.

She was proud, she had a passion for the human anatomy and it gleamed in her eyes as she spoke about it. Something I envied. I don't think I'd live long enough to be passionate about a career.

"So Max brought home Doctor Death, how ironic." Lily sneered from across the table, taking a sarcastic bite of her ham and smiling on the rim of her glass. My mother's eyes widened as she smacked Lily's shoulder.

Harriet just laughed, completely missing the point. "Potentially."

"How did you two meet?" My mother said kindly. Making the conversation steer right when it was clearly about to go left.

Before Harriet could even contemplate what she was going to say, I spoke up. Webbing another lie to avoid further ammunition for my family to use on me later.

"Coffee shop on campus." I looked toward Harriet, bowing my head at her stunning presence, making sure she knew to follow my lead. I was in awe at her beauty when Lily decided to open her fucking mouth.

"Bullshit." She laughed, thinking she was keeping the conversation light. She can be so bone-headed sometimes.

Harriet tensed beside me. She wasn't exactly eager for my parents to know how we spent the first night we met.

"Enough, Lily." *Thank you, Dad.* "We're happy you have joined us. Hopefully your family is alright with that."

Harriet shoved a large piece of ham in her mouth and nodded playfully. Her mother was probably with her boyfriend. The rest of the family scattered with the people in their own lives. Harriet was alone. But not tonight.

My father met her with a nod and a soft chuckle. It was calming to see my family relax in her presence. She was an unknowing servant in our distraction. Distraction from my brother, distraction from me. She gave us a reason to fake a smile on the holidays.

However, my father is not *sir*. I am.

CHAPTER

16

Maximus

The rest of the dinner was more lighthearted, including a less awkward interrogation for Harriet. By the time we all had several drinks, she was innocently manipulated into taking funny videos with Lily. Laughing and dancing on the kitchen floor. My parents were cuddling on the couch watching *The Grinch* and I was sitting at the table just watching her.

"Last one! I need to breathe!" Harriet panted. They'd been standing there laughing for half an hour over the clips they were filming. Lily threw her head back and laughed.

I muttered against the rim of my glass before swallowing my whiskey whole, intently watching her dance horribly. My stomach rolled as I watched her fold herself within my family perfectly. I was trying not to hate it.

"What was that?" Harriet's head turned as she wobbled toward me, trying to look as naturally stiff as possible but the gin had gotten to her and giggle attacks were creeping up.

She was laughing by the time she got to me. She put both hands on the arms of my chair to steady herself. I took one look toward my parents fifteen feet away from us.

"Enjoying your evening I see." Lifting my chin to stare at the blue eyes above me.

"I think I might love her." Turning her head to take one more glance at Lily before turning back.

I put my hands on her wrists guarding my chair. "Seems like she might love you too." I grinned uncomfortably.

"I like your family."

I felt the pang in my chest. It wasn't supposed to skip a beat. Skipping a beat could kill me before I hit the floor, another side of the addiction forming in my pants, but that's what addictions are. They revive you before they kill you.

It was a simple sentence. My family had been through the ringer, and here was this random chick—woman—who liked my family without knowing anything about them. She's been with them less than six hours and already is fond of them. This, I hated her for.

Just for that, I wanted to punish her all night. Keep her locked in my room and devour her all at once. Silently thankful for her distraction.

"Ready for bed?" I asked. With absolutely no intention of sleeping until morning.

"Bed? I should go home." Harriet laughed.

"You're drunk. You are not going anywhere but upstairs with me."

"Upstairs?" She giggled. "You're allowed girls in your room?"

"He's always been allowed girls in his room. It's a shock he wasn't a teen dad." Lily interrupted. "The same fairness doesn't go for both children. It's annoying and unfair!" Emphasizing so our parents could hear.

"The answer is still no, Lily!" My father called from the couch, not bothering to look back at us.

I just laughed. Lily had been trying to convince our parents to let her have boys sleepover for a while now, even if there were no prospects. Needless to say they haven't budged on the topic. Something about her being their little girl, how it's different for girls than it is for guys. They don't want her getting pregnant, as if I don't run the same risk behind my doors.

"Shut up. I should've been born with a penis." she scoffed, marching upstairs.

"I heard that!" Laura turned from the couch, shaking her head as Lily disappeared up the stairs.

"She would've been blessed," Harriet whispered in my ear. And my cock instantly hardened at the hem of my jeans. I couldn't help myself. I pulled one of her wrists to show her what she had done, and I put the other in between herself. She smiled softly, silent adrenaline pumping through her veins with my parents only mere feet away.

"Time's up. I'm tired of sharing you with everyone else." I demanded, gesturing toward the stairs.

As I rose out of my chair she didn't bother to move, I towered over her and her chest was hot against my abdomen. I looked down at her and saw the mischief in her eyes.

Blood replaced with gin, girl replaced with slut.

I laced my fingers in hers and led her up the stairs. She let out low giggles all the way until we reached my door. She pushed passed me, eager to see my den of inequity.

"The *Game of Thrones* posters seem to be a theme with you." Her head angled toward the slope in my ceiling covered with the posters of Tyrion Lannister and Daenerys Targaryen.

"I drink and I know things." She read before turning to me with a sly grin. "You know nothing, Jon Snow."

So she's a fan too. "You're sassy when you drink gin." I started taking off my shirt before her hands landed on mine, continuing the work for me.

"Allow me, sir." She kissed the tips of my fingers. Both my heads going wild with imagination. *Sir.*

"About that…" I started, feeling the switch. I leaned forward to grab under her chin to force her to look at me. "My father is not your sir..." I wrapped my fingers around her delicate throat. I laughed lowly and shook my hair.

I leaned closer. "I am." My throat growled, as I tightened my grip.

She smiled, nodding while pulling her bottom lip between her teeth. One after another the buttons came undone and she started at the button on my jeans. I tugged at her shirt, but she pushed me away.

"Let me," I pleaded, searching for her eyes.

"No."

"No?" My voice raised with a light laugh. "You don't get to tell me no. This is my house."

"Oh well." Her sass was turning taunting. She knew what she was doing.

I did not feel the same playfulness. I hated her in this moment. My eyes darkened. I leaned down to her eye level again, building the tension by softly holding her throat. I let out a few deep breaths. "I'm going to fuck that attitude out of you."

I lifted her shirt over her head and unclasped her bra. Her tits fell hard, exposed to the cold air in my room. She pushed away from me, turning around to pull down her own pants while bending over to expose her ass to me. *Slut,* my brain smiled. I was eager to punish her for being so good with my family, for *liking* them. I gave her ass a light tap before flicking the switch on the wall and in my head.

"Turn that back on."

With the sound of her voice, both switches flipped back. She was staring at me with her sweater in my hands. "What's this?" Her voice was low and gentle. *Well, fuck.*

What was I supposed to say? It reminds me of the man I've manipulated you into thinking I am? I had no response. I just stood there, glaring at her. Hoping she wouldn't press further since even I didn't fully understand why I brought it home. To my annoyance, her intuition stepped in.

"You brought it home with you." It wasn't a question. "Why?" She stepped closer to me and it took everything I had not to back into my door. I didn't want to answer that. I didn't want her to see the vulnerability she held. My urge to hate-fuck her into tomorrow dissolved by the second.

"I-I found it in my bag. I must've scooped it up by accident when I was packing to come home." I stuttered quickly.

She just stared at me. Silently calling my bluff. Grinning widely and biting her bottom lip before glancing down at the sweater in her hands. She hugged it and rolled her eyes at me.

That I could not hold back from.

I lunged, grabbing her face in my hands and kissing her. Her kiss was intoxicating. She gasped beneath my lips, and it only ignited us more. I leaned into the electricity and wrapped her arms around my neck as her breasts pressed against my chest. I could feel her hard nipples against my skin, amplifying the pulse running through my veins.

She pulled away, palming my cheeks and just stared at me. I didn't have the courage to ask, in fear she would say something I didn't want to admit. Her smile had vanished and all that was left was curiosity. She got lost in my eyes, and I in hers. It was terrifying. Too compelling. In one look, my ego crumbled and my fight subdued.

I scooped my arms under her thighs and straddled her around my waist, walking us over to my bed and leaving her on her back.

I stood up, pulling down the rest of my pants to free myself from restraint. She leaned up on her elbows and never broke her stare. I could see the thoughts passing behind her eyes, begging to be voiced but she wouldn't dare. Wouldn't dare ruin what was coming to her. Her now princess treatment for dealing with my family, for liking them, for noticing my vulnerability to her. All the things I wish I could tell her.

I'm so confused with myself.

I spread her legs and landed right between them. Licking her opening so softly I felt her push into me with demand. *Patience, woman. Patience.* Her pussy was warm on my mouth and eager for more. Sucking her clit is her kryptonite. The little bundle of nerves so delicate that when I push too hard, pleasure and pain become one.

Her hands were combing through my hair as she grinned against me, releasing quiet whimpers as I circled her clit, her opening, the inside of her thighs and everywhere in between before she filled my mouth, soothing my throat. *I have never craved such a taste so fiercely.*

I licked my way up to her neck and sucked on the hollow of her throat, feeling her vocal chords call for me under my touch. It only made me ache for her more. She slid her hand between us, reaching for my cock and guiding me into her. She wasn't patient but I was at my breaking point so I let her.

Before I knew it, I was lost in my mind, in her eyes, in her body. I released. *Oh, shit.*

She gasped as the heat of it warmed her. Her eyes widened. We stopped dead in our tracks. Both frozen, refusing to move in acknowledgement of what just happened. I didn't want to speak. I didn't want to move. I had no idea what I had done, or what was going to come of it. I couldn't move. My body seized and my heart quickened with panic.

I slowly glanced down. I was still pouring out of her. Before I could open my mouth to speak, to apologize, to say anything, I leaped off the bed and stood. Heaving panicked breaths as I stared at her splayed pussy still oozing my come. I held my chest, begging it for air.

Silently, she got to her knees and crawled to where I was standing at the edge. She forced my face to look at her, she knew I was panicking. I knew she was too. It was an unspoken mishap between us, and nothing else.

She pulled my hand from her hair and kissed my fingertips before getting up to go to the bathroom. No doubt my warmth leaking down her legs. A feeling I'm sure felt good for the moment, perhaps not the eighteen years afterward.

I flopped on the bed, wiping the panic from my face.

"What have I done..." I whispered into my shaking hands. *I want to do it again.*

"What is happening..." my voice cracked. It wasn't about how I came in her, how good it felt to fill her. No. It was the terrifying shift in my mind.

"Maximus, shh." Her voice was hushed.

I wiped the remaining panic from my eyes and sat up to greet her.

"I'm so sorr—" My breath quickened. She didn't need to say anything more. Her touch was answer enough. She could sense the tension and although I knew she was in panic too, she pulled me into her and kissed the top of my head. Slowly twirling my hair between her fingers.

You're pathetic, I thought to myself. *Fuck her.*

I felt the tether tighten. *I want to do it again.*

CHAPTER

17

Harriet

The room was blanketed in wet white paint. Dripping down the walls like the tears on my cheeks. My family turned to me and once again, began laughing at me. Their wide white smiles gleamed at me. Their eyes were pools of jet black and bleeding the same tune. Their faces drained of color as if blending in the walls.

My drunk sleep was deep. But not deep enough. My horror world launched and sent me jolting upward to an unfamiliar room in an unfamiliar house with unfamiliar people.

Gasping for air, I glanced beside me. Trying to recognize where I was. Who I was with. Sleeping peacefully beside me, his skin glowed in the cracked light of the curtain. *He's beautiful.* His chest was rising and falling to a calming melody. I followed his breaths to pace my own heartbeat while forcing the images of my nightmare into a quieter place in my mind.

His lips were parted ever so slightly. If his chest wasn't rising, I would think he was dead. *Mouth breather,* I giggled out loud.

He stirred in the sheets and yawned himself awake. Before he even opened his eyes, the corners of his lips lifted, and his hands started searching the covers.

I let him find my hands. He was warm with the morning. His forehead was beaded with sweat as he moved his hand from my palm to the small of my back, eventually making its way between the mattress and my ass.

The sheet covering him started to rise and his eyes finally fluttered open, smile in full force.

"Good morning." He yawned. "Oh, maybe not. Jesus, look at that hair!" He barked a loud laugh.

"That's what happens when I'm on my back all night." I bit back. Remembering how he refused me into any other position rather than low missionary. Trying to block out the thought that there was now a palpable chance I could be growing a human life.

The images flooded my mind. His hands in my hair. His tongue between my thighs. His trailing touch across my body. His bites over my nipples. The feeling of his come filling me, calmly caressing my insides as it leaked out of me. *That could become addictive.* I scared myself. I shouldn't have liked that, I know the consequences. But fuck, did it ever feel amazing. Like black market crack.

I tried to reel in the wetness beginning to form between my thighs. But before I could change the channel, his hand slid out from under me, over the brow of my thigh and right into the hollow of my pussy.

He gave a wicked chuckle. "Mmm. Good morning, indeed."

He pulled himself over and hooked himself around my waist, lowering his head into my lap. Pressing gentle kisses on the sides of my thighs while stroking me and himself under the sheet. My smile spread and I tilted my head back, vanquishing my nightmare entirely. Releasing a small huff of air, I turn him over and straddle his thighs.

"Are we going to—" he began.

"Nope." I didn't want to talk about what happened last night. If I was good at anything, it was letting my mind wander to the worst possible places. We will cross that bridge when we come to it.

"We—There are—"

I slapped a hand on his mouth to shut him up. "I said no. I'll deal with it."

My answer was clear enough as he bit the inside of my hand and reached for the creases in my hips, but I swatted him away with a daring smile. Grabbing his wrists and forcing them beside his head.

I kept his hands pinned and folded my lips around his cock beneath me. It wouldn't do much for him, but it would do plenty for me. I started grinding against him, letting go of his wrists to lean back on his knees for stability.

My morning wet soaked his tip and he started curling his hips against me as he leaned back, his hands folded behind his head with a proud smile on his face, watching me work my body over his. My head fell back and my mouth opened in a gasp. My clit grinding against the head of his cock, I gained speed and my gasps turned into quiet whimpers. Quiet whimpers became low groans, and low groans became—

His hand clamped over my mouth.

"Shut the fuck up." He dug between our thighs and pointed himself upward into me. Thrusting so hard, he hit my hilt. I would've gasped loudly in agony if it wasn't for the hand over my mouth or bites on my neck to drown it out. He wasn't being nearly as gentle as he was last night, that's for sure.

He whipped us over, landing me flat on my stomach and pummeled into me like jackhammer. It was one quick motion, catching me off guard. He wedged his two front fingers as far down my throat as he could. Filling my mouth with his knuckles, silencing my tight gags around his fingers.

"Oh..." he breathed. "Please."

He stopped pumping. Pulling my hips and twisting me to face him. Staring at me, he grabbed my jaw and pulled me inches from his face. He took one deep breath, squeezing my jaw open. Quickly, he glanced between my eyes and mouth, gritting his teeth. He growled one last demand before we'd have to brave his family below.

His eyes darkened. But no wicked grin this time.

"Gag on it."

———◈◈———

I couldn't catch my footing until the last stair into the kitchen. I was grateful for the railing. Regardless if his parents knew we were fuck buddies, knowing it and seeing it are two very different things. Especially in my household with my mother and her boyfriend. You can have one, but I don't want to see jack shit.

"Pancakes okay with you, Harriet?" Andrew turned to smile at me from the pan. He was across the kitchen, with his back to us. A blue and red striped towel over his shoulder and an apron that read "Kiss The Chef" on it.

"Absolutely, I'm starving." I relieved a happy sigh.

"I'm sure you are." Lily snickered over her glass of iced tea. She sat on the bar stool at the countertop, facing her dad's back. Spinning on the chair with a devilish stare.

Maximus took one stride from behind me and smacked her upside the head. I almost laughed but thought better of it when I saw the look on their mother's face when she turned from her spot on the couch, hearing the smack from across the house. "Hey!"

"Do you absolutely fucking mind?" She growled at him, rubbing the back of her head. I'm sure that hurt.

"These comments are going to come back and bite you in the ass one day." He bit back before getting a smack to the arm.

"Oh that's it—" and they lunged at each other.

"That's enough! You're like a pack of animals. Eat your damn breakfast." Andrew yelled from the stove in the corner of the kitchen.

I just stood there. Not moving. *Was that normal?*

Laura had gotten up from the couch and walked toward us, empty coffee cup in hand, book in another. "I'm sorry for the lack of decency my children have." Setting down her coffee cup and book to smack them across the back of the head at the same time.

She was much shorter than them, but you knew who held authority. They wouldn't dare cross her, regardless of her soft appearance and warm smile. Devastatingly similar to the way my mom's appears. The siblings just glanced at each other and made silly faces.

"Please sit. Breakfast is ready." she demanded. Her tone was directed to me, but the nasty glare was for her children. A silent promise that they were going to hear about it later. For fighting. For what Lily said. And for what Lily said to be true.

As I sat down in my spot, I thought about how my mom would react to me having sex under her roof. And finding out about it through another person. Immediate death came to mind. For me and him. I pushed out the thought and forked two blueberry pancakes and bacon onto my plate.

"Did you sleep well?" His sister asked me with her kind smile again. But her eyes were a promise.

"I did, yes. Thank you. You?" I replied softly, clearing my throat.

"Couldn't get to sleep for a while, but I managed eventually."
Yikes.

Thankfully, their father stepped in. "So, will we be seeing you for New Year's?"

"Uh…" I glanced toward Maximus to see his expression. It gave me nothing. *Help me.*

"Do—do, uh, you want to come for New Year's?" He coughed over his glass of juice.

I turned back to his father. "If my mom's going out, I'd love to join you." I said, shoving a pancake in my face.

I should've said no. If Maximus wanted me here for New Year's, wouldn't he mention it by now? Or maybe we were too busy *creating life* in the sheets upstairs. I shook my head.

"You okay?" He asked me. His eyes were filled with concern.

"Always." I couldn't tell him how much that scared me. I know it caught him off guard too and he wasn't expecting it but I don't think he knew what he was doing. Part of me thought he has never had sex like that before. You know, normal. *Without his mask.*

Something was going on inside his head. I could see his thoughts spinning behind his eyes. He kept his eyes on mine for far too long. I knew what it looked like to get lost in someone, but I think it's foreign to him. And when he spilled into me, it shocked him out of it. Forcing him into a state of panic he'd never been taught how to handle.

Women always get stuck with it. I'd have to take the morning after pill. I'd have to carry a child for months. I'd have to have an abortion. I'd have to push a monstrosity out of a very small hole. Everything comes down to the woman. And that is something he will just never understand. I can't let that happen again, my own peace of mind is way more important than how *euphoric* his come felt inside me.

⸺◈◈⸺

Maximus is different around his family. He's not as talkative or as lighthearted when he's enveloped in their presence. He was shy, timid even. He was nervous by the sounds of it; I was the first girl he had ever brought home that wasn't his ex, Eve.

His father, a weathered man, didn't seem to really notice my being, but Lily was ever more embracing. She was beautiful, sassy, welcoming, and just an overall joy. Laura was your typical mom, short speckled gray hair with rectangle reading glasses. A creased warm smile with eyes that hide pain.

In fact, they all do. Their smiles are bright and genuine, but their eyes betray them all. They're sad, like their looking for something. I don't have the slightest clue of what it could be, but I know something happened to the four of them.

I haven't been *friends* with Maximus for long, so I won't pry about his family issues. The last thing I want is to talk about my own, so I can imagine how he would feel if I asked what happened to them.

CHAPTER

18

Harriet

I spent most of the drive home in silence. Overthinking about how I was overthinking. I stopped along the way to grab a morning-after pill and a bottle of water. I had been on birth control for almost ten years at that point, but I still felt like I needed to cover all my bases. And if nothing worked, I would take a test behind closed doors. I have never let anyone do that before, and now I remember why. Although it was one of the best experiences I have ever had, the fear was not worth it. I could barely feed and take care of myself. Ain't no way I was going to keep a child alive. Even if I wanted to.

When I walked into the kitchen, Elton John filled the air. Along with the delicious smell of chocolate banana muffins.

"Still baking?" I shouted at my mom, who was startled by my voice. The music was so loud she hadn't heard me come in. She was dancing at the oven, waiting for the timer to beep.

"They're almost done. I tried a new recipe so let's hope these taste good or else we're out of snacks. There's a snowstorm coming in so I hope you don't have plans tonight."

"I don't. How was your night with Paul?" Opening the fridge to grab myself some water. As if that would wash away the potential life in my uterus right now.

"It was lovely. I met his kids, he has a son just about your age." She winked at me.

"Moooom." I groaned. "Stop playing match maker." I laughed.

"I'm not, I'm not..." she trailed off.

"But..." I tilted my head at her, waiting for the rest of that sentence.

"But he has a good career, he's really nice, only a couple years older than you. And he has tattoos." She lingered.

My ears perked at the tattoo comment. I loved men with tattoos. Something about them was just so erotic. As long as they weren't explicit or degrading, I loved any. Maximus doesn't even have one, but I'm okay with that. He's talked about it, but not until he can afford them. I can wait but I'm afraid if he even gets a smiley face on the bottom of his toe, I won't be able to keep my hands off him.

My mom caught me shuddering at the thought.

"What's wrong? How was your night?"

"It was lovely. His family is really nice. I like his sister, her name is Lily. His parents are Laura and Andrew."

"What do they do?"

What do they do? I have no idea. I don't think I ever asked. Something I noted to ask Maximus on New Year's.

New Year's.

"I'm not sure. I can ask when I see them next. Which by the way, they invited me for New Year's, but I said I want to know what you're doing first."

"I figured you had plans, so I made plans of my own. Is that alright?" She asked, her warm smile spreading across her gentle eyes as she pulled the muffins from the oven. She still had her pajamas on, even though it was two p.m. in the afternoon.

"Yeah. I'll probably sleepover and then drive home in the morning. If I'm not too hungover." I laughed.

Sleepover. She did not like that. I was half expecting a lecture about me sleeping in the same bed as Maximus but my mother has always been very good about other people's households. What happens in their household is okay because it's not hers. Everyone has different rules and different values. Even though she was reluctant about us sleeping in the same room, let alone the same bed.

Her eyes cocked at the word and she pressed her lips into a thin line.

"Do you sleep in his—you know what? I don't want to know." She paused for a moment. Looking at the ceiling with her hand on her hip.

"Just please be careful and use—"

I immediately covered my ears. "Yes Mom, yes." *Even though we didn't last night.* "Can we please just drink and play some card games?" I laughed, lightening the topic, hoping she wouldn't say I was giving her attitude.

I poured myself a gin and tonic while she marched to the wine fridge and pulled out her favorite box of wine.

Five drinks later, she started asking questions about Maximus. I had to stop my mouth from watering at the thought of him. And then I had to stop myself from vomiting at the thought of the come stain in my panties.

My answers were short and simple. "He's nice." "He's guarded." "He's funny." ...Sometimes he makes me want to pull my hair out by the root...and sometimes he makes me question my life choices.

All in truth but none in full.

He is nice. In the wicked-perhaps-toxic way. In the way that he will make his entire world about you for one evening. Fall in love at night, just to fall out of it in the morning. The type to pretend to be your boyfriend just to be your stranger. Which is why he was funny.

He is guarded, not necessarily in a bad way. In the way he won't talk about some things. Which is typical of many people. I wasn't surprised he wasn't truthful about how my sweater came to be in his possession. It has been all the rage for girls to take their boyfriend's sweater, their boyfriend's boxers. Not once have I ever come across the reverse. I didn't know what to make of it. Was it a sign? Eventually, I would figure that out. The underlying message of what he was trying to tell me, maybe even himself.

I went to bed that night thinking of everything that happened. His hand on my shaking knee. How he avoided answering how he was. How he hesitated to let me in. Dancing with his sister. The adrenaline from my hand on his pants with his parents in the room. My jealousy when I saw his parents cuddling on the couch. How his eye sockets have sunken half an inch.

And then my mind wandered to a different place. The images of him over me, staring so deep in my eyes I thought they were going fall out. The unexpected light touch all over my body. Crimping the veins in my groin, making me squirm under his touch. The slower pace of his cock working in me. His hands in my hair. His hands running down my arms and lacing his fingers in mine.

My hand found its way into my tiny lace panties. Swirling and curling my clit between my two fore fingers.

His lips.

His eyes.

His calm smile.

His touch.

His cock.

Second after second, twirl after twirl. Everything went black, stars danced in my vision, golden magic encompassed my body. Euphoria.

The urge to text him what I had done was immense. But I refrained.

CHAPTER

19

Maximus

The days after she left were a blur. Because of the pills being rammed down my throat, I didn't even notice when it was New Year's Eve.

The moment I turned the corner, my father was standing at the bottom of the stairs with pills in one hand and water in the other. I tried to walk past him but before I even stepped one toe on the floor he was pushing me against the wall. Setting the water down on the bench beside us, keeping me in place with his elbow at my throat.

"Take them, son." He demanded. His eyes were scared, he didn't like what he was doing but the fear of my impending death was overpowering the guilt of physically jamming pills down my throat. He may be shorter than me, but his years as a construction foreman had built double the muscle. I struggled beneath his grip, it was useless.

My eyes started to swell. "Dad, please…" I begged. Not today. Not New Year's Eve. Harriet was coming over, I wanted my mind. I wanted to be alive.

"Take them!" *Please, Dad.*

He squeezed my jaw open, forcing the pills on my tongue and closing my mouth.

"I hate you." My words were harsh and unwavering. His face didn't move a muscle. He pushed himself off me with a huff and a smirk as he patted my arm. He didn't take the words to heart because he's justified himself. He's prolonging my life. He's saving me. This is what I need. This makes him a good parent. This will be worth it.

Tears fell as I glanced toward my mother standing at the edge of the countertop. She didn't do anything to stop him. She just stood there, bowing her head so she didn't have to watch him force medication on me.

If it meant saving my life, they would hang me.

All I could think about was Harriet while we sat down for dinner. I had called her earlier in the day to tell her I would let her know what time to come, so when we finally sat down for dinner, I picked up my phone.

"Put your phone down. We're eating dinner, Max." My father warned. I didn't want to push, so I obeyed, not wanting to risk him forbidding Harriet's invite.

"Lily! Get down here! Dinner!" Laura shouted, bringing a pot of peas to the table. Lily rushed down in an outfit I wish I never saw.

"Um... where do you think you're going wearing that?"

Her tiny-ass skirt and tiny-ass shirt was blinding against her pale-ass skin. I wanted to barf. I took one glance and immediately kept my eyes on my plate.

"You look like a slut." I mumbled over my food.

"Hey, don't say that about your sister. But he's right, you look like a stripper."

Ironically, my dad and I both barked a laugh, but my mom's glare silenced us both.

Lily scoffed. "I'm going to a party with my friends. Gonna land me a New Year's kiss." She finished that sentence with a kick in the air.

"Hey, hey, hey. I'm still your dad." My dad grumbled, revolted by her outfit.

She ignored that comment. "Max, can you drive me, please? Before Harriet comes and you guys drink your livers to death."

"No."

"I'll do your laundry for a month."

"Fine."

I shoved the rest of the meat and peas in my mouth and marched toward the key rack hanging on the wall by the door. Threw on some slippers, and grabbed a coat. Lily followed me out to the car, plunked herself down and a clinking black backpack at her feet.

"You're not slick." I laughed, remembering when I used to do the same thing.

"I know but I don't care. And neither do they. It's New Year's." she leaned down and grabbed a bottle of vodka, downing two shots like it was pumpkin juice.

We drove ten minutes down the street to a house that was filled with eighteen-year-olds who stole their parents liquor and cigarettes. People were sprawled out all over the lawn and in the house. Girls were dressed in the smallest outfits that money could buy, and guys were just looking about. Like predators hunting prey. I bet they were all thinking they would get lucky tonight. Or I'm just psychotic and they're only wanting a kiss at midnight.

Who am I kidding? They're all hypersexual teenagers. Just waiting to become hypersexual twenty-year-olds. If they're anything like me, they'll be hypersexual eighty-year-olds.

As if I will make it eighty.

Lily took one last swig of the vodka bottle as soon as we parked out front and reached for the handle.

"Be safe, okay? Call me if you need me, Harriet and I will come get you right away." I was sincere. I know the two of us fight like dogs—literally—but I would do anything for my sister. After everything that has happened in our lives, we have remained best friends. She is my whole world and over my soon-to-be dead body would I let anyone hurt her.

God help anyone who did.

"Thank you, big brother. I appreciate the drive. Have fun with Harriet and Mom and Dad tonight." She smiled. Opening the car door and leaning out, her skirt rode up and I felt my meat and peas begging to come back up.

"You still look like a slut!" I called out the window.

She bent down, peering through the window.

"For the love of God, will you please stop telling me I look like your type?"

I couldn't help but howl a laugh.

———⋄⦁⋄———

By the time I got back to my house, leftovers were packed away, dishes were done, and my parents were sitting at the table with a glass of wine.

"Everything go okay? How bad was it?" My mom asked, meaning the state of the house I just dropped my eighteen-year-old sister at.

"Typical. Bunch of teenagers drinking stolen booze and sucking face." I chuckled. I knew they wouldn't want to hear that but I find joy in antagonizing them about my sister's activities every now and then.

"Did you give her the talk?" Andrew piped in.

"No, Dad. That's your job. My job is to be her brother." I said lightly.

He just laughed and pulled out the chair next to him. A glass of whiskey already poured for me. I slid in next to them and took it in one gulp. My father quickly refilled it from the bottle sitting in front of him.

"Where's Harriet?" They both said in unison and then laughed with each other. After forty years together, thirty-five of them married, three children, and one catastrophic death, my parents were still so in love. I was in awe of them, I wasn't sure I'd live long enough to find what they had.

I wanted to have what they had; still finding joy in the same person after four decades, always laughing, always cuddling. Always happy. Like every couple, they fight but they always resolve it and come back stronger than before. They both have that one person they can hold at night and wake up with. Right now, I'll just settle for this drink.

"I'll text her after this." I hesitated, tipping my glass in their direction. Being in sync as they are, they both noticed.

"Something on your mind, honey?" My mom was gentle around the subject. I hadn't spoken to them about who she was to me, even the days after she left. No one brought her up other than they thought she was lovely and laughed about her love for gin.

Truth is, I still don't know what she is. All I know is I enjoy her company and she brings peace to my world. She silences the tsunami with her own waves. Without knowing it.

"She makes me nervous." I said bluntly.

"*She* doesn't make you nervous. What she, or what she *could be* makes you nervous."

Unfortunately, he was spot on with that one. She as a person didn't make me nervous at all. I could quite literally be my naked self with her and not a hint of judgement would come from it. I could be anyone, say anything, do anything I wanted with her and she would just smile. And suck my cock under my desk.

But what she could become is what made me nervous. Last time I had someone even remotely important, I got cheated on. Multiple times. With me in the vicinity. I was heartbroken for months. Even then, what I felt for Eve wasn't even a fraction of what I'm beginning to feel for Harriet. So if I were to be broken like that again with the power Harriet has over me, I don't know what I would do.

My mom leaned across the table and grabbed my hand. "You won't know anything unless you invite her over. Midnight is in a few hours and I'm sure she's waiting for your call."

"I will." I appreciated their comfort. It wasn't like them to encourage me toward something so dangerous. But I guess their sympathies were growing from this morning's medication mishap.

I continued, downing my glass once more. With my parents kindness, and my liquid courage, I get up to retrieve my phone from the kitchen counter. There was an anxious jolt in my chest.

Or so I thought. I coughed. "Here goes nothing—" I coughed again.

I coughed one last time before I felt my chest give out. I hunched over in pain, clutching my heart as my ribs cried out.

Every breath I took was shallow and sharp, I wasn't getting enough air, which means my heart wasn't pumping enough blood. My heart was pounding so fast I thought it was going to erupt out of my throat. My veins burned, my head went heavy. While I gasped for air between my cries, I felt my body go limp.

"Max!"

The last thing I remember was my mom screeching to call an ambulance while my dad tried to break my fall. Everything went black as I heard my knees crack on the tile floor.

CHAPTER

20

Harriet

It was embarrassing how long I waited by my phone.

I was like a thirteen-year-old laying on her bed with her feet in the air. My fuzzy socks were cheetah print and my hair wet in a claw clip. All I needed was a fake flip phone with lip stick and a sponge applicator and I was your typical crush-crazed middle schooler.

My make-up was already done and my hair mask was almost ready to be washed out, leaving my hair silky enough to slide through his fingers.

My mom helped me pick my outfit. We had gone over dozens of options. The right balance between pretty, hot, and appropriate for his family.

Three skirts, four body suits, and two sweater combinations later, we settled on my staple black jeans and a cream bodysuit top to accent my shoulders and collarbones. No cleavage, but it had enough skin for him to fawn over while he watched me smile and make conversation with his family. Slowly making him fall in love with me, one shoulder at a time.

But it never came.

My phone never lit up. Never buzzed. No matter how many times I checked it, his name never popped up. As if I kept checking, it would appear.

I wasn't sure how I should feel. Was it me? Did his family not like me? Did I say too much? Too little? Too loud? The questions flooded my mind. There was nothing I could do to stop them.

It struck eleven p.m. and my mom knocked on my door to find me pacing the perimeter of my room.

"Still nothing?" Her voice was calm and soothing. She knew how excited I was, dependent on the number of outfits we went through six hours ago.

I just shook my head, not wanting to speak anything into the universe.

"I'm sorry, honey." she huffed.

I drew a breath. "I just... I just thought—"

"I know. I know." She sighed, leaning against the doorframe. "I'd be more than happy—"

I cut her off. I didn't want her to bail on her plans just because mine *forgot* about me. She deserved a good night out, to get her New Year's kiss. It sickened me to my stomach at the thought of my mother kissing another man but I couldn't help the jealousy rolling around my stomach, weighing me down like a boulder.

"No, Mom. You definitely should go. He's just a boy, right?"

"Are you sure?"

I know she was trying to contain her happiness but her giddy smile and little chuckle betrayed her immediately. I forced a smile. Just because I was bummed out, doesn't mean I should transfer it to her.

"Absolutely. I'm going to text Kim and see if I can join her if it's not too late."

She sighed in relief at the thought of me not being alone. She didn't need to know that I had no intention of texting anyone. Kim wasn't even in the country. She was visiting her family in Japan.

"There's nothing a cup of tea can't fix." She smiled. She was so right about that. Tea had always been my go-to. The soft, warm liquid falling down my throat fixed everything about me.

But tonight? Tequila. Shots of it.

I heard the back door slam and the garage door going down. I waited a few extra minutes just in case she forgot something. In the time being, I took apart my entire appearance. My make-up, my outfit, and I just left my hair in the mask. I wasn't up for washing it out now. I threw on some old sweatpants and hoodie.

I made my way down the stairs, around the corner and into the kitchen. Hanging a hard right to the tiny counter against the wall. I barrelled through the cupboard and begged for the tequila to just call my name.

Harriet, Harriet...... I want you to drink meeeeee...

My mother's fancy Patron tequila was hiding in the back of the cupboard. It was for special occasions. Christmas, Thanksgiving, when Elton John came out with a new song.

Tonight seemed like quite the occasion. I grabbed some a shot glass and the neck of the bottle like I was John Wick reloading his favorite gun. I made my way to the corner of the kitchen to hop up on the counter. One leg toward the sink, one leg toward the stove.

I laughed at the sight of my legs spread with the absence of his head between them. I tilted my head back in shame of the thought.

"Ow!"

The handle of the cupboard above me carved a dent into the back of my skull. I laughed again at the pain it brought me. The difference between physical pain and mental pain was something I was familiar with.

My first broken bone in grade three. My shoulder. That was air-depleting. It took everything from me to gasp for air.

My second broken bone in grade five. My left leg. That was insane.

My third broken bone in grade nine. My right wrist.

And then my first heartbreak in grade ten. The death of an uncle I never met in grade twelve. My parents' divorce a few months later.

Nothing compared. No cast to protect my brain. No sling to rest my thoughts. Just the cracks in my chest.

This was not one of those times. I was not heartbroken. I was not in pain. I was not sad. I was embarrassed. He's just a boy. He means nothing. We have nothing in common. We are nothing. But he didn't text me like he said he would?

"You fucking idiot." I grumbled to myself as I threw back the first shot.

The golden liquid burned my throat. The exact opposite of the tea my mother recommended. Tea was for relaxing, sour moods, or just because. Tequila is for lonely nights sitting by the phone waiting for no one to light up the screen.

My phone was on the counter in front of me. It was in my sight but not close enough for me to reach. I didn't want to embarrass myself further by continuing to check it every twenty seconds.

"God, you're ridiculous." I spoke out loud. No one was here to tell me I was a crazy person so I just started my own monologue.

"You really thought you were getting that invite, huh?" I huffed.

"He's probably partying with some other girl. God, this is so stupid. He's out getting a midnight kiss from some random bimbo with a big ass and bouncing tits, while I'm..."

I glanced at the only friend I had that night. Patron. I couldn't stop laughing at how pathetic this was getting. I had a very serious conversation with myself while I was preparing to move to university. No distractions. No boys. Nothing of consequence.

"What a joke that became." And downed my second shot.

I double swallowed, and the liquid shot up my nose before going back down my throat.

"Ah, gross." I coughed. Still laughing at myself.

"Music. We need music."

"Hey Alexa! Play..." she waited for my demand but I came up short. What music do you listen to when you get stood up by no one? When you get forgotten by someone who has no obligation to you yet you planned your evening around their assumptions?

I settled for a throwbacks playlist of the early two thousands. If I was going to be alone, I might as well dance. The songs went on, I started bouncing around the kitchen. Taking shot after shot. By the time I got to my fifth shot, I had completely ditched the glass and just started sipping from the bottle. This—this was my downfall. I should not have done that. But who cares, right?

Definitely not him!

"Woohoo!" I swung myself around the island chairs, down the hallway, through rooms, acting like I was in a goddamn music video.

"God, what is wrong with me? This is starting to get pathetic."

"AH!" My foot kicked something fury and small. "Ruby!"

I looked down at my dog staring at me. I apologized to her profusely, begging for her to understand I had no idea she was even here, let alone mean to kick her straight in the side. She must've been following me this whole time. Where did she come from?

"Mom didn't take you with her?" She cocked her head at me and just gave me her big black eyes in response. I picked her up and patted her head, walking back to the kitchen where we keep her treats. She needed to know I didn't mean to punt her ass to the moon a minute ago.

"Here you go. I'm sorry." She snatched the treat from my hand and I patted her head again before setting her down. As I was trying to walk away to find my bottle, she took a seat right on my feet. *I guess Mom knew I wasn't going out.*

My whole vibe changed. I told the music to shut up, I picked Ruby back up and went to sit on the bench banking the left side of my kitchen island. Still managing to grab the Patron bottle which was more than half empty by now.

I glanced at the stove, secretly hating myself for searching for the time. But there it was…blaring its face at me.

12:01 a.m.

Realistically, I stopped caring—more like forgot—that I was supposed to get kissed by a tall glass of water this evening but the moment I saw my dog, I didn't care. Nothing else mattered more than this little chunk of meat curled in my lap.

I shoved Maximus out of my thoughts and decided to grab a canvas. It won't be my typical set up; canvas, paint, lit candle and a cup of tea with my favorite podcast playing in the background. Tonight, it will just be me, my brush, Ruby, and my emotions.

I grabbed a blanket from the couch for Ruby and collected all my necessities. I filled my stained mason jar with warm water and a dab of soap, lightly setting it down out of reach of Ruby's face. And my liquor bottle. The amount of times I have drank my water cup over my teacup is embarrassing.

Once, I even put my used brushes in my tea. I still drank it…

I unwrapped my canvas and dolloped my paints in my palette, quickly settling in my spot on the bench and Ruby into the blanket. Took one last swig of my tequila bottle, deciding to play one of my comfort podcasts, Dr. Death.

I completely blanked. What emotion do you paint for how I'm feeling? Considering I don't know what I was feeling, I looked at the time again.

12:09 a.m.

"Oh, fuck you!" I yelled, jolting Ruby from her slumber beside me.

"Sorry, my love. What the hell do I paint? I don't even know what I'm feeling…" I laughed at myself quickly. I knew exactly what I was feeling.

Drunk.

My grin widened and I grabbed my first brush and dipped it into an inky black. I smirked to myself, *the perfect color.* Where I was usually a perfectionist with my strokes, the tequila rumbling through my veins paid no attention. I twisted, pulled, dotted my brush all over the canvas. So far, this was a drunken mess, and I just continued laughing for stooping so low in my principles.

I dabbed a striking gold over the bristles of my brush and twirled it over the black streaks, complimenting it nicely but being careful not to overpower the black and the cream of canvas prime.

I heavily contemplated adding a pop of color, but I wasn't exactly feeling colorful or joyous so I stuck with my black, white and gold, unsure on where to go next.

After several minutes of growing frustration and my paint brush not reacting the way I would've liked, I set it down. I pushed back, glaring at the ugly painting sprawled out on the counter in front of me.

"What do you think, Ruby?" I pouted, cocking my head, begging for it to look better at this angle. She glanced up at me tilting her head as if she knew this painting was ridiculous.

"Ugh!" I smacked my canvas, getting black, gold and white all over my hands. "Wait a minute… Hey, Alexa!" She chimed to the sound of my voice and did as I commanded.

As soon as the first beat to "Kill the Lights" by Alex Newell blasted through the speakers, my smile could've blinded the room. My favorite song in the entire world, it never failed to lift my mood and as of right now, it did the exact trick I needed it too.

I slammed my hands on my painting and started running my fingers through the wet paint. Ruby noticed the change in my mood and sat up with her tail wagging and her pink tongue panting at me. I beamed with delight and my fingers flowed over the canvas like water succumbing to a current.

Maximus had completely left my mind, and I went right back to feeling like myself. Someone who could control her environment and her moods. Someone who didn't need another person to feel alive when all she needed was Ruby and brushes. The tequila was still thrumming through my veins, but that only heightened my point. Me, Ruby, painting, and an almost-empty tequila bottle was my core. My heart quickened and my lungs squeezed with joy.

I finally started liking my painting. But it was missing something. It had everything written all over it, my emotions, my environment. Except the one thing that influenced the recklessness and *freedom* laying in front of me.

I grabbed the bottle with my hand, almost dropping it from how slippery my hands were. As gently and calculating as I possibly could, I poured the remaining liquid over my canvas. The separation of the paint versus the liquid brought me renowned joy. I had separated from the painting's emotion hours ago. I was no longer confused about Maximus not following through with his—our—plan.

Instead, the piece spoke of freedom, capability, strength, and overall… separation.

Deciding to take my separation one step further, I searched my kitchen for a grocery bag, dug through my garage for a hammer and plugged in my hot glue gun. This was about to get explosive.

I wrapped the empty tequila bottle in a tea towel and threw it in the bag. With one hard swing, I brought the hammer down on the bottle. Down on my emotions. Hearing them crack under the mallet filled me with revenge and utter relief. My evil laugh echoed in my mind as I brought the hammer down again, hearing them shatter for the second time.

When the pieces were of the right size, I tugged out the tequila-stenched tea towel and carried the bag to my canvas where my hot glue gun waits for me.

——◦❧◦——

By the end of my evening, I somehow had created two of the exact same pieces. And apparently got a doppelgänger of Ruby, who had eight legs and a hollowing bark. My laugh was ricocheting through the halls of my house by the time I set Ruby back on the floor and my paint set up was cleared.

I hadn't even noticed my mother gracefully stumble into the house with a bright smile on her face. She immediately saw me, fumbling through the fridge next to an empty bag of Miss Vickie's Salt and Vinegar and... uncooked pasta?

"Harriet!" My mom's voice was drenched in worry.

"Thas me!" I stumbled from the fridge, pulling out the mustard bottle for my uncooked pasta. The look on her face pulled me to a halt.

"What?" My smile faded as she rushed toward me. In particular, my hands, and the fact they were covered in dried blood.

"Harriet, no!" She brought my hands to her face, I knew she was seeing double too.

I repeated, "What?" The realization punched me in the face when I felt her trail her finger up my forearms, the scarred white lines highlighting a troubled part of my past.

"Uh ma god, no, Mom!" I struggled but I was sure I got my point across. "Mom, I made a pa-painting. I broke the bottle on... on... purpose!"

I guess I wasn't as careful as I thought. She just looked at me, her eyes were questioning enough to know she wasn't sure if she believed me.

"Look!" I ushered her over to the part of the counter that housed the painting I made and her shoulders fell in relief.

"Oh, thank god! Let's drink! And you can tell your mother why you didn't end up going out tonight." She cheered, throwing her hands in the air but quickly rethinking her thoughts and opted for water instead.

CHAPTER

21

Harriet

If I knew he was going to ghost me for almost two weeks I would've gone out on New Year's.

When I moved back into my house in the first week of January, I made a rash decision—gin might've been involved. Maximus hadn't gotten back to me and although I told myself not to obsess over it, the gin pumping through my veins told me it was okay.

"Fuck it!" I jumped up from my couch, my roommates flinching. "I'm texting him." And I immediately wobbled down again.

Jane and Mia stumbled, "No!"

"Why not? All we do is fuck, so texting him about meeting up isn't like...like..." I didn't know where I was going with that.

"Like being clingy?" Jane piped in. I could tell from the look on her face, she didn't approve of my drunken idea. Mia just giggled and Kim gave me a funny look.

"Whaaaat?!"

"I think you should do it." She covered her mouth with the sleeve of her sweater to cover her smile. She always loved balancing on the edge.

I bolted up the stairs as fast as my drunk legs could carry me. "I'm doing it!"

"No!"

"No!"

"Yes!"

The three of them chased after me, fumbling their way up the stairs until we got to my room in the corner.

"Harriet… I don't think you should—"

Kim slapped Jane's arm and laughed. "She definitely should. There's no way he wouldn't answer a text like that." Her eyebrow cocked and she playfully nudged Mia to her right. Eventually, they walked out and closed my bedroom door, leaving me to make my decision in peace.

I scrambled through my closet, looking for something that could entice him to answer me. *Think, Harriet. Think. What do you send someone when all they want is sex?*

Then my hands hit them. *Got it.*

Old hand cuffs from a costume back when I was in high school, playing the naughty police officer one Halloween. I smiled softly at the memories of getting drunk in someone's basement and handcuffing myself to my friend so she couldn't hook up with that ugly guy.

Piece by piece my clothes came off and perhaps piece by piece my sanity. I took one look at myself in my bathroom mirror and just smiled at myself.

I sat down on my bed and got in his favorite position. Grabbing my phone from my desk and snapping a few photos. Bending, twisting, arching. Of course I had to figure out which one he would succumb to.

"I did it!" I yelled, stumbling down the curling staircase. My roommates all cheered, despite their hesitations earlier.

"Has he answered?" Kim questioned. "No, I'm sure he's going to want to make it look like he's cool, calm and collected." I giggled back, waving my arms and scrunching my face.

We continued drinking that night, practicing our beer pong skills. We sure needed the practice but somehow the drunker we got, the better we got. We laughed and moved our bodies to the overhead music while we pounded back drink after drink.

Knock, knock!

"Shit..." Mia whispered, trying to hide her smile. "How much you want to bet they're here to tell us to turn it down?" We all walked to the front door. We were having fun and we didn't want our neighbors to ruin it.

"What if we didn't open the door?" I suggested, hoping the people behind the door would tire.

"We heard that!" *Shit.* Kim opened the door and the downstairs tenants were staring back at us.

Tori and Lori were the girls a year ahead of us. Cade was the guy who knocked on the door, who was in a few of my classes.

"Hey, guys!" I cheered sarcastically. If we were going to keep our night going, we'd have to make them like us. I side glanced at Jane and she just shrugged.

"We're trying to study, can you please keep it down?" Tori asked, crossing her arms across her chest. "Study? It's the first week back, all we got is syllabi. Relax!" Kim said, throwing her arms up in the air trying to seem inviting.

Lori just tilted her head and scoffed. Cade stiffened beside her and scratched the back of his head while thinning his lips. Tori just stared straight into Jane's soul.

"Okay, okay, okay. How about this?"

All of us turned toward Mia. Wondering where she was going with that. I knew she was going to invite them in, but I didn't stop her despite me being wary of it. We haven't spoken to them since the night of the party.

"We'll turn down the music for an hour," she exhaled. We all turned back toward the incomers and then we all turned back to her. "And then how about you join us?" Our eyes widened but we let it happen anyway.

The three of them contemplated it, eventually shrugging their shoulders in agreement before walking down the steps and around the corner to the basement door.

I closed the door behind them and turned to my roommates. "So this is happening, I guess." Laughing off my worry. "Oh well!" Kim said, grabbing my hand to pull me toward the kitchen where our beer pong game was waiting.

—⟨⟩—

"Whooooo!" Kim and I cheered as our ball sunk the last cup, high-fiving in the air. "That's game! Let's—"

The knock at the door stopped us all in our tracks. Had it already been an hour?

The seven of us didn't really speak much at the party so this was feeling rather official. I've often been told my first impression was hard to swallow, I didn't mean to come off so distant. Which wasn't helpful when enrolling in a university where no one knows you, so I had to make this work. I wanted to make sure I had some lifelong friends when I leave.

Maximus...doesn't count. Unfortunately, it was looking like that wasn't going to last so...

"Looks like the party is about to get started." Jane yelled behind her while walking to open the door. She dramatically swung it open and moved aside to allow our guests to make their way through the frame.

Tori came to the kitchen first, holding a six-pack of coolers. Wearing tight black leggings and light blue crop top, drenched in jewelry, with her hair up in a tight bun. Lori came second with an unopened bottle of vodka in sweatpants and a hoodie. Cade sauntered in last, wearing a formfitting white t-shirt and black jeans, pocketing a mickey of rum with a six-pack of a beer I didn't recognize clutched under his arm.

"Hello again, girls." He smirked. His black hair and black eyes were piercing. The cigarette between his teeth twitching with the curve of his lips.

His presence unnerved me. His lean body was a frame against the side of our fridge. He moved in swift motions as he placed his beer on the counter and pulled the mickey out of his pocket, cracking the seal before taking a sip.

"So what are we playing?" I asked, avoiding Cade's eyes.

"Flip cup? Round of pong?" Mia answered from behind me. I was standing at one end of the table and she was sitting in the chair against the balcony door.

"What about an icebreaker? King's Cup?" Lori smiled. She seemed nice, approachable. We all nodded and grabbed chairs for the table, cleaning it off to spread a deck of cards around a red solo cup. I pulled up my chair to the end of the table and everyone sat down accordingly. Lori to my left, Tori to her left, then Mia, Kim, Jane, and finally, Cade spun a chair around and sat on it backward, leaning his strong forearms on the table.

"Oldest goes first!" Jane yelled over the speakers. "Who would that be?"

"Me."

We all turned to him, surprise across our faces. I thought he was our age considering he was in a few of my classes. But that's the thing about university, anyone at any age can come—and go—at any time.

Without even blinking the words just came out of my mouth. "How old are you?" He offered me a small smile and picked up the first card. A Queen. Rule Maker.

"My rule is," his eyes lingered over all of us, his roommates were smiling but mine were eyeing me, all of us wondering what the hell he was about to say.

"Every time you have to drink, you drink twice." His smile was bright, and straight. "Pft," came from Lori across the table. "Baby food."

"Your turn, Harriet." He smiled on the rim of his beer can. I pulled my card, a King. *Boring.* I poured some of my gin and tonic into the middle cup.

"Lame! My turn!" Lori pulled her card, a ten. Categories. We all went around saying types of chocolate bars until Mia choked and had to take two drinks, thanks to Cade's rule. We continued playing and I could tell we were starting to actually enjoy ourselves. The alcohol was making our first encounter a lot easier than I expected.

As it turned out, I really enjoyed the company of our downstairs tenants. They were rowdy, sure, but they were fun and whenever anything was spilled, they immediately cleaned it up. This had potential to become a ritual. Cade was a bit of an ass, and a bit wild in the scary sense, but overall he was a positive contribution to our evening.

When it came back around for my third turn, I pulled a Jack. Never Have I Ever. *Great, I'm either going to look like a slut, a criminal, or all out insane.*

"Jack." I laughed, knowing in the next few minutes we were all about to get really close. I could lie. But where's the fun in that? I decided to go with something light, not wanting to start the kinky shit straight away.

"Never have I ever had jet black hair."

Cade drank and put a finger down. So did Jane, and Mia, and Lori. I guess they had all dyed their hair at one point in their lives. Lori was blonde, Jane and Mia were brunettes. Tori sat there smiling with her natural ginger, proud of never bleaching her hair.

"Never have I ever... had a threesome."

I never have. I've thought about it, had opportunities for it, but never went through with it. I smiled when Lori said something I actually hadn't done. *Relief.*

"Never have I ever smoked weed!" Tori cheered. My roommates and I gaped at her, then all caught each other's eye. We threw our heads back. To my surprise, Cade didn't drink. "You've never smoked before?"

"Nah." He was nonchalant about it, like it never crossed his mind. Charming.

Never have I ever had blue eyes. Mine and Tori's fingers went down and drinks went up. Never have I ever been out of the country. Again my fingers went down.

Then it was Jane's turn. "Never have I ever kissed a girl."

"Well shit..." Cade laughed, putting a finger down and taking a big final gulp of his beer. Only he noticed my finger went down too.

"Damn, angel. Did not see that coming." He muttered, turning his whole body to me. I tensed. His presence made me feel something I couldn't put my finger on. Whatever it was made my nerves flame. I tried to shrug it off.

"Leave me be," I smiled. "Lips are lips?" And everyone laughed. *Thank fuck.*

"I mean you're not exactly wrong, was it good?" Jane asked me.

"What?" I almost spat. "I guess. A kiss is a kiss." I shrugged. I was drunk with my friends at a party one night and made out with one of the girls. It didn't seem like that big a deal to me. I wasn't romantically involved with this chick, it was just a kiss.

"Hot."

Before I could even think, I smacked Cade upside the head. "Get that image out of your mind, right now." I joked, standing up to make myself another gin and tonic.

My phone sat on the counter and I couldn't bear to look at it. I didn't want to see that Maximus hadn't answered me. I was enjoying myself tonight and no way was I going to let a nobody ruin my evening.

Cade walked over to me and grabbed another beer from where I was standing. I could feel his body heat and it bothered me that I noticed. He caught me staring at my phone.

"Waiting for a text back from your boyfriend?" He asked, popping the tab on his beer with his teeth.

"Doesn't matter. I don't care."

"Shame on him." He smiled, it was sincere like he meant it.

"And I don't have a boyfriend." I don't know why I wanted him to know that but it just came out anyway.

"Doesn't matter." It was firm. He nodded and turned away to get back to the table. He got to his seat before me and as soon as I went to sit down, he yanked the chair from beneath me and I fell flat on my ass.

"Asshat!" I yelled. I wasn't as annoyed about the fall, I was pissed because my drink was spilled all over my chest. *Ugh.*

"You made me spill my drink!" I stood and slapped his beer out of his hand, it poured all over the hardwood. I couldn't help but laugh.

He was flabbergasted, had to catch his breath even. He gasped and before my brain could register, his arms were around my thighs and I was hanging upside down over his shoulders. I hadn't realized how tall he was until I was dangling four feet from the floor. The girls were laughing and cheering him on.

"Well now what the fuck are you gonna do?" He laughed. Smacking the back of my thighs, careful not to touch my ass.

"Put me down, Cade!" I laughed. My drinks were swirling in my stomach. I had to tense my muscles to stop them from coming up. "My world is spinning!" I was serious, but kept laughing. This was fun.

"Say you're sorry and I will!"

"You made the first move, dickhead!" I started pounding on his back, across the top of his jeans.

"Girl say sorry, he's gonna keep you up there until you lose your drinks!" Kim yelled from the end of the table. Ain't no way in hell was I going to apologize! I didn't do fuck all!

"No!" And then it hit me. The tricks of grade six. Good old middle school.

I pulled up his shirt and yanked the top of his boxers as hard as I could. I could almost feel them slicing between his ass cheeks. He immediately threw me from his shoulders and I fell backward, miraculously landing on my feet.

"Dirty move!" He wasn't mad. He almost seemed impressed.

He shook his head and patted me on the back as we made our way back to our seats. His hands were big and warm. They were strong too.

The game resumed. Five, drive. Ace, waterfall. Four, whores. Six, dicks. Seven, heaven. Eight, mate. Queen. King. King. Nine, rhyme. Two, you. Three, me. The solo cup was almost at the rim, filled with gin, beer, coolers, and vodka. Nasty combo.

"Thank god!" Jane threw her hands up. She wasn't going to have to drink all that. Three remaining cards. It was either Cade, me, or Lori.

Cade pulled a card. A two. He picked me to drink.

Then it was my turn. To my relief, I picked a seven and shot my hands in the sky, quietly thanking the lord I didn't have to drink the jungle juice sitting in the center of the table.

"Fuck me!" Lori slammed her hands on the table standing herself up. She had to drink that monstrosity.

"Go Lori! Go Lori! Go Lori!" All of us cheered her on. Her hand was shaking as she lifted the cup and put the rim to her lips. She took one deep breath, squeezed her eyes shut and started chugging.

"Yeah, Lori!" We screamed at her, all standing up at the champ that was her.

She slammed it back in less than ten seconds and threw the empty cup on the table. *Damn, girl. Respect.*

"How was it?" I asked, planting my wobbly ass back in my chair, almost missing it completely. "I think I'm drunk cuz it actually wasn't that bad." She laughed and wiped the remaining liquid off her chin.

The rest of the night didn't last much longer than that. Lori was getting sloppy. Mia disappeared, Jane and Kim were half passed out over the table, and Cade was on the balcony smoking a cigarette when I came back from the bathroom. Tori was no where to be found. I opened the door to the balcony.

"Where's Tori?"

"She went downstairs." He said. I let out a sigh of relief and glanced back at Lori wobbling to the front door.

"Me go home!" She yelled at no one. I glanced behind me from the doorway and gave her a thumbs up. I could watch her from around the balcony to the basement door. "I had too much fun! See you next Friday!"

I just waved in agreement. They were a lot nicer than I gave them credit for. If she wanted to come back next Friday, my first impression must've not been that bad. I stepped out onto the balcony and walked over to Cade who had his elbows resting on the railing, cigarette limp in his right hand. I peered around the corner to watch Lori stumble her way through their door before making my way to his side. Contemplating on stealing that cigarette.

"You good, dude?" I questioned, taking his side. We both had a lot of drinks tonight but at least we were at home. No danger this evening.

"Oh, I'm mighty dandy, darling."

Angel. Darling. I snatched that cigarette right out his hand and put it to my lips. "Hey!"

"Don't worry about it, *darling*." I mocked. He just narrowed his eyes at me and locked them ominously. All of sudden, I got insecure.

"What?"

I didn't expect him to answer. Nor did I want him to. The amount of drinks sloshing through our brains wouldn't allow such a complex conversation. He watched me finish his cigarette, moving his eyes back and forth between my eyes and the cigarette between my teeth. I flung the butt over the edge of the balcony and leaned over to watch it put itself out on the concrete below.

Cade disappeared from my right. I leaned back and turned around, becoming pinned between his chest and the railing. I gripped the edge of the railing and gasped. Everything in me went cold. I met his gaze, it was ominous, but sure.

He reaffirmed his hold on the banister. He sucked his lips between his teeth and smiled. His lips were wet and his dark hair was hanging in his eyes but he never lost my glare. *Why isn't he saying anything?*

Over my dead body was I going to be the first one to say something. Other than maybe it was time for him to leave, it was getting late and his gaze was sobering.

He moved closer, our noses just inches away from touching. He inhaled deeply and closed his eyes before pushing off the railing and heading for the door.

I rushed past him and put my hand on the handle, meeting his gaze once again. I said nothing, he said nothing. Pinching my eyebrows together, I slowly slid the door open and moved aside to let him pass me.

He marched to the front of the house, in no obvious rush. I followed, walking out my own guest seemed courteous after all. As he bent down to put on his boots, I scanned his whole body.

He was lean but I could see his muscle through his white shirt, constricting around his biceps. His jawline was soft as his skin and his legs were long. He was all legs.

He pulled himself up in one swift roll and shook his black hair before pulling out another cigarette and holding it between his teeth. Finally, he spoke.

"Thank you for a memorable evening, Harriet. I will be seeing you again." His tone was soft but conspicuous.

"See you next Friday, Cade." I offered a small smile in exchange, pondering what he meant.

Opening the front door, we both stopped in our tracks, eyes wide.

CHAPTER

22

Maximus

Coming back to Greenlake was a relief. After my spill with the hospital, I needed a break from my family's worry. Yeah I collapsed, but I'm not dying today. Or tomorrow. I may be deteriorating faster than we thought, but I still have loads of time to fuck around. I can't stand being around fragile eyes and constant worry that if I stand up too quickly, or cough once, I'm going to have a heart attack. Mind over matter and all that bullshit.

Running away from my problems is so much easier than dealing with them, so as soon as I got back to Greenlake, I went straight for Harriet. She would provide me with a mind blowing distraction. If it was anything like that photo she sent me, I was in for a wild ride.

Who knew she had that in her? She could only go two weeks without reaching out to me. Granted, it wasn't on purpose, mostly. My parents didn't allow me to have my phone so I just sat and watched bad hospital tv while the doctors ran test after test and talked to a student nurse. Inevitably finding out that—surprise!— I'm still friends with death.

Nothing like a conjugal visit from death and a naked photo from the hottest chick ever to get your dick pumping. As soon as I got my bags inside and had a few drinks with my friends, I made my way to Harriet's front door. Completely ignoring what I had tried to convince myself to do while I was in the hospital.

Only to be confronted by an unfortunately great looking dude. He was tall with messy black hair and dark eyes, wearing a tight white shirt and black jeans. Both of them had a stunned look on their face when he opened the door just as I was about to knock. Harriet was dressed in black sweatpants with her nipples poking through a dark green tank top. Her make-up was done and her hair was pulled into a loose bun. My teeth clenched.

"Um... I'm just heading home. Have a good night." He said, barely making eye contact with me as he snuck past, sneaking another glance at her. I didn't even bother to move aside, he could walk around. Harriet had some answering to do. I watched him walk down the steps and to the side of the house. *Where exactly is home?*

"I see you've been busy." I sneered at her, making my way through the front door and taking off my boots, trying to relax.

"We met our neighbors. Turns out they're a lot of fun," she giggled. "Lori, Tori, and that was Cade."

"Tori and Lori?" I repeated. "What a combo."

"I know right. What are you doing here?"

"Well... I had to have some sort of response after you sent me a naked picture of you bent over with your hands cuffed behind your back."

She just stared at me. Her cheeks flushed and I could tell she was getting embarrassed about the photo. It was probably a drunk decision no one talked her out of.

"I—uh..." she started but I couldn't let her finish. I stepped closer to her, hovering above my favorite set of eyes.

"You left out the best part." I smiled. She was smart enough not to put her face in the photo. No one would know it was her unless they knew what her pretty little puss looked like and how she did her nails.

She turned from me and walked to the kitchen. Evidently getting some water to mask to smell of gin on her breath. *Fun night indeed, Miss Harriet.*

She closed the fridge to find me leaning against it staring at her with narrowed eyes. I didn't like the fact their was another guy here. Anyone who had eyes could see how beautiful she was, no doubt wanting to make their way into her pants. Over my soon-to-be-dead body would she sleep with another man ever again.

"What?" Her tone was sassy.

Blood replaced with gin, girl replaced with slut.

She had every right to question me like that, she had no reason to grant me exclusive loyalty. We weren't together. Doesn't change the fact I'm not letting another man get close enough to even sniff her.

"You fucked him." It wasn't a question. And it came out exactly how I wanted it to. Cold. Harsh. Painful.

She scoffed. "Excuse me? I just met the guy." She raised her voice in shock and slammed the empty water glass on the counter.

Check.

I didn't say anything, I just cocked my eyebrow and glared at her. After all, she practically leaped into bed with me before she could even speak my name.

"I know how that sounded," she huffed to herself. "But no, I didn't sleep with him. All of us just played drinking games and got to know one another. They live downstairs. They're nice."

For the first time I glanced around the room. Her roommates were drooling on the dinner table and what looked like the King's Cup was toppled over in front of them. Before I could observe anything else, she stepped close enough that I could feel her warmth.

"Not that I care," she swallowed. "But we had plans. And you ditched me without a word. So I'll ask again, what are you doing here?"

I grinned. *She cares.*

"I spent the evening with my family instead." It wasn't exactly a lie, I did spend it with them. And twelve doctors, nurses, and cardiologists.

"Not good enough." *I tried, they wouldn't let me have my phone, plus...*

"Let it go. It doesn't matter." I bit through my teeth. I wasn't liking this line of questioning, no matter how much she deserved to know the truth. I know I ditched our plans, I would've liked to spend New Year's with her.

Unfortunately, that just wasn't in the cards this year.

She didn't answer and turned her face away from me but I grabbed her chin in my fingers and forced her to look at me again. I towered over her so I slouched my neck to get to her eye level.

"I'm sorry," I whispered, unblinking. The look in her eye told me she didn't want to forgive me, but she knew she'd have to. I moved in to kiss her but she tore out of my grip and pushed herself off my chest.

"You're going to have to earn that." She scolded, moving around me and going up the stairs to her room.

She opened her door, picked up the clothes spread everywhere and went digging in her closet for what I'm sure would be her pajamas. She pulled out black silk shorts and a matching spaghetti strap top.

"You're not going to need those." I mumbled, take two big strides to sit on her bed. She held my eyes while she pulled on her pajamas before going to the bathroom and closing the door. I heard the lock click as I reached for it.

Damn it.

I undressed myself and got in her sheets. They were silky and light blue this time. Her one black pillow was undoubtedly her favorite so I threw it behind my head. She'd protest, and in her fight for it, I'd fuck the shit out of her. *Good plan.*

She opened the door and halted in the frame. "You got a tattoo!" Her smile lit up the room. She was staring at the rose that I had a done on my chest. "I did." I smiled back.

"It's beautiful. Why did you get it?" *I can't tell you.*

"Had extra Christmas money and wanted to start." I nodded at the black and white art piece on the left side of my chest. It was pretty large, took up most of my left peck. But it had to be to cover the scar from my procedure on New Year's.

I had to get an ICD. Implantable cardiac defibrillator. The tattoo artist gave me a warning look when I asked for the tattoo over the scar. She voted against it and blabbed about something to do with the healing process but the extra hundred I slid in her hand did the job.

Harriet didn't give it another thought. After registering my new ink, she went back to the case in hand.

"That's my pillow," she demanded. I didn't budge. "That's my pillow," she repeated, stepping closer to the edge of the bed.

"And?"

"And give it back. There's like four others you can *sleep* with." She emphasized sleep, as if I wasn't going to fuck her senseless. What a joke.

"Come get it." I smirked. The wicked in my eye gleamed and she tried her best to hold back her grin but I saw the corners of her mouth twitch. She climbed in bed and sat on her knees next to me, pulling at the pillow. Still didn't budge.

And then my plan clicked into place. She rolled over and straddled me, taking her pillow from my head with ease and replacing it with another one. Softly putting it down on her side of the bed. When she started getting off, I gripped her thighs and stopped her in her stead.

"Maximus…" She looked down at me, her eyes were filled with lingering fury. *Oh please, I can feel your thighs clenching.*

She swatted at my hands but I wasn't giving out. Not happening. She gave up and crossed her arms over her chest and just gave me an annoyed look.

"Got a problem?" I asked, planning my next three moves in my head. I'd force her to succumb the way I did when I saw that photo. It still ingrained in my mind, sitting peacefully in my favorite place inside my head.

"You—"

I darted up and grabbed her jaw to kiss her neck but she dodged me and moved her pawn in our little game. She dodged my mouth and put her hands between us, pushing hard as she could as she slammed me into the mattress. I grinned, which just ticked her off more.

"You ditched me and think you get to just show up at my house and have your way?" She hissed. Her tone was defiant and pouty all at once. My dick hardened under the comforter, no doubt she was going to feel it in about three seconds.

She shifted her hips.

Yep.

Our faces were only inches apart but her eyes were solely on my lips. She wanted to devour them so bad but her stubborn streak forbade it. She wouldn't give in until her body betrayed her.

"Obviously." I coughed from under her hand. She was stronger than I remember, or maybe I was getting weaker.

"No." It was stern. Her mind meant it, but her hips were ever so slightly rolling over my cock beneath her. I narrowed my eyes at her and she started to ease up. *That was a mistake, Miss Harriet.*

Before she could get her bearings again, I grabbed her by the throat with both hands and flipped her over.

I forced myself between her thighs and nuzzled in tightly. My cock was full-blown erect and it was pressing against her thin shorts.

"No," she demanded again.

I smiled. "Yes."

"No!" She laughed, thrashing under me, but there was no use. She had the advantage when she was on top of me, but once prey is under predator, it's game over.

"No?" I softened my tone and ran my tongue over my teeth. If she was being serious, I didn't care. Her body was betraying her, one muscle at a time. Her eyes darted back and forth between my lips and my eyes with a smile and I knew right there. No meant yes.

"Say it again," I demanded. "Say no one more time."

Her legs wrapped around my waist and her hands softly stroked my hands still on her throat.

Her eyes went dark. The crazy in her was coming out to play. I wasn't a stranger to a little bit of darkness. I'd welcome it.

"You didn't speak to me for weeks." She snapped in my face.

"And what are you going to do about it?" I mocked her. There was confusion spread all over her face. She was furious about New Year's, but she wanted me so badly. It was a battle of the mind and pussy.

I leaned my neck down to her face. "Do it." I demanded. I had no idea what to expect but I was testing her waters.

The shock of the sting sent my brain for a spin. My neck snapped to the side and I rolled my neck on my shoulders, my hair fell over my eyes. *Mmmm...*

I didn't know she had that in her. She looked just as shocked at it as I was. Even she didn't think she had that slap in her. Angry drunk Harriet might be my favorite version.

As soon I came to reality, that was it.

I released her throat and pinned her wrists above her head with one hand, pulling at her silky shorts with the other. She moved her hips to help me and as soon as they were off, I was palming her breast under her shirt. My dick was painfully hard, not needing to guide it. I needed release.

One thrust was all it took for her to melt under my touch. Her body softened, her muscles relaxed.

I leaned down to her ear. "That's what I fucking thought."

She huffed under her breath. Trying not to show her wounded pride, she moved her head away from me. But it was no use. I could feel how bad she wanted it. Her shorts were soaked, her nipples were rocks. Her body couldn't have been further from her thoughts.

Even though she succumbed, she still wasn't going to get away with trying to deny me.

I flipped her over on her hands and knees and shoved her down on her stomach. Her hands curled in the sheets like she was begging for restrain. I thought I should remedy that.

"Handcuffs." I ordered, a hint of deviance in my voice. I fisted her hair and yanked her head back, demanding an answer.

"Drawer."

I held her down firmly and reached over to her side table, digging around in the drawer. I was pleasantly surprised to find they were made of metal rather than the plastic dinky ones from Halloween costumes. *Where did she get these?*

One by one I cuffed her wrists. Twisting the chain in the middle around my fist and balling her hair in my other.

Three, two... one.

I drove inside her with one hard launch. *Fuck, yes.* She tried to get one up on me, and before she faltered... it was working.

She let out a loud moan, and I pushed her head in the pillow. "I can't hear you. Speak up." I taunted.

I thrusted into her relentlessly. Never giving her a break. I knew how to edge myself so every time I felt my orgasm rim the edge, I pulled out and poked her asshole with my tip. She flinched every time, fear tensing her muscles when she thinks I'm going to plant myself in there.

Not yet.

I could see her back rising and falling quickly, knowing she wasn't getting enough oxygen from the pillow. Too bad.

I yanked the chain in my hands and lifted half her body off the bed, she inhaled with a loud gasp. Silently thanking God—me— for letting her breathe again.

Her knees were spread and she looked beautiful. Everything was bared to me and she was completely helpless. It was amazing. I pulled her head back and leaned forward in her ear.

"You're so pretty when you beg for air." I whispered in her ear before biting her earlobe. I nipped at her neck, her shoulders, her back. Leaving heavier marks than I normally would but I couldn't help myself. Her skin tasted so sweet. The feeling of her muscles tensing between my teeth made me feel powerful, primal even.

When she didn't say anything my anger grew. I let go of her hair and the chain in my fist. She fell face down into the pillow and shot up to her knees. When she tried to turn around to face me, I forced her back against her headboard.

"Fuck you," she snapped. It was the only thing she could get out between heaving for air and pleasure. I laughed at the torture. *Damn straight, bitch.*

"That's how you're going to talk to me?" I purred back.

I hoisted her up on her knees and drove into her from beneath. There was no way she was going to be treated like a princess after speaking that way to the one in control.

I reached around her dragging my hand up her groin, between her tits and to her throat. Her muscles released and contracted from my touch. I squeezed as hard as I could. Bitch won't even get a cough out if she fucking tried. My other hand went to town on her clit while I jackhammered her soaking pussy. She scratched at my hands, no doubt drawing blood but I didn't care. She'll regret speaking to me that way.

I twirled my fingers in a tight circle until I felt her hips buck and her thighs tighten around my wrist. She let out frustrated grunts, she was fighting her orgasm, refusing to succumb to me. Her defiance was not part of this plan.

My orgasm was building low in my stomach, begging to be released. I couldn't hold onto it much longer. This was just too fucking good. She always felt too fucking good.

But I had to fight, she *had* to go first. I needed to win this.

We moved in unison as she rolled her hips on my fingers and I continued to circle her clit. Finally I felt her pussy muscles clench around me. She started vibrating in my arms, letting out a frustrated laugh.

"Use your words, baby." I whispered in her ear.

She panted in my arms and curled her lips into a smile of defeat. I tightened my hold on her throat to stop her from breathing.

I let out an angry growl before allowing her enough room to speak for me. My fingers were still circling her clit and in no time at all she was pulsating around me again.

"I said use your words, bitch." I said sharply in her ear as she leaked into my hand.

The way her body was shaking sent small jolts of pride through my limbs. She took a few breaths, "Thank you..."

"Thank you..." I repeated, silently begging my release to wait.

"Thank you, sir." She panted softly. Her entire body fell limp in my arms.

Unable to hold myself back, I throbbed inside her and pulled out.

I slowly released her throat as she buckled over but I caught her, gently this time. I brought my fingers up to her mouth.

"God..." was all she could get out. I grinned in her neck. *You're welcome.*

"Suck them," I challenged.

She caught her breath. "What?"

"Taste yourself."

She didn't have much fight left in her so she obeyed. She needed to know what defeat tasted like.

I unlatched the cuffs and laid her down on her back gently. She was exhausted. Her orgasms took the life out of her.

Checkmate.

She rolled into her sheets and pulled them up to her face. "Maximus White..." she breathed.

Fuck after fuck, she keeps surprising me. I had no idea the depth of her potential until now. I gave her a soft smile and kissed her forehead, just to remind her. Her eyes were half-lidded as she gave me one last smirk before closing her eyes.

I went to the bathroom to clean myself up. When I closed the door I tried to catch myself on the sink but it was no use, my knees were weak.

I needed a minute. Maybe several minutes. That was a lot of exertion. Even my new scar was aching a bit.

You're okay. You're okay. You're okay. Breathe.

My body went limp as my knees caved beneath me. I grabbed toilet paper from my spot on the floor and wiped myself up. I'll just lay down for a minute to catch my breath.

"Oh my god!" I heard above me, and then a door slam. *Shit. Oops.*

I forced myself to my hands and knees, then my knees, one knee, hesitating on one leg, two legs, and I was up.

I opened the door to find her fast asleep. She was so beautiful when she slept. That naughty mouth of hers couldn't do any damage while it was dreaming. I got in beside her, sliding an arm underneath her head and pulling her into my chest.

"Checkmate." I whispered into her hair. She moved slightly, and I hissed when her cute nose brushed my tattoo.

I knew we were dreaming of the same thing.

Answers.

CHAPTER

23

Harriet

I woke to find his entire body curled around me. How can someone be so brutally gentle yet so painfully kind?

Carefully slinking out of his hold, I grabbed my shorts and tank from the floor and walked into the bathroom holding my head. It was pounding so hard, I was convinced it was going to explode. I ran through the course of events last night, remembering the fun I had with our neighbors.

Cade's stare stuck with me. It frustrated me.

Not nearly as much as when Maximus stormed through my front door demanding to fuck, regardless of giving me an insufficient answer as to why he left me hanging on New Year's. Let alone not speaking to me for two weeks. I planned on pinning him with questions about that eventually.

For now, Advil. Tylenol. Orange juice. Greasy breakfast.

I didn't even know what time it was, but the Saturday morning was already beautiful.

Not as beautiful as the sleeping boy laying naked in my bed just a few feet away. My body abandoned my mind last night. The moment he stepped in the front door I knew I wanted him but I was still determined to know the truth.

I balanced on the frame of my bathroom door and stared at him. So peaceful. So full of grace. His beauty was astounding. I often wondered what he dreamed about. Chocolate? Games? His future? A dream job? Endless pussy?

Me?

Sweat beamed across his forehead. Everything about him was so alluring you'd think he was a vampire. His skin bone white, his eyes dark blue, his hair messy, his angled jaw. I couldn't tell him how hot his tattoo got me, it was immaculately done and made him that more attractive. As if he needed that. He was nothing short of gorgeous. Any guy would kill to look like him.

How easily someone could fall for his charm, his voice, his secrets. Why did he pick someone so flimsy like me? *What did I have to offer?*

He tossed and turned in my sheets, mumbling something. He even talked in his sleep. I walked closer to him to see if I could make out what he was saying.

"Don't... don... can't... Won't di...die," he mumbled under his breath.

What? Don't, can't, won't die? What is he dreaming about?

"NO!" he yelped.

"Maximus? Maximus. Hey, hey, hey." I tried to soothe him quietly without startling him. I knew you weren't supposed to wake sleepwalkers, but what about nightmares? Just because he's been an asshole doesn't mean he didn't deserve his own peace of mind, especially some place such as sleep.

I sat down and wrapped my arms around the half of his body above the sheets. He jolted awake, immediately clutching my arms and folding himself into me. He was panting, unable to catch his breath for more than a minute.

Even for a nightmare he was heaving pretty heavily. Abnormally even. What was going on?

"Maximus? Hey, Maximus." I whispered. He peered up through the opening in our tangled limbs. I wasn't sure he could see me. Tears brimmed his eyes and his chin quivered. I'd never seen him like this before. What was happening inside his head?

"You—thank you," he choked out. He squeezed his eyes and his tears vanished.

"Are you okay?"

He didn't answer me. Just melted back in my arms. I held him tightly, hopefully conveying he wasn't alone.

"I got you," I whispered, not knowing if he fell back asleep or not. I didn't care. There was a vulnerable piece of his puzzle and I just became witness.

"Home" by Good Neighbours was softly playing around the kitchen while I cooked one of only things I can. Crepes!

Kim was still passed out for as far as I knew, Mia and Jane were prepping the table for breakfast, and Maximus was still lying comfortably in my bed.

The smell alone was keeping my hangover at bay. It was almost gone now that the drugs I took were kicking in. Didn't do much for the twang between my legs though. I pulled my bottom lip between my teeth at the thought of his fingers between my thighs. Heat stirred in my lower stomach and my thighs clenched at the stove. My muscles were really sore today.

Everything about last night was a lesson. The main one being there was something inside me that was either morally fucked up, or I was way kinkier than I believed myself to be. Maximus couldn't have handled it more perfectly, from positions, to his grip, everything was perfect.

Those orgasms sent my veins aflame. I was learning to love the mask.

I made fifteen crepes, hoping that would be enough. For me. Cream cheese, jam, syrup, Nutella, strawberries, bananas, and grapes were all set out on the table with the relative cutlery. It was the perfect morning. A delicious breakfast, my friends around the table, and a toe-curling man in my bed.

I heard the creak of the last few steps on the stairs and turned to find Maximus wobbling in the kitchen. Only it wasn't him. It was some guy with no shirt on, but a rocking set of abs. Plaid pajama pants sat low on his waistline, showing off the carved V poking out the top of the pants.

"Well, hello…" I lingered, itching for his name. "And who might you be?" I turned to my roommates. "One of yours?" I laughed at both of them.

"Mine," Mia smirked on the rim of her glass.

"Very nice, Mia." Jane applauded, staring at Ryan's graceful raven-toned appearance and vibrant smile.

"I'm standing right here," the guy said. "I'm Ryan."

"Nice to meet you, Ryan." Jane and I said in unison, watching his thoughts spin behind his deep brown eyes.

Maximus appeared from behind him and walked over to stand behind me. He wrapped his arms around my waist and dove his head in my neck landing a few soft kisses in the area between my ear and my shoulder.

"Good morning, Maximus." I said quietly so only he could hear.

"Morning, beautiful." He whispered on my skin. He picked up one of my crepes, shoving the whole thing in his mouth before I could protest. "Hey! Those are for everyone!" I barked at him happily.

He shrugged with a smile. "Oh well." His morning voice made my pussy clench. I parted my lips and gasped. After all these mornings, his voice still took me by surprise.

I rolled my eyes and went to work on replacing the crepe. He didn't stray far, but he turned and leaned against the counter while I worked, eyeing Ryan. He went back and forth between him and Mia.

Ryan, who stood very still in the center of the kitchen with no directive, eyed Maximus.

"I'm Ryan," he offered his hand. "You are?"

"No one."

Ryan just thinned his lips and gave a partial nod. I nudged Maximus in the ribs. *Play nice.* "Anyone know if Kim is awake?" Turning around they both stopped and stared at each other.

"What?"

"She's not here, actually." Jane tiptoed lightly around those words.

"Why not?"

"Cuz when she saw a naked man curled up in a ball on her bathroom floor she went to Riley's." She crossed her arms and cocked her eyebrow at Maximus. He didn't flinch.

Shit. Bathroom floor?

"Does she not know what university—"

I cut him off. "Bathroom floor? Why were you on the bathroom floor?"

"No reason. Just to catch my breath. I had a few drinks last night too, you know." He chuckled. He leaned down and kissed the top of my head before making his way to the table, careful not to sit in my seat at the end.

Mia walked over to me. "I think she was just shocked and probably wanted to give you privacy. No one knew he came over last night."

"That's because you disappeared on us last night." I pointed a fork at her, turning to laugh in Ryan's direction. "Now I know why."

"And you passed out drooling over the table." I snorted at Jane, who covered her face with her hands in embarrassment and chuckled.

We all bellowed in laughter. "Let's eat!"

CHAPTER

24

Maximus

Harriet grilled me the whole way back to my house about why I was on the bathroom floor but I just stuck to my story. I saw it in her eyes that she didn't believe me but I was grateful she let it go eventually.

I didn't bother to kiss her before I got out the car and I went inside. Dylan, Chase and Banks were spread out on the couches playing Fortnite, blasting Drake's latest hit album.

"Hey! The man is back!" Dylan cheered from the couch along the far wall. "So... how was it? You were in a rush to get to her last night."

"Woah woah. Not too much of a rush. I had to pre-game before I showed my face to her." I said, setting down my backpack and slumping into the spot beside him. They all knew I didn't follow through with our New Year's plan, but didn't know why. I scrunched my nose.

Our house was disgusting. The table was covered in crunched beer cans, old food wrappers, and multiple dirty bongs. It was like a tornado blew through this place one night after another. It was nice being in her house. They always had the dishes done, tables wiped, everything was in order.

"But it was good. She didn't press me too long about New Year's. Didn't really give her a chance." I smirked, stealing an unopened bottle of water from the case on the floor. "You know who walked in this morning though?"

"Who?" Banks focused his eyes on me. There was a bunch of people it could've been, all that hate us for the shit we pulled in first year.

"Ryan."

"No..." Chase gasped. "No fucking way, did he recognize you?"

"Surprisingly, no." And thank fuck for that. He didn't need to remember I beat the shit out of his roommate for absolutely no reason. I was having a tough week, I had a bad doctors appointment, and it was my brother's birthday but that wasn't a reason to break a guy's face. He simply just looked at me the wrong way, and I snapped. I beat the shit out of him so badly, Banks thought I was going to kill him. It was an unfair advantage, I stood six-foot-four, and he was lucky if he was five-ten.

"Oh shit. You're lucky." Dylan resumed the game but gave me a lucky nod.

Guilt coursed through me. "I know." He didn't deserve that. He wasn't the one who told me the remainder of my lifespan. Or the ghost of February fifth. He just happened to be in the wrong place at the wrong time... giving me the wrong look.

Turns out, I fucked his girlfriend. Before she was his girlfriend. Still, he didn't like me around her. *Fair enough. That girl begged for it.*

"Alright, it's *League of Legends* time for me, boys. Banks, kick their asses."

They all moaned in protest, they much preferred me staying out here and playing their game, but my friends were waiting for me online.

"I'll leave my door open!" I laughed as Chase tried to grab my legs to keep me in the living room.

"I promise!" I laughed again. I could see the main area of the living room from my desk chair. It was the perfect set up.

I closed my door and they all yelled at me thinking I was full of shit.

"I'm changing! Jesus!" I yelled back, yanking off my pants, shirt, and finally boxers. I lifted my arms.

"Oof." I gagged. "I need a shower, actually." I grabbed the towel from the back of my door and wrapped it around my waist.

"Is anyone in the shower?" I asked, opening the door a crack.

"No, you're good. We're out of shampoo though."

Of course you are. I, however, have my own I keep hidden in my closet.

The stairs creaked under my feet as I skipped two at a time. I needed some serious burning sensation right now. Harriet was starting to get comfortable enough to question my actions. It was becoming a fucking problem.

Lying to her had become increasingly more difficult, strictly because I was starting to feel bad. I didn't want to lie to her, but I couldn't tell her.

I stepped into the shower and immediately winced at the boiling droplets hitting my back. My hands stung from where Harriet ripped her nails. I couldn't help the smile.

She was getting feistier and feistier. It was so sexy. Thinking about her slap got me hard, relieving myself in a few short strokes. I closed my eyes and all I could see behind them was her. Her tits. Her beautiful little ass and that gorgeous smile. Her eyes come off so innocent, no one would know she's becoming my sex demon.

I sat down and hung my head between my knees, taking a few deep breaths to calm my nerves and remind myself I woke up today. That was a good start.

Knock, knock, creak!

"Hey, you okay, buddy?" Banks opened the door a crack.

Right, no lock up here.

"Yeah, I'm good, thanks man." I appreciated his friendship. I had no one like him. He was a hard son of a bitch, but when Banks decided he gave a fuck about you, good luck getting rid of him.

I must've dissociated because when the water ran cold it felt like I had been woken up. I turned the knob of the shower and stepped out onto the makeshift mat on the floor.

Wiped down my face, my arms, my legs with the towel, and wrapped my lower half in it. I moved my hand over the fogged mirror and saw exactly what I felt.

Exhaustion stared back at me while expiry loomed over me like a cloud. At least I was pink in the face—looked alive—thanks to the burning water.

It was nice to look alive considering that's the last thing I felt. I ran my hand over my tattoo and lowered my head. I couldn't feel it or see it, but knowing it was there, my muscles slowly growing through it like vines on a house. It was a weird feeling.

The steps creaked under me again and when I turned the corner in the hallway all the guys turned to look at me.

"Yo, you good, bro?" Chase asked, his eyes were wide and his mouth was slightly hanging open. They had paused the game when they heard me coming.

"Yeah…why?" They all looked at each other. What?

"You were in there for over an hour."

What?

"I didn't even realize. Yeah, I just needed a good wash. I smelt like—" I coughed and gave a slimy smile. They knew what I meant. They all chuckled and gave me an approving nod.

I smelled like sex.

CHAPTER

25

Harriet

I needed to have a conversation with Kim.

Knock, knock.

"Hey... just wanted to apologize for the tall ball of skin and bones you walked in on in the bathroom last Friday. I still haven't gotten a straight answer as to why he did that." I spoke kindly.

Kim peered up from her computer and turned her chair to look at me. I was leaning against our bathroom doorframe.

"It was a jumpscare, that's for sure." She chuckled lightly. "It's okay. What time did he come over? I could've sworn Tori and them were here until like midnight."

"He just showed up on our porch as they were leaving. I didn't even check the time." I answered, rubbing my eyebrows together.

"Why?" She seemed genuinely curious.

"Long story short?" I huffed a breath and made my way to sit on the edge of her bed. Her bed was in the far corner of her bedroom with her desk at the foot under the window. Her closet was on the same wall as our bathroom and she had a champagne candle lit.

"Yes, please. What happened?" She turned back toward her computer, I knew she could multitask.

When I got back to school, the only thing I told them was Maximus hadn't talked to me in a couple of weeks. The rest I kept to myself, mainly out of confusion.

"So..." I began. *Where do I start?* "I met his family on Christmas break—"

"YOU WHAT?!" She immediately spun on her chair to face me again, eyes wide.

"I know, right? Super weird but I actually had a lot of fun with them."

"Okay..."

"Not only did I meet his family, but I also joined them for Christmas dinner and slept over. My mom was with her boyfriend, my dad was away and my siblings have their own families so pretty much I was alone on Christmas past three o'clock. I was just painting and talking to Ruby when he texted me."

She looked down at her hands in her lap, she knew my life had changed. Before she would join me after Christmas dinner to come party with me and forty of my family members.

Now I somehow ended up alone.

She muttered *oh my god* under her breath while I continued, "One thing led to another and his dad asked me what I was doing for New Year's."

"What did you say? What did Max say?"

"Honestly, he looked like he was going to shit his pants. His face was white, and it was the first time I'd seen him lost for words. I eventually said I would see what my mom was doing, but if she had plans, I would join them."

"Okay so his *father* invited you to New Year's, not even him. That's interesting. Sounds like you made quite the impression. Shocking." She made fun of me. I rolled my eyes and smiled at her. *Yeah, yeah.*

She continued. "So how was New Year's then?"

"That's the thing. He stood me up. No text, no call. Nothing. I didn't hear from him until he showed up on our porch on Friday night after I sent that photo."

She started to say something, but I cut her off. "Do you think it's because his dad invited me and he was blindsided?" I rose from her bed and started pacing her room. My mind was going a mile a minute.

"Like yes I can see he was blindsided but does that really warrant no texting and completely ghosting you for two weeks?" She had a good point. That wasn't a good enough reason for him to practically ignore me.

"Men can't communicate," she continued softly. "Maybe you should just confront him about it. Sometimes they don't even know things until it hits them smack dab in the middle of their forehead. They're stupid like that." She laughed. She was right.

"I did! All he told me was that he spent it with his family. I guess he lost track of time?" It was a question I knew she couldn't answer, I was thinking out loud at this point. "Ugh! Why do I care this much?"

"Because he's a puzzle and you like figuring things out." She raised a brunette brow at me.

I threw my hands up in the air and let out a grunt while I fell back on her bed. She leaned on my knees and offered me a devilish expression.

"What?" I sat up on my elbows, studying her face to see what she was thinking.

"You know what would help?" She wiggled my knees and offered a playful tone.

"Let me guess—" I started.

"A party." We both said in unison. She continued, "Ben is having another party at his house tonight and I think we should go! Let off some steam, get him out of that pretty little head of yours and get absolutely gobsmacking drunk."

I sighed, "I could be convinced."

———◈◈———

I got convinced. The seven of us walked into Ben's house. Mia, Kim, Jane, and I in the first cab and Tori, Lori, and Cade were behind us getting out of the other.

"Drink?" Jane grabbed Kim's hand and started walking. Mia grabbed mine and we formed a conga line all the way into the kitchen where drinks were laid out. We lost Lori, Tori, and Cade to the chaos but we were confident we were all going home together when the time came.

CHAPTER

26

Maximus

I was on my last round of beer pong when I watched her walk into the party. God, she was breathtaking. She was wearing a short black skirt and a black low-cut top that annunciated her breasts perfectly, I could see her nipple piercings through the fabric. I couldn't help but feel the growl forming at the back of my throat. I wanted to bite them until she screamed.

I sunk the last ball and Ben high-fived me before setting up the cups for the next couple to play us.

"Hey, can I play with you next?" A familiar voice that made my stomach scream pulled my attention.

She was here. How was that possible? Last time I saw her was New Year's. *This can't be happening.*

"Nicole." I was stunned. I looked around for Ben, my actual partner, but he was nowhere to be found. *Shit.*

"Yes, Maximus?" She batted her eyelashes at me and brushed her hair over her shoulder.

"Max." I corrected. "What are you doing here?" I was stern and I didn't need to look at her to notice she was pouting beside me. I did not want to play with her. I did not want to even be seen with her, not with Harriet walking around this house.

Then she stepped up to the table. With the guy who opened the door at her house. My chuckle was sinister as I made eye contact with her. She was slouched on one hip with a drink in her hand. She was eye-fucking me and when her gaze switched to Nicole who was now clutching my arm, her expression hardened. *Shit. Shit. Shit.*

"Well, are we going to play or what?!" Nicole's annoying voice echoed in my ear. I never took my eyes off Harriet, and she me.

"Oh, we're going to play alright." Harriet's voice was sly as she picked up the first ball. Nicole reached for the ball on our side of the table, but I snatched it first. No way was I letting her do eye-to-eye with Harriet when it was clear I was the one she was challenging.

Cade bent down, whispering something in her ear, she smiled and laughed, turning toward him to whisper something back. I couldn't hear it over the music but I had a feeling it was only going to make my blood boil faster. I fucking hated the way he looked at her. I could sense him salivating from across the table.

She looked back at me and then to Nicole, I knew she was not liking my partner being so attached to my arm. She was shaking with jealous rage but it made my smile widen. I'll win this game and happily deal with her attitude later.

She counted down to three, and we shot our balls. Neither of them sunk. Nicole and Cade head off and his ball sunk. Harriet shot first and sunk a cup. I took a shot out of the bottle of Jamieson I was holding. Cade sunk another, and Nicole took a swig out of her cooler.

"Damn, they got balls back. I thought you were supposed to be good at this game?" She squeaked beside me.

"I am." I gritted back through my teeth, not taking my eyes off Harriet.

Harriet sunk another ball but Cade missed his second shot. He turned to apologize and put his hands on both her arms. My teeth were grinding together. I thought my skin was going to catch fire. I was about to leap across the table before Nicole put her hand on mine trying to guide my swing.

"I got it." I said sharply, this girl was really getting on my nerves.

I shot my ball and finally sunk one. But before Nicole could shoot hers, I grabbed it from her hand and sunk it as well. She scoffed at me but I paid no attention to her pouty face. I couldn't deny she was attractive, but she wasn't the magnet I was looking for.

My magnet across the table took two shots out of a tequila bottle she must've found in the kitchen and kept her glare on me. She was not pleased about Nicole's presence. Something I would have to lie about later.

The game continued until we each had one final cup. Nicole took her shot and missed, Cade took his shot and missed. Harriet stepped up to the table and Cade moved to stand behind her. Way too fucking close. He leaned down and whispered something else in her hair. *Is he dense?*

I physically moved Nicole out of my fucking way and stepped up to eye Harriet. She pulled her top down an inch and squatted down so her tits and her eyes were staring at me over the tops of the cups. She was trying to distract me, it wasn't going to work.

"Aw... is *sir* not confident he can make the shot?" She mocked.

"*Sir?*" Nicole squished her eyebrows together and made a face that made me want to scream in her face. "Mind your own fucking business." I growled at her. She backed off immediately but still wouldn't walk away. Have I not made myself clear?

Harriet and I weren't shy around our roommates, but we weren't like... "out". Not many people knew we were fucking, but they were about to find out if she keeps testing me like this.

The tension to bend her over this table was building in my jeans.

I focused only on the cup, but I could see her breasts in my peripheral. I shot and sunk it. *Yes.*

Then she shot and sunk it too. *Shit. Redemption.*

She squatted lower so it was only her eyes staring at me now and when I shot it, I missed. *Fuck.* She laughed and Cade threw his hands up in the air in victory. *Not yet, douchebag.*

She shot the ball and it sunk right into the cup with an easy splash. Damn. She actually won against me. Cade cheered and picked her up, spinning her in a tight circle. I wanted to drag his ass outside by the neck.

Harriet gave me a wicked grin, pulling her bottom lip between her teeth. Nicole put her arm around my waist and Harriet's expression went sour. I yanked Nicole's arm off me when Harriet made her way around, staring at me while she dragged the tip of her finger across the table.

She stopped to my right and glanced at Nicole on my left. She tilted her head and narrowed her eyes. "Hi." Her tone was plastic but Nicole was dumb enough not to notice.

"Hi, I'm Nicole." Her voice was screechy and Harriet chuckled at it. This conversation was about get really bad if Harriet pushes.

"How do you guys know each other?" Nicole asked politely. *Well, fuck.*

"We met at a party I had at my house. We've been friends ever since, what about you two?" She responded. *Friends.* I scoffed, jumping in now, I couldn't have Harriet hearing that answer. "Let's get out of here. Want to go home?"

"No."

"I'd love to."

They both answered and Harriet's eyebrows raised as she looked between us. This just got really bad. Harriet crossed her arms over her chest.

"I'm sorry, how do you guys know each other again?"

"Harriet please, let's go." I pleaded with her, turning my back to Nicole.

"No."

"We met on New Year's. I guess he didn't know I was also a student here."

SHIT. FUCK. SHIT FUCK. Harriet's eyes widened and immediately her face fell. This was not panning out well for me and I had no idea how I was going to get myself out of it.

"Wooowwwwww..." was all she could manage before she turned on her heels and started walking away. She didn't get far before I grabbed her arm and turned her toward me. "Harriet, please. Let's go home."

"Not a fucking chance." And she ripped out of my grip. She rushed over to Cade and pulled him toward the kitchen. I began reaching for her again when Nicole got between.

"What the fuck is the matter with you?" I snapped.

"That's her, isn't it? The girl you were telling me about in the hospital. That's the girl you were trying to see on New Year's."

My jaw clenched. "I don't know what you're talking about." I turned to walk away but she spun me around again.

"I'm sorry. I was just messing with you—"

"Well, don't. You don't know what you're playing at. Stay out of it, and stay the hell away from my girl." I snapped. It came out worse than I meant it. Maybe.

"Jesus, okay. But you should tell her." She bit back.

"Tell her what?" What could I possibly have to tell Harriet that wouldn't hurt her?

"The reason you missed New Year's, and the fact that you're crazy about her."

I leaned down to her eye level and slid my hands into my pockets.

"Keep. Your. Fucking. Mouth. Shut." I couldn't make an enemy out of this girl, but my temper was getting in my way. She might have overheard the doctors while I was unconscious. I shook away my anger. "Please."

"Fine. But she deserves to know. Both things." She sounded smarter in that sentence. She waddled away and went to annoy another group of guys standing by the front door.

More people were coming through the door as I lowered into my seat on the couch, Jamieson clutched in my hand. My knuckles were turning white around the neck of the bottle and my legs were slouched. I took a hefty chug from my drink before setting it between my legs and leaning forward to put my head between my hands. I couldn't think straight.

I couldn't decide which was worse, the lie I was going to tell Harriet about Nicole or if Harriet found out the truth to New Year's.

She was a student nurse at the hospital I was taken to in my hometown, Moore. Almost three hours from our school. I never thought it was a possibility she was a student at Greenlake.

She wasn't working my case but came to sit by my bed when the doctors were running their tests and my family was getting coffee. We talked for a while, I confided in her about Harriet and how much I wished things could be different. She didn't know about my disease directly but she had every liberty to find out. Overall, she knew where I was on New Year's.

Now she was here.

And she threatened everything I had with Harriet.

CHAPTER

27

Maximus

I was so over this party. I rose off the couch and started walking around looking for my roommates. I found Banks making out with some girl in the bathroom, Dylan was playing flip cup, and Chase was talking on the phone by the staircase. One by one, I grabbed them all to drag them outside. We were pretty hammered, but I couldn't notice over the constant angst I was feeling surrounding Harriet and Nicole.

I got them outside before sending off one last glance toward Harriet dancing in the middle of the living room. She made eye contact with me and stopped dancing. Her face dropped and she looked like she was about to say something when Cade appeared next to her with yet another drink.

"I'll be right out. Call that cab." I couldn't help myself. I stormed back in the house and headed straight for them. Maybe I was drunk. I'd had enough of his antics. He wasn't going home with Harriet—well, upstairs—if I had anything to do with it.

I made my way to the middle of the dance floor and reached for Harriet's arm. She looked up at me with narrowed eyes, they were angry now.

"Come home with me. Now," I demanded.

"Don't you have your hands full? There can't possibly be enough room in your bed for all three of us." She snapped. I knew she had enough to drink but her words were sharp with ice. "Let's go, now."

"Hey, she said no, dude." Cade stuck his arm out. *Oh no, no, no, no, no. You do not want to get in my way right now—dude.*

I glared at him and stepped up closer when I pulled Harriet behind me. The people around us quieted and stepped back. They were expecting a fight and if this guy was going to push more of my buttons, they were going to get one.

"She's drunk. She's coming home with me." I bit, he was almost my height so I'll give him that. I may be skinny, I may be sick, but no one comes between me and her. *No one.*

"I think," he rubbed his chin. "I think she lives closer to me, so maybe she should actually come home with *me.*" He tilted his head slightly and clasped his fists in front of him, he was showing off.

For my Harriet.

I got right in his face, inches between our noses. "No."

I turned around to a wobbling Harriet, I slid my hand around her waist to stabilize her.

She mumbled something about her roommates and I looked around for them. They were huddled together on the couch, staring at Mia's phone in the middle. "If I get them home safely, will you come with me now?"

She was looking out for her roommates, and honestly after a few movie nights and that breakfast we all had, I liked them too. They came as a pack and they would leave as a pack. That much I knew about girls.

She nodded slightly, and I turned back to walk toward them but Cade stepped in my path. "Do we have an issue here, Cade?" I glared at him. I didn't want to fight this *dude* in the middle of my friend's party but he was starting to go a bit unchecked.

"Not if you listen to her," he said as he gestured to Harriet still wobbling further behind me. "You can't just boss her around. If she wants to stay, she's going to stay."

"That's not what she told me." I stood firm.

"Guys, enough. It's late anyway, we can go now." She appeared below us and turned back to me. "But I'm not going home with you," she slurred. "I'm not even sure if I'm allowed to be mad at yo...you. But I am."

Technically, she wasn't allowed to be mad because we were only fucking, but I felt bad enough like we weren't. Her being mad meant she cared. I liked that.

I didn't exactly wrong her, she just doesn't know the whole story. I still wasn't sure what I was going to let her believe. She thinks I fucked Nicole. If this were first year, I definitely would lie to one girl so I could fuck another.

But something changed when I met Harriet.

Cade and I stared at each other for another minute, contemplating Harriet's words. *Fuck this.* I shook my head and turned to walk away but now it was Harriet in my path. This one I welcomed. She didn't say anything, just stared at me with her glossy eyes.

"Just get home safely." I kissed the top of her head quickly and walked out the door into the cab where my friends were waiting for me.

We got home and the guys went straight to their rooms. I brought each of them a glass of water and an Advil tablet for the morning. The usual stairs creaked under my footsteps. When I reached the bottom, I saw a shadow standing at the door.

I opened the door and there she was. Just standing on my front porch with her arms on either side of the frame to stabilize herself.

"Were you not going to knock?" I made sure to keep my voice low. Not that I would wake the guys, but I didn't want to scare away the baby bird standing in my doorway.

"You were with her on New Year's." Her voice was hard. Scary bird.

"Harriet—"

"You were with *her* on New Year's!" She snapped her head up and pushed off the doorframe to get in my face. Those big, beautiful blue eyes filled with green jealousy.

"You were with—" I stopped her in her tracks by grabbing her face and kissing her. It was the only thing I could think of to give myself enough time to think about what to say. She pushed off my chest as I quickly closed the door behind her.

"I'm leaving." She barked but I put my hands on the door and caged her in. "No, you're not." We were nose to nose and I could smell the tequila on her breath. She wasn't going anywhere, even if I had to throw her over my shoulder and strap her to my bed myself. Her defiance was already turning me on so when I thought about her tied up on my bed my dick was full-blown erect.

"Explain." Was all she could squeak out of that dirty little mouth of hers.

"Would you believe me if I told you nothing happened with Nicole?"

"No."

"Then what's the point of explaining?"

She didn't bother to answer that. "You ghosted me for weeks! You bailed on New Year's! You—" She pounded her fists on my chest but I didn't budge, regardless of how much it jostled my ribs, sending heavy shocks of pain through my chest. I deserved this.

I'd let her get her anger out and then make her tea. I learned that about her over the last couple of months. All she needed was tea to settle her nerves and it instantly made her feel better.

"I know. I'm so sorry." I spoke quickly, hoping the chest pain I was feeling wouldn't show in my words. "If you want the full story, we can talk about it in the morning."

She turned to jiggle the door handle but I wasn't letting it open.

"Like I said. You're not leaving."

Before she could protest, I dropped to her thighs and threw her over my shoulder. She started pawing at my back and yelling to put her down but I wasn't listening.

My cock was still hard so I knew what my next move was. I kicked open my bedroom door and tossed Harriet's thrashing body on my bed. She got out one breath before I was strapping her wrists and ankles to the frame.

I took off my shirt and climbed on the bed. I straddled her rib cage and leaned down to her face, grabbing her by the jaw. "Are you done?"

She immediately stopped thrashing to spit in my face.

CHAPTER

28

Harriet

His laugh echoed through my skull.

He gave me that wicked grin and licked my saliva off his lips. His erection was poking me and my pussy immediately started clenching under his weight.

I was so mad at him when I learned about Nicole. Did I believe he didn't fuck her? I wasn't sure. The only thing clouding my brain now was the fact that I needed him. If he reached down and under, he was going to find out just how bad.

My jaw was locked in his grip. Despite my attempts to buck him off, my energy was draining. He was taking all of it. He was patiently waiting for me to tire myself out before he could have his way with me.

And if the heat in my lower stomach were to attest to that, I was going to let him.

I closed my eyes to collect myself. He lightly tapped my cheek with his hand.

"Look at me, Hare."

Hare.

I opened my eyes. His entire demeanor shifted and his face softened. I needed this whole situation to change before the tequila leaves my system and I see my actions from a sober perspective. Finally, I spoke, feeling the Velcro against my skin.

"Are we fucking?"

"No."

"No?!" I repeated. *Oh you have got to be kidding*. "Fine," I snapped. "I believe you. You did not stick your pretty little dick in another bitch." I tilted my head at him, my voice dripping with sarcasm.

He only heard one part of that sentence. "Excuse me? Did you just call me little?"

"I also called you pretty. Did you hear that?" I snapped.

He rolled his eyes and relaxed his shoulders as I began to struggle against his restraints. "Hare..."

I was frustrated now. "Get me out of these." I demanded. He didn't move, "Hare, you're drunk and as much as I would love to use that to my advantage, you're upset with me, rightfully so, but not in the fun way."

He was right. I was drunk, and not in the cute, fun way. More like the jealous, enraged way. I should probably leave.

"I did not sleep with Nicole." He didn't blink. I grunted in response, fighting a silent war between anger and arousal.

"Do you need me to say it again?" He asked softly, tilting his head. "I need you to get me out of these restraints," I demanded again. Again, he ignored me.

He took a deep breath before continuing, "Hare. I did not fuck Nicole. I promise." I could hear the sincerity in his voice, but that was the only thing he was saying. I got nothing else. No explanation.

"Hare?" Was that concern I hear?

I just stared at him. *I want out.*

"Fine. I'll just keeping saying it until you believe me." He started. Real slow, he repeated himself. "I did not fuck that girl."

He trailed his fingers over my neck, sending shivers down my spine as he kissed me between his words.

"I…did…not…fuck…Nicole…" he whispered, finalizing his tease with a bite at the bottom of my throat.

I rolled my eyes, the silent war raging on. I jerked my chin toward the restraints and gave him a look. He untied my wrists. *Thank you.*

Quietly, he got off me but stumbled off the bed, suddenly winded. He started coughing and clutching his chest while fumbling at the straps around my ankles.

"I got it, I got it." I said, untying the straps. The heat in my stomach quickly turned to ice. For a brief moment, I thought he was having a panic attack but then it stopped. He refused to look me in the eye as I followed his movements around the room.

"Maximus? What was—" I began. He interrupted me, avoiding my question entirely.

"Do you believe me?" He inhaled, catching his breath.

"Yes but you were with her when you were supposed to be with me." I didn't stutter.

He opened his mouth to speak, but closed it again.

I'm confused. What just happened?

"Okay…I'm gonna go to sleep now." I said quietly, the tequila draining from my body and eyes half-lidded, half-confused. He nodded. He could tell me the rest tomorrow.

For whatever reason, he was adamant on making me believe his innocence. He convinced me for now, but it was fun to watch him squirm.

I knew I wasn't supposed to care if he fucked other women, but there was no hiding it now.

I showed up unannounced.

CHAPTER

29

Harriet

When I woke, I rolled over to find him gone and a mug filled with steaming hot earl grey, beside it was a little note.

Please stay. I will be back soon. MW XO.

It was 10:15 a.m. on the Saturday after the party. The party where Cade was all over me like a dirty shirt and I hadn't minded. Not since I saw Nicole standing beside Maximus with those fuck-me eyes and beautiful long brown hair and brown eyes. She was gorgeous and it made my stomach do somersaults. So when Cade happened to get a little too close, I allowed it. Gave Maximus a taste of his own medicine.

Although I could tell from his demeanor that he was having no part of her existence. It really did bring me joy, but I kept wondering why. She was gorgeous. Even if it was just to fuck, why did he seem so disinterested?

Then I learned how they met. New Year's. The night we were supposed to spend together with his family. Not only did he ditch me, he ghosted me for weeks afterward until randomly showing up on my front porch after I sent him a risqué photo.

Even with the alcohol slowly leaving my system, I still wasn't sure if I fully believed him. He was persuasive, but even then my suspicion was there. *I didn't fuck Nicole. I promise,* echoed in my head. If he didn't fuck Nicole what the hell was he doing with her? Arts and crafts?

That made my blood boil more. A quick fix is one thing, each party is there for one reason and one reason only. One and done. Fuck and chuck.

Talking seemed more intimate, more permanent. I hated that I felt like this. He wasn't supposed to mean anything after our own one-night stand. I wasn't supposed to care.

But I do. I care so much.

I sat up, my hangover was not nearly as bad as last time. The time I made breakfast for all of us. I swung my legs over his bed, feeling woozy and having to lay back down. Maybe it was just as bad. The anxiety wasn't helping. I reached for my tea and took a sip. It was singeing hot, just how I like it.

I read the note again and sighed, putting my head between my hands and closing my eyes. I felt guilty his erection went untouched, regardless of it being his own damn fault. That's what our relationship's purpose was. To get each other off. We hadn't fulfilled our duties last night. Instead, I cabbed over to his house like a scorned desperate housewife practically demanding to be the chosen one.

The thing is, he didn't seem to mind.

———⬧⬧⬧———

I decided to stay and wait for him. I needed to know the truth. Fifteen minutes passed and he came through his bedroom door with another tea and a breakfast that smelled delicious. His face lit up when he saw me still curled in his blankets.

"You're still here!" He set down a breakfast tray across from my lap. I hesitated to sit up but caved anyway.

Crepes. He recreated the breakfast I made last week. Little ceramic bowls of Nutella, bananas, strawberries, and grapes were dispersed around the tray. A bucket of cream cheese and a jam jar sat on the side of the white plate that held about five crepes.

Along with a little mason jar filled with purple and yellow flowers.

"Maximus..." I mumbled to myself, I had no words for him. "This is lovely. Thank you." He just gleamed at me with sorry eyes and a big smile. He felt like he was walking on eggshells. One short breath and thought he would blow me away. I wasn't going anywhere, not after this. This was just too cute to pass up. I settled in my blanket and picked up a crepe, spreading cream cheese and jam all over it before shoving it in my mouth.

It tasted like ass. But I wasn't going to tell him that, it would break his little heart and I didn't want to do that after this display of undeniable effort. I smiled and made a *mmmm* sound with my mouth before chewing on some grapes. Crepes was not his forte.

"Are they good? I think I fucked up the recipe." He winced, closing one eye waiting for my response. "How could you possibly fuck up *instructions*?" I laughed at him. He definitely figured out how, they tasted like wet sand. "They taste delicious. Thank you."

One by one I ate the crepes and started feeling better. My hangover wasn't as bad as it could be but it disappeared after I ate the second crepe. He shoved one in his mouth and gasped, spitting it back out on the plate.

"Oh my god, these taste like dog shit!" He burst out in laughter. "I can't believe you told me these were good! Just eat the fruit."

"It's not the food that's delicious." I smirked at him, trying to wash down the cement left from the crepe. He looked up at me and smirked back. My breath caught when he dipped his finger into the cream cheese and spread it on my lips with his thumb.

Frozen in my spot, he leaned over the tray and licked it clean from my lips. He kissed me gently and mumbled something about how good I tasted. I couldn't focus on his words when his tongue ran over my lips.

"What was that for?" I licked my lips, the taste of remaining cream cheese and Maximus's lips filled my mouth. It was heaven. I loved cream cheese probably a little too much. I thought it went with everything. Crepes, waffles, pancakes, bagels, toast... the list goes on. And don't even get me started on jam.

"Just because," He shrugged. "You looked like you'd taste good with cream on your lips." The corners of his lips curled when he spoke.

I reached for his hand and pulled it in my lap, tracing my fingers over the wrinkles in his knuckles and kissing them gently. Time to confront the elephant in the room.

"Maximus, what happened on New Year's?" My voice was soft, my eyes were on our hands. I wanted an explanation. I wanted the truth. Even if it hurt, I wouldn't let it.

With a cough, he hesitated. He squeezed the hand in my lap and tugged on my chin with the other, forcing me to look him in the eye.

"Harriet... I did spend time with my family on New Year's, but it was at the hospital in Moore."

My eyes narrowed, what hospital? "Hospital? What happened?" Nicole was the last thought on my mind now. What happened with his family?

"We—I—my grandpa collapsed. There was a lot of chaos and I just couldn't find the time to let you know. Nicole was there, she's a student nurse. She wasn't working his case, but she came and sat with me while we were waiting for the tests."

I immediately felt like an idiot. *Ugh, why did I have to make everything a big deal?* This was a perfectly reasonable explanation for why he didn't reach out.

"And the two weeks afterward?" I tried to sound as plain as I could but empathy slipped through the cracks in my words. "I was taking care of him, and my guilt for ditching you was eating away at me so I avoided it. Until I just showed up on your doorstep."

"After I sent you a naked photo." I crossed my arms over my chest. This part sounded fishy.

He threw his hands up in surrender. "I swear that was a coincidence. I was going to come knocking at your doorstep to apologize either way, but I loooooved the photo." He leaned forward but I backed away.

"Uh huh."

He stayed right in my face, he wasn't backing down until he got a kiss, so I kissed his cheek. A comfortable compromise. He saw the sass in my eyes and gently wrapped his hand around my throat.

"What kind of shitty kiss was that? Try again." he demanded. He sounded playful but the sternness in his voice told me he was serious. I planted a doozy on his lips before pushing him back into his spot on the bed. I gave him a light chuckle and a slight shrug to ease him.

"I'm sorry about your grandpa. Is he okay now?" I asked cautiously. He gave me a nod and put the breakfast tray between us onto his desk a few feet away. He seemed to have relaxed a significant amount which caused for alarm but if his grandpa had a health scare, I could understand the tension.

Now that we were both at ease, his next words almost sent me into another dimension. "I'll fuck you now."

I laughed at him but shook my head. "Too late. I gotta go, actually."

I needed to catch up on my lecture notes from the second week of class. I hadn't done much other than my assignments that were due, the actual lecture notes I often forgot to do.

"I need to go to the library and do my notes from my classes this week. But maybe you'll get lucky tonight if you have space in your *availability*." I started to get off the bed, but he pushed me back down and got on top of me. "Last chance." His knee was pressed between my legs and his hands were in my hair. His dark blue eyes were staring into my soul and my thighs started to pinch again. I hated the power he had over my body. Any whiff of him and my common sense became not so common.

I whispered in his mouth, "I need to study." I gave him a light kiss and used all my force to buck him off me. Not sure if he let me or if I actually got the one up on him this time, but he went flying to the side and flopped down on his bed again.

I gathered my belongings and stuffed them into my pockets. I came here with nothing so I got redressed in last night's clothes but kept my thong in my pocket. Wearing a day old thong just didn't sit right with me. I'd rather go commando than feel old fabric against my skin. I made my way to the front of the house and slid my shoes on. When I reached for the door, I heard a shuffling behind me.

"What are you doing?" My eyebrow raised and my hand hesitated on the handle.

"I'm coming with you." No...

"No, you're not, I'm going to study."

"Me too. We can be study buddies." He slung his black backpack over his right shoulder and started walking toward me.

"Maximus, you are quite literally the most distracting thing to me on this entire campus. You cannot possibly think you coming with me is a good idea!" I half-laughed, half-shouted.

He had no part of that. He wrapped his arms around me and lifted me up on my toes. "I'm. Coming. With. You." He kissed between words. "Besides, how fun would it be to play footsies under the table then fuck in the bathroom?" He headbutted me. I rolled my eyes and turned for the door again.

"Fine. But I need to go home first, I smell like old tequila and... wet sand..." I laughed to myself. I walked out, down the steps and headed for the street. I obviously didn't drive here so I guess I was walking home.

He ran after me down the steps of his house. "What do you mean wet sand?"

CHAPTER

30

Harriet

Somehow I convinced him to sit at another table of the library while I worked. I couldn't have any distractions. My Embalming Theory and Procedures class was an important class for my career as a mortician, funeral director, and coroner.

I sipped my coffee and took my notes on the process for embalming a cadaver. How to drain their blood, where to place the tube for the embalming fluid they call formaldehyde. A chemical that has a very distinctive scent often found in the bowels of morgues. A place I can't wait to hide in.

I've always been consumed with the idea of death. A lot of people thought me weird for such a thing, but someone has to do it right? I tell people they just happen to know someone who is willing to do the job. I've been called morbid, crazy, disturbed, all the names you can think of, but they never bothered me. If anything, they made me feel different. Not someone who was going to fall into a mind-numbing-nine-to-five desk job that has them wishing for exactly that, death. Going home to my basic apartment with a boring husband and a child that doesn't feel loved by me because I couldn't love myself enough to pursue my dream job.

Luckily enough, I was given the opportunity to study my dream job. The thought of a boring job for the rest of my life was distant. The husband however... I would have to work on that. Finding someone who can keep the spark *and* the butterflies going for the next sixty years would be tricky. And if I've begun to learn anything about myself with Maximus, the sex needs to be top tier, something to keep me on my toes at all times.

Lori and Tori stopped by my table to say hi before getting their coffees and asking to join. They got their classic pumpkin spice lattes, surprising that they were still in season considering it was January but what did I know about Starbucks rotations?

The three of us didn't speak for the next two hours, we each had our headphones in and scribbling away in our notebooks. Lori was in business, and Tori was in agriculture. My prof was hammering away in my ear when a text slid over the top of my computer screen.

I think you need a break. It was Maximus. I looked over to him and he was resting his head on his hands staring at me with a innocently cute grin. *What do you want?*

I think I need to finish these lecture notes. I replied. I focused again on the video on my screen, frantically scribbling notes to distract me from him.

Tap, tap.

"I wasn't asking." He bent down over my shoulder and said it loud enough for me to hear over my headphones, which means Lori and Tori might have heard him as well. I looked over to them and they exchanged a look between each other before angling their heads back at me.

"Hi! I'm Tori, this is Lori." She smiled and flipped her hair over her shoulders. She looked Maximus up and down as he was bent over my shoulder. *Was she flirting?*

I moved one of my headphones off my ear to see if I heard that correctly. *Again, was she flirting?* I turned my head to look at Maximus but he didn't move. My cheek collided with the side of his face, he was smiling. His skin brushed mine and it lit my stomach on fire.

"Hi." His grin was childish, playful. It made the heat in stomach feel gentle. I can never guess what mood he's in when he switches up like this. "Hi! Can I help you?" I replied back with a sarcastic grin.

He moved my hair to the side to get a better angle at my ear, "Bathroom. Three minutes." And he sauntered away down the hall and around the corner toward the gender neutral single bathrooms. *Ugh. Fine. Maybe I could do with stretching my... legs.*

⸻ ·❖· ⸻

I knocked twice, hoping this was the one he was in. The latch clicked and I opened the door, briefly checking the hallway before entering. Maximus was standing in the middle of the bathroom waiting. The room was decently large, it had to be for accessibility students. Anyone can be gender neutral so they had to accommodate for every human being. I appreciated that about my university. The inclusivity here was refreshing in a world full of hate toward anyone who didn't follow societal norms.

I opened my mouth to speak. He allowed no chance. He slammed me against the wall by my throat, his hands running through my hair and fisting it as he yanked my head back to bite my neck.

"I've been waiting three hours for this," he growled in my ear. "All I could think about was that sweet spot between your thighs. Give it to me." He panted. *Yes, sir.*

I responded with taking off my shorts and moving my black lace panties to the side. He would have to make due. "That's my girl." It was a low whisper, but I heard it all the same. *My girl.*

I twisted the bottom of his shirt and yanked on it. It slipped off with ease and I stuffed it in his back pocket so it wouldn't get dirty on the floor. He parted his lips for mine and kissed me as hard as he could. He felt primal. If I wasn't obedient, he might go feral on me. *Not that I would mind.*

He lapped his tongue over my teeth and I swirled my tongue over his lips. He felt so warm and welcoming yet so dangerous all at once. He pulled my bottom lip between his teeth before backing up and holding my face in his hands.

"You... what—" He panted, I lunged for him. Dragging my hands through his hair and brushing the sides of his face with my fingers. He moved us over to the sink and bent me over it. I looked back at him as he unbuckled his jeans and set himself free. I've seen his dick before but in public it seemed that much more intimidating.

He grabbed my jaw and turned my face forward. "Watch." Was all he said before burying himself in me. My knuckles went white around the edge of the sink and his hand covered my mouth to silence my moans.

"Bend your knees, baby. Let me all the way in."

I obeyed and he slid deeper, stretching me as I let out a cry in his palm.

"That's it," he growled behind me. "Oh... finally. Yes, baby."

I mumbled beneath his palm to speak, but when he didn't let me get a word out, I bit him. He winced, but didn't budge.

My orgasm was already building in my stomach from his voice as his dick curved to hit that perfect spot. I squeezed my eyes shut begging for my release but he grabbed my face again with his hand. "Watch us."

I made eye contact with him in the mirror, watching his hands over my mouth and tugging my hair. His teeth were bared and his Adam's apple was bobbing in his throat. His bicep and forearm veins were bulging at the seams as he continued pounding into me. He wasted no time. He didn't allow for my pussy to adjust to his girth but I welcomed the roughness.

Eventually the slickness between my thighs melted my walls and allowed him to dive deeper and deeper, hitting my cervix with each blissful pump. It barely hurt anymore. I missed the pain.

I moaned in his palm as he pulled out and forced me to my knees on the bathroom floor. "Take it," he said.

I nodded and placed my hands flat on my thighs. He gripped the back of my head, staring me right in the eye as he stroked himself to his breaking point before using his hand to pry my jaw open. He spilled into my throat and I swallowed every ounce of him. He tasted like a creamy heaven.

He threw his head back as the last of him dripped down my throat. He was still throbbing over my tongue when I gave myself a sneaky smile.

"Fuck...I needed that." He panted. He picked me up under my arms and kissed my lips softly. Landing light kisses over my cheeks, neck, shoulders, before landing the softest one on my forehead.

I pleasantly shook the webs from my head. "Oh my god." I laughed in shock. "Why was that so good?"

"I know right." He huffed back in his normal demeanor, giving himself a shocked laugh too. "I guess you have a thing for public indecency. Good to know." He winked, putting his shirt back on. I gave him a face, to which he smiled and raised an eyebrow at me. If I had to survive on one thing...

"I'll leave you undisturbed until you're ready to go home, I promise." He smiled before opening the door and checking the hallway. He kissed my cheek and rushed me out before anyone saw.

My cheeks were blushing with arousal. I felt the wobble in my knees as I made for my table. I tried to make it come off as naturally as I could but I utterly failed. When I got to my table, Cade had joined the girls waiting for me.

Before I could even sit down, Maximus pulled up a chair at our table and sat on it backward with his hands resting on the table. Just like Cade did the night I met him.

"Wait, did you guys just like, fuck in there?" Lori pointed between us and Cade's expression fell. He turned to Maximus and gave him a look down.

"No."

"Maybe."

I shot a disapproving look to Maximus, but he wasn't looking at me. He hadn't blinked since he sat down, I thought his eyes were going to pop out if he kept staring at Cade.

"What's happening right now?" Tori said from in front of me.

"Great question," I piped in. "What's going on with you guys?"

"Nothing." They both said in unison but didn't look away from each other. A game of chicken between alphas was going down in the middle of the goddamn library. Over what I had no clue. I knew they squabbled at the party last night but I didn't think it ran this deep.

"Okay...well I think I'm done studying for the day. It's Saturday and I want to go shopping for a new outfit before tonight's party." Lori said, her voice was wary and Tori starting packing her things too. The tension at this table was unbearable, so I followed suit.

"Are we leaving?" Maximus finally broke eye contact with Cade and I responded with a slight nod, asking him questions with my eyes. He ignored my look and rose from the chair, returning it to its table to stand directly beside me.

Cade smirked, walking away with Tori and Lori and sending Maximus one last glance before leaving the library.

I slowly closed my laptop. "Would you like to stand directly on top of me?" I joked, Maximus didn't budge or take his eyes off the library doors.

"Oookay then…" I muttered, quickly throwing everything else in my bag. I left the library with a few good hours of studying under my wing and a very tense Maximus.

He slid into my passenger and with a slam I turned to him. "What the hell was that? Was that about what happened at the party?"

"It was nothing." He kept his head turned toward the window.

I didn't believe him one bit. "Nothing? You were practically standing on my toes!"

He said nothing. I accepted that as my answer and started my car. It took a few minutes before he noticed we were headed for his house, not mine. If he wasn't going to answer my questions honestly, I had nothing to say.

"Where are we going?" He broke the silence.

"I'm taking you home," I said sternly.

"Why?" he protested.

"Because I'm hungry. I'm taking you home and then going back to my house to eat dinner."

———⟨♦⟩———

It was already six p.m. and my tummy was rumbling under the hem of my pants. I fantasized about the ramen noodles waiting for me back at my house. I dropped Maximus off and as soon as I closed my front door behind me, I found my roommates sitting at the kitchen table eating the same thing.

"Hey, you okay? You look flustered." Kim slurped her noodles and gave me a concerned look. "Yeah, I'm good, I'm fucking starving. How was your guys' day?" I opened the ramen package and poured water into the cup before yanking open the microwave door.

"I had a very interesting day. You won't believe what I found out." Mia swallowed her noodles and drank a sip of her water before continuing.

I sat down, each of us listening intently. University drama was something I guiltily lived for. Not my own, of course. But other people? I was in there like a dirty shirt. I loved being in the know, even though I never did anything with it.

"Remember that guy I slept with a couple weeks ago?"

"Ryan." The three of us rolled our eyes and giggled at her. He was cute, but a total surprise. No one knew who he was or where he came from.

"So apparently, his roommate, Cory, got beaten up pretty badly last year and was sent to the hospital with a broken eye socket, nose, and jaw." We all gasped, that sounded awful.

"Do we think he deserved it?" I asked. They all gave me weird looks. "What? Sometimes guys need a beat down. That's how they handle their shit." I shrugged. They pouted their lips and nodded. They knew I was right.

"Apparently he gave the wrong guy a wrong look. Turns out the guy fucked Cory's girlfriend before they were dating but he had a bad rep for sleeping with a bunch of girls and kicking them out after."

"Pft. Typical men. Always fighting over women." Kim muttered over the rim of her water glass. "Do we know who beat the shit out of him?"

"Actually, yeah. We all do." We instantly turned our whole bodies to her. Our ears perked. I chomped down on my noodles, antsy for her answer. "Harriet knows him the best."

I choked immediately, coughing up a full noodle. There was no way. I knew he got into fights last year but I never knew he was capable of putting someone in the hospital with *broken bones*.

"Maximus?" I blurted out, throat still stinging from choking on my noodle.

Mia just shrugged at me and gave me a worried look. "Yeah."

Oh my god.

CHAPTER

31

Harriet

I had no words. I wasn't *entirely* shocked at Maximus's actions, but this seemed way out of proportion. He beat a guy half to death over a look and an old fuck?

"I don't even know what to say." I started rising out of my seat to put my bowl in the dishwasher. I wasn't hungry anymore.

"That's not all." Mia's voice was sad and sharp at the same time.

"There's more?" Jane finally spoke up. She had been silently drinking in the drama from the end of the table.

"What else could there be?" I said, sitting back down instantly.

"It's about Maximus. I'm not sure if it's true but..." she trailed off. I couldn't take the suspense any longer. "But what?!" They all turned their heads to me. "Sorry, sorry, I'm just— I'm..."

Kim put her hand on my arm. "We know. It's okay."

I was getting worked up over this, I wasn't sure why I cared so much. But after all, this was the man I had been sleeping with for months at this point. The man who made me a horrible breakfast with flowers in a mason jar. The man who called me his girl and had a massive thing for cuddling.

"Ryan told me Maximus had a brother." She swallowed. "Apparently he died tragically when he and his sister were younger and it screwed him up really bad."

He had a brother? Now I was shocked and confused. This was a huge piece of information about Maximus life that he separated me from.

The girls gasped. I just sat there in silence staring at my noodles. I definitely wasn't finishing them now. My stomach was in knots.

"Did you know?" Jane turned to me, her hand on my arm brought me back to reality.

"What?" I was still lost in thought. Her question registered in my brain a few seconds later. "No, no, I didn't. He never told me. I can't believe he didn't tell me."

"Are you gonna ask him about it?" Mia asked me gently. "I don't know. Should I? We're just fuck buddies. It's not like he has any obligation to tell me. Wouldn't he have told me if he wanted to?"

"Oh girl, please. That tall, lanky motherfucker is obsessed with you." Kim chuckled. The other girls joined in before shutting up at my confused expression.

"What do you mean?"

Kim looked me dead in the eye and her words hit true. "You met his *family*. You went to his house for Christmas *dinner*."

"You did what?!" Mia and Jane stood from their chairs and covered their mouths. "Yeah, I did do that, didn't I?" I couldn't make eye contact with anyone. My nerves were on fire and I thought I was going to fill my noodle bowl with vomit. *Why is this hitting so hard? Poor Maximus... he had a brother?*

It clicked. The sadness in his family's eyes. The thing I thought was missing wasn't a thing at all. It was a who. I scanned my memories of his Christmas decorations over the break. They had a fifth stocking and an unopened present under the tree. I couldn't remember the name but I remember the drunk thought that it was weird they had an extra stocking when they only had the four of them.

He did have a brother.

"Maybe I'll ask him about it. *Gently*. In time." I huffed. I didn't want them expecting answers in twenty minutes. This would be a delicate topic for Maximus and a very good chance he would blow up at me. I would have to be extremely soft and mindful.

"Be careful. Don't want you to end up in the hospital next with a broken neck."

I shot Kim a dirty glare. She shuffled in her seat, instantly regretting her words. I didn't give her the privilege of a response. Maximus would never hurt me like that, and I didn't appreciate the implication that he would.

I stood from my chair and emptied my bowl for the dishwasher. I headed upstairs to my room and closed the door.

CHAPTER

32

Maximus

Banks, Dylan, and Chase were exactly where I left them. On the couch playing video games. I slouched beside Chase on the couch, digging under my ass for the remote I just sat on.

"Yo, you good?" Banks looked up from his controller to look me in my eye. He knew something was up. He always knew.

"You guys ever see a guy around campus named Cade?" I ignored Banks's question.

"What does he look like?" Dylan asked from his spot on the far couch. He finished what looked like his fifth beer and set the bottle down on the glass of the table.

"Almost the same height as me. Dark hair. Dark eyes. Asian. Kind of muscular."

"That's not much to go on." Chase huffed beside me. I shot him a glance but he continued. "Why? What's he done?"

"He's pining for Harriet."

The room went silent. They all shared silent glances. "What?"

"I know this is going to be hard to hear, but she's not your girlfriend, man. She's still free game. If he's interested, he has every right to pursue her, ya know?"

I shot Banks a glare. *Say that again.* "Doesn't mean I want another man eye-fucking her. He lives in her house. He's one of the downstairs tenants. And after that bullshit at that party last night, the idea of him being around her annoys the fuck out of me."

"Then claim her," Chase said under his breath before chugging what looked like his fifth beer too.

"It's not like that." I replied sharply.

"I'm going to say this as lightly as possible," Dylan said calmly, opening his sixth beer. "You're kinda obsessed with her, man."

"Am not."

"Are too."

"Am not!"

"Are too!" They all yelled at me and then laughed. "It's okay, Max. She's awesome. We like having her around. She's super chill and actually funny."

"Not to mention she's great to look at."

My jaw clenched and I punched Chase straight in the upper arm. "Ow! I'm just saying she's hot! Good job!" He punched me right back. We both grinned and shrugged.

They were right. She was awesome. She was chill. She was funny. And she definitely was hot. Most divine woman I've ever seen in my goddamn life, actually. *And she was probably going to be the last.*

"Alright, enough with the bitch talk. Let's get fucked up." I patted Chase on the back and headed for the kitchen to open my first beer. Dylan and Banks called after me to get them another and I obliged. Then they yelled over the music, "Invite her over! Tell her to come get fucked up with us! It's Saturday night!"

I stumbled, letting out a gasp before catching myself on the fridge door handle. "Gah... shit. Not now."

The medication in my backpack flashed through my mind. I hadn't been taking them again. I wanted to feel alive. Harriet was the only thing I needed for that. She made me want to be alive, she *kept* me alive.

Those stupid drugs fuzzed my head, but they did stop my chest pain. It was a constant struggle. Take them... don't take them...

The idea of her coming over to hang with me and my boys brought me back. *Mind over matter.* They really enjoyed her company and she seemed freer around them. She doesn't have many guy friends, all the guys I've seen talking to her have the fuck-me eyes. So they're not really her friends. Mine know their places. They stay in their lanes. They look to Harriet as a friend and a friend only.

After a few deep breaths, I retake my seat next to Chase and pop the beer cap with my molars. The guys persuaded me, so I sent a text.

Hope you had a good dinner. The guys wanna hang. Come over?

I set my phone down and grabbed a controller to select my character on FIFA. I'd come to the realization I could probably figure out any video game, so after twenty minutes of playing with the guys I was already starting to kick their asses. They grunted and groaned every time I made a move they didn't think of. I thought it was funny because I loved winning, but they didn't share the same humor.

I loved being the best at something. Even if it was something as simple as FIFA, it meant a great deal to me that I would leave this planet with people knowing they can't beat me at video games. Or sex. It was no secret I'd slept with a bunch of girls, and it was no secret that they kept coming back for more.

I didn't mind coming off as the "fuckboy" or "manwhore". No one knew why, no one needed to know why. As shallow as it sounded, I wanted to fuck as many women possible before my heart gave out.

Until Harriet. God, this girl was really messing with my head. I was young, I was decently attractive, and I knew I was packing inches. No way I wasn't going to stop myself from getting some tail. But when she said *fuck it* that night we met and climbed on top of me, I had a feeling I was done for. She was so curious, so full of questions...I couldn't help myself.

I told her my entire life story—ish—and I didn't even mean to, it just came out. She had that effect on me. Even the guys noticed it the first few times they hung out with her. They felt like they could tell her anything. There was no judgment, no fear. Honestly, I think it might be one of her superpowers. The other being her immaculate blow job skills. That shit drove me crazy. It was starting to get unbearable. I wanted to be around her constantly.

Is this how the girls felt when they wanted more from me?

I didn't want her to drop me off at the house after the library. Not being around her reminds me I'm dying. Also maybe I should take my medication. Everything is so clear when I'm with her, so when I'm not... the medication rotting in my backpack shows itself.

She's becoming my lifeline, someone I'm incapable of letting go, someone I need to protect. So when I saw Cade get too close at the party, and then again in the library...

I knew how it came off: possessive, crooked, crazy. I couldn't help it. He was making moves on what was mine.

Ugh. It's terrifying me. The more I'm around her, the more I feel guilty about not telling her what's wrong with me. That lie I spun about my grandpa has stuck with me, often making me feel like I'm going to hurl. I felt horrible, and I almost let it slip it was me but I just couldn't. I couldn't break her heart like that. I couldn't sit there and watch her future dissipate. If she thought of me that way.

Come to think of it, I don't actually know how Harriet feels about me at all. *Knowing would only make it worse.*

---·◈·---

I took a break from playing the game and Chase asked me if I could use my free time to get him another beer. These guys are like kegs, they can hold their beer like champions. I opened the fridge door and made eye contact with the month-old sandwich that's been sitting there for a week. *Disgusting,* I shivered. Not my sandwich, not my problem. I wouldn't bring it up until it started growing things. And since it's safely under the protection of saran wrap, I'd say we're in the clear for about another month.

"Here." I handed him the beer, and he cracked it with his index finger.

Knock, knock!

"Oh shit, she's here. Quick, tidy up the table." Dylan lunged forward to grab all the dirty wrappers and empty beer cans off the table as if our house could look even the slightest bit presentable in the time I walked to the front door and back.

I leaned against the wall and watched my roommates scuffle around trying to make the place look less disgusting. I smiled at my feet, I liked that they cared so much about what she thought. Guys show their care in different ways than women, and for my roommates... I think this was the biggest one.

"Okay, we're ready." They were panting and sweating beer from their skin. "Open the door."

I chuckled to myself and walked to the door. Only it wasn't Harriet.

"Nicole. What are you doing here?"

"I came to see if you wanted to hang out and go to a party with me?"

"Not tonight. I'm hanging with the boys, sorry."

And I shut the door in her face. *Okay, I admit, that was rude.* But why does this chick keep popping up everywhere? She seemed like she didn't care I wasn't into her at the party and now she's just showing up at my house? I don't work like that. You come when you're invited. Period.

She knocked again. I swung the door open. "Are you kidding me—" I halted. My eyes widened. "Oh hi..." I picked my jaw up off the floor as those big blue eyes gave me a look of idiocy.

"Did you want me to get her back here or..."

She begun to shout Nicole's name, but I lunged forward and clamped my hand over her mouth, spinning her inside and slamming the door behind me. I pinned her to my chest and growled in her ear, "If you ever think you can invite that chick to my house... you got another thing coming, Hare." The last thing I needed was Harriet making friends with Nicole and trying to push her toward me in some taunt game. She had to have known I only wanted her.

She was laughing under my palm. "Are you done?" I panted. The corners of her lips turned and she shook her head in my palm. Slowly, I lowered my hand and gave her throat a little squeeze for good measure.

Instead, she opened her mouth again. "If you didn't fuck her, what's the big—" She was joking, but I clamped her mouth shut again.

I rolled my eyes and let her go again. The tips of my fingers were barely brushing her by the time she spun around and slammed me against the door. She launched herself into my arms and kissed me hard. I laughed under her lips and kissed her back as hard as I could.

God, this woman is going to be the life of me.

"Let's go, you big buffoon!" She laughed in my face. She used all her weight to haul us forward through the hallway to the living room. I did as she directed and marched us into the living room, her body light around my waist.

"Hey, fuckers!" she shouted from my arms.

"Hey, bitch!" They all shouted back. "Welcome to the party. Can I offer you a beer, milady?" Banks cracked a bottle and handed it to her. Her legs fell down, and she took a seat beside him. The beer bottle was huge in her little hands. One of the many things I liked about her. She was so tiny, yet her personality could dominate a room in a matter of seconds. I sunk into the open spot on the couch and pulled Harriet in my lap.

She nodded in thanks and offered him a wink. Chase regretfully asked her some questions about her degree, Banks offered up a story about her roommate and Dylan just paced the room staring at her.

"Yes?" She finally answered his stare. Her legs were draped over Banks's thighs with her hands wrapped around the neck of the Corona in her lap. He continued pacing and I could tell he was itching to ask her something.

"You're making me dizzy, boy!" She said in a playful tone. I agreed, his pacing was getting annoying.

He stopped pacing and took his spot on the far couch. Harriet's eyebrow cocked and she crossed her arms over her chest. The way she squeezed the beer between her legs made my mouth water. I want to be between those legs so badly, an ache between mine was starting to grow. She turned her head, no doubt feeling my cock swelling underneath her ass. She pressed a light kiss to my temple and turned back to Dylan.

The sound of her voice broke my thoughts. "What's her name?" She looked so motherly. Surrounded by four of her children. Well, three. I'm *definitely* out of that equation. The sparkle in her eye told me she really cared about my friends. That thought alone made my chest warm with pride.

"Amy." He put his head between his knees and took a hefty swig from his hundredth beer.

She rose from my lap and plunked her tight little ass beside Dylan. I had to adjust my position to hide my erection.

"Okay... what's your question?"

"I think I want to take her on a date, but I don't even know what girls like these days. Our generation is so annoying. Hot.

Cold. Everything. Nothing. Y'all are fucking confusing, you know that?" He scoffed. Harriet laughed over his voice.

He really did like this girl. He talked about her frequently and she'd been to the house a couple times. I felt for the guy. He's socially awkward around girls. Around us, he's one of the most outgoing fuckers you'll ever meet. But any girls around and he clams up like a feather duster. Except for Harriet.

To my knowledge, none of the guys saw Harriet as a girl... as respectfully as possible. She wasn't a sexual target for any of them, I made sure of that when I gave them stern talkin' to the first time she came over.

We've shared girls before, this was not the case. It's clear Harriet is a catch. With her porcelain skin, sprayed freckles, bright blue eyes and blonde hair, who wouldn't want a piece? Not to mention the fucking perky kahunas that sit on her chest. Yeah, Chase makes his comments, but no one dared to make a move. None of them could take me and they knew that.

So the only thing left was to be her friend. Or in this conversation, mother.

"Oh, I know we're annoying. I can be quite demanding myself." She shot a look my way. Her eyes were twinkling and she offered me a smug grin, hoisting her shoulders up and shaking back and forth for a minute. Banks smiled and shook his head, he turned to me and mouthed, *you're screwed.*

"So how do I tell her I like her? And where do I take her on a date?" He stood again and started to pace, running his hands through his hair and rubbing his eyes.

"She already knows." Harriet grinned. "We always know." Another grin flashed across the room. She continued, "As for the date, Valentine's Day is in a few weeks, so you gotta play your cards right if you're gonna get lucky on the fourteenth. Try the movies. Get some snacks, a slushie. Don't be shy to touch her."

"Woah, woah, woah." Chase's sarcasm was paramount. "You mean there's *touching*?"

Banks leaned over and smacked him upside the head, whispering something about shutting up. Dylan really liking this girl put him a little on edge, so Chase's quips wasn't great timing.

Harriet went into detail about the date, Dylan listened. Chase tossed me his controller and I took over playing Dylan's character, creaming them every single round of the game. Eventually, they'd grow tired and opt for a drinking game instead.

CHAPTER

33

Maximus

As I guessed, the drinking game was opted for. We played a round of beer pong that's permanently set up in kitchen, a round of cards and even Never Have I Ever. That never lasts with us, we've done a lot of shit. And apparently, so had Harriet. She's snuck out, smoked, drank during school hours, stolen a car, and fucked more than six people. I angled my head at that one. *What's her count?*

Of course, there were things she'd hadn't done. Slept with a professor, had a sexually transmitted disease and a threesome. I made a mental note to talk to her about that last one. The thought of pleasing her with another girl made my stomach hot. *Would she want two girls or two guys? One of both? Four?*

The thoughts were racing through my mind and she shifted her ass over me. The head of my cock was rubbing against the inside of my jeans and I felt the growl grow in my throat. We needed to get out of here. Now.

"Hare, get up. We're going to bed," I whispered in her ear. She didn't even look at me when she mumbled back. "But we're having so much fun!"

"Yeah! Don't take her yet, man." Chase protested. I made up my mind, no one was going to stop me from dragging her ass into my room by her hair and strip her naked while I suck the life out of her clit.

But I made it interesting anyway.

"Fine. If you can beat Dylan in a round, we can chill a bit longer. Deal?" She squirmed and squealed on top of me and Banks passed her the controller. It flopped on the fuzzy blanket Dylan had given her, she picked it up and fumbled with it. She didn't know anything about a controller that wasn't attached to a Wii system or Nintendo. I made fun of her and she elbowed me in the ribs. I knew she was going to lose.

Except she didn't. The bitch fucking won. Entirely by luck. Dylan was hammered, and it gave her an advantage. She figured out the controls relatively fast for someone who was also drunk. Cheering after every shot and turning to me to see the look on my face. Was I proud? Of course I was. My girl playing video games? Are you kidding? I don't think she could get any better. *Except if I was buried in her pussy.* My dick ached beneath her and she moved her ass over me.

"One more! One more! Chase, let's go, bitch." She cheered and spread her legs over mine, lifting her knees to place her feet in the space between Banks and I.

As they played their round, I couldn't hold back. The arm I had wrapped around her slid under the blanket. I circled her pussy over her pants and she adjusted her position for my reach. She rolled her head and her neck cracked in my ear. *God, she's into this too?*

Once I started, I couldn't stop. I tugged at the waistband and slid my hand into her panties. I felt the lace. Black, I guessed. I inched my middle fingers down her slit. *She's soaked. Right here. And no one knew.* I circled her bare clit and she tilted her head back into my neck.

"Ha! Score!"

She jolted her head up and tried to focus again. Chase's score sent him ahead. I slid my fingers up her pussy. Her slickness coated my fingers as I pumped in her slowly. I moved her hair over her shoulder with my other hand and bit the space between her ear and her shoulder. She winced, trying to get me to back off while she gamed. I wasn't taking no for an answer, I pulled my coated fingers out and pinched her clit in between my fingers. She let out a frustrated growl as Chase landed his last goal and the game concluded. *Finally. Play time.*

"I'll get you back for that one day, that's a promise." She tilted her beer bottle in his direction and turned to me, landing a hungry kiss on my lips as she whispered against me. "I'm ready, sir."

My heart instantly jumped and I felt my smile go wicked. I couldn't take my eyes off her. My hand retreated, and I scooped her up in my arms. I carried her to my bedroom and closed the door with my foot behind me.

I accidentally chucked her on my bed with far too much force, she went flying and hit her head on the wall. "Oh my god! I'm so—" *She's laughing?*

She burst into a howl, clutching her head and falling over on her side. I leaned down to cradle her head, she pulled my arm to force me to sit down. "I'm sorry!" I laughed with her, not sure what she was feeling right now. She continued to laugh. She was fine. I knew she liked it rough but we haven't gotten there yet.

"You're okay?" I gave her a soft smile. "Eager much?" She snorted, smiling wide and bright. Those pearly whites could light up any room. "Maximus, there's something I have to ask you." Her tone turned serious and I knew we were over the head-to-wall smack.

"Anything," I lied. "Anything, at all." I lied again.

She sat up on my bed and crossed her legs, similar to our breakfast set up. "Did you beat the shit out of Cory? Ryan's roommate?"

Fuck. This I can't lie about.

"Yes." I kept it as simple as possible. She looked down at her hands and fiddled with her fingernails. She wasn't sure what to do with my answer. After a few minutes, she looked up at me.

"Because he looked at you the wrong way after he found out you fucked his girlfriend?" Her voice lifted at the end like she knew there was something else going on. *What did she know?*

I took a minute, conjuring an answer that would make me sound the least dick-ish. "I was having an extremely bad day, he pushed my buttons and I just snapped. I haven't beaten anyone up like that ever, and for sure not since." It was the truth. The week I had was unbearable. It was my brother's birthday that night, plus the doctor appointment the weekend before. *She doesn't need to know that.* I was on edge from the moment I woke up. I tried not to leave my room to keep my bomb from going off, but when I got drunk, I exploded at the first person who breathed in my direction. I pummeled his face until I was torn off him and he was sent to the hospital with a broken orbital bone in two places, nose and jaw. I fucked him up *good*.

"I felt ashamed the next morning and went to the hospital to apologize to him. He pressed charges but eventually dropped them from all the time the system takes. He had to get back to school, I guess. I thanked him as he left the hospital, *healed,* and haven't seen or talked to him since." That was the truth, too. I stared at my legs crossed under me. Cold thin fingers pulled my chin up, her eyes were glossy. *Are you ashamed of me? Are you disappointed?*

"Say something," I pleaded. She closed her eyes and played out a long sigh. She looked at the ceiling before moving her face inches from mine. There was a chance the immediate future with her was going to be interesting. It was clear she gave no third chances, but she was so understanding, so forgiving. I couldn't fuck this up. I couldn't lose someone like this.

Thankfully, she just shrugged. "Shit happens, Maximus. We live and we learn is what my mama would say. Everyone has bad days," She released my chin and kissed my cheek.

"But that's not a great way to handle them!" She tapped my cheek twice, and I launched myself. Falling on top of her to bury my face in her chest and hold her. She giggled and circled her arms around my neck.

"Thank you," I whispered, the fabric of her sweater muffled my voice. She didn't hear me, but she didn't have to. "Thank you," I repeated. *Thank you, Hare.*

I wasn't complaining about the position we were in, or the moment we were sharing, but I needed to stop this memory from lingering in the air like a hot fart. "Let's fuck?" I mumbled in her chest, louder this time.

She rolled her eyes and tightened her hold on me. "Be so honest, right now. This turned you on?"

I scoffed jokingly. "Bitch, please. You could blow air at me and I'd be bursting at the seams."

Her laugh vibrated my head, and I peered up between her breasts into her eyes. My chin was hard on her sternum as she ran her hands through my hair just staring at me with mischief. "What?"

There was a quick, small puff of air that pushed through my hair.

She blew at me.

I burst out laughing, tightening my grip on her sweater. She really just did that.

"Well, let's go then." I snorted, backing off her immediately to undress.

Goddamn it, Hare.

CHAPTER

34

Harriet

"It's true." I plopped down on the couch in our living room and they all lifted their heads from their computer screens.

"What is?"

I didn't answer, just toyed with my fingernails. "Oh." They let out a sigh and closed their laptops.

"He did beat the shit out of Cory," Jane confirmed. I looked up, there was no judgment on their faces, no relief the gossip was true. Just mouths pressed into hard lines. Jane and Kim opened their laptops again.

"Did you ask him about his brother?"

They closed with a quick *snap*.

"Yeah, did you?" Jane peered over her glasses. "No, I didn't. He didn't offer it up either. That's such a touchy subject, guys." However, my curiosity was fucking feral. Deep down I knew from the fifth stocking, but I needed confirmation.

"You think his mom would post anything on her Facebook?" I wondered. I was talking out loud more than anything else. I pulled my phone from my pocket and typed in my Facebook login.

"Do you know his mom's name?" Mia asked, opening her laptop too.

"Laura White."

"Basic as fuck." We all laughed, sure as hell was.

There she was. *Oh shit.* Her smile bright in her display photo, along with the *three* children at her side, with her husband standing over them from behind.

"Holy shit. I found it." They piled in next to me as we stalked his mother's Facebook page. We found old baby photos of Maximus, all saying *awwww* in unison. Damn, he was even a cute baby. A fat baby. *God, I love fat babies.* I made sure to save a few photos to haunt him with.

"Oh my god…" Kim muttered practically in my ear. His brother's death post. May eleventh. He was eighteen. There was hashtags about MADD. *Mothers Against Drunk Driving.*

He was hit by a drunk driver.

"Poor Maximus… his poor family. That's awful." All of us slouched further into the couch as if that would take away the horror. His brother was tall, like Maximus and Lily. He had darker hair and light green eyes, like Lily's, with a short stubble. He was a buff guy, and according to the posts I found, he was a football star. Best on the team.

We kept reading the novel his mother posted about him to find out he was buried not too far from here. Rosemary Cemetery. Jane looked up the directions, and it was only a half an hour from our house. *Is that why Maximus came to Greenlake?*

We scrolled for a few more minutes. Accomplishment posts, Christmas, Easter, Valentine's Day, and finally… Sam's birthday. February 5th, 2013. His last birthday. Wow, it's been eight years since he passed. The moment Maximus turned nineteen last year, he became older than his older brother. That means…

"When did Maximus beat up Cory again?" I turned my head to Mia. She shrugged. "February last year, I think."

It clicked for her. "Oh shit."

I exhaled. "He beat the shit out of Cory on his brother's birthday."

"I can't believe we're doing this." Mia sunk into her seat in the middle of my car. "It feels like an invasion of privacy."

Kim shrugged in my passenger seat. "Cemeteries are public spaces. We can visit whoever the hell we want."

Jane snorted behind me and opened her door to get out. "Wait." I turned to slam her door closed. I was freaking out. "Should we be doing this? The post confirmed his death."

"It's a little late now!" Kim shouted in my ear. I narrowed my eyes at her and grinned. It was too late. We were already sitting in the parking lot with our all black outfits and baseball caps. We looked like the ultimate burglars, minus the ski masks.

"Fuck it." I got out of the car first. Kim followed then Mia and Jane. We made head way for the rows and rows of headstones. Some old, some new. It was heartbreaking to see death dates the same year as birth dates. Babies who never got their first breath. Adolescents who never got to be adults. Adults who never got to grow old, have families, or find the best wrinkle cream on the market.

It was mesmerizing to think I would be working here one day. My handiwork would be buried in a place like this. The care, attention, and respect I would put into each loved one. I'd ask their family what their favorite music genre was so I could play it for them as I prepared their bodies for eternal rest. I paused at the top of the first row. There had to be hundreds of headstones here. The administration building was to my right, winding roads between chunks of headstones so people could access their loved ones via cars. Benches were spread out evenly through the field.

We passed by a five-year-old, the flowers were fresh. The headstone said last month. The headstone beside it had the death date 2008. The flowers were dead.

"According to their website, they organize the stones by last name. This row is A. So we have to keep walking down. His last name is White, right? The brother?"

"To my knowledge, yeah." We walked for what felt like a kilometer until we reached the beginning of W. The road took a turn and as we begun to approach the section, we saw a tall dark figure standing over one of the graves. We gasped, pushing each other back around the corner and ducking behind four gravestones.

"Sorry Miss...Varman?" Kim whispered behind her grave. We chuckled, if it came off disrespectful, we paid no attention.

"I think it's the groundskeeper. Should we keep going?" Jane asked from behind Mr. Valdez.

"We drove all the way out here, I am not leaving until we find that grave." Mia whisper-shouted from behind Mrs. Vincent.

"Agreed." I confirmed, patting Miss Van on the head. I pulled my sweater sleeve over my mouth to stop from chuckling. *Hey, at least they still got purpose in their rest.*

This is why people call you disturbed, Harriet.

One by one, we slid out from behind the stones, hiding in the next row. Slowly creeping our way down the line of W's. Until we reached WH. My breath hitched as I creeped closer to the marked grave. It was worn down by years of weather and nature, but the flowers were fresh. *Purple and yellow flowers.*

The man in front of the grave rubbed the crack in the cement with his fingers. It was dark, so I couldn't get a good look of his face until he'd turned around.

I couldn't move.

What's he doing here at this hour? *And I thought we were wild.*

I gasped, covering my mouth with my sleeve as quickly as I could before he heard me. He bent down and put his forehead to the name on the grave.

Samson Andrew White
Beloved son, brother and friend.
02/05/1995 — 05/11/2013.

He was here at one in the morning. Faintly, I could hear him speaking. My heart fluttered. He was talking to his brother.

Forever eighteen as his younger brother stood over him at twenty.

I put a hand on my chest and slowly lowered my body to the ground. I curled my legs under me, listening to the wind and supporting him from afar. My stare could've burned a hole in the back of his head.

I am so sorry, Maximus. I am so sorry for your loss. I'm right here.

Maximus leaned back and pulled his legs to his face, holding his head between his knees. He fell on his side and curled himself into a ball at the foot of his brother's grave. Even in the dark, I could see his shoulders shake.

In the silence of the grave, I could hear his tears.

He clamped his sleeve over his mouth, but I could hear him whimpering anyway. The wind picked up as his whimpers turned into sobs, carrying them to a place only the broken can go.

I couldn't see his face, but the longer he laid there the tighter he pulled into himself. Eventually, he let loose. He got on his hands and knees and bowed his head. His entire body was shaking as he let out a guttural scream that could've cracked the ground beneath him.

The birds in the trees flew away as fast as they could from the predator crying brother between the headstones. Another scream. Another cry. He was dry heaving and clutching his chest before falling over on his side again. I'd seen him do that before. This seemed different.

I heard him take shallow breaths, it felt like he was preparing for something. His last breath was long, like it was final. He crawled back up to his knees. When he threw his head back into the night sky, he screamed his name. The name of the brother who didn't mean to leave him behind.

My instinct was to rush to him, to hold him, but he couldn't know I was here. If he caught me here, I'd be joining his brother six feet below. So I moved up a row as silently as I could. Even if he did turn around, it was dark, and I was hidden behind someone named Molly Wheeler.

I weaved my hand through the grass, feeling the condensation between my fingers, searching for the part of his soul that was missing.

All I could do was sit in silence and wait. One day, he won't be alone on a night like this.

Between the cracks in the headstones and the brother calling brother, a promise was made.

I'm right here.

CHAPTER

35

Maximus

I came to his grave every other Sunday. I allowed myself one hour to feel my feelings about Sam. Anything after that, I shut them off.

Banks always allowed me to borrow his car. He's the only one who knew I had a brother. My mother let a couple of things slip when she visited in the first few months. He was the only one who heard and I made him swear to keep his mouth shut or I'd put him in the grave with Sam.

Now it's just a unspoken ritual between us. I would knock on his door and he would point to his keys on his nightstand. It was a silent exchange, but an exchange I would never forget.

We used to have a cottage near Greenlake, his favorite place, where he spent most of his free time if he could. He loved football and his friends, but football plus his friends at the cottage was his real-world version of heaven. He never forgot to take me with him. No matter how old and "cool" he got, he was never too old or too cool for me.

I mean, I wasn't allowed to drink the beer they snuck in, but I was allowed to throw the ball around with them.

I loved him so much. Even the six-year difference didn't do much to affect our relationship. He was my best friend, only acting like my brother when I had an outburst or made impulsive decisions. He always brothered Lily, but that's because she was still little. Sometimes he would bring her to the cottage, but she often opted to stay home with her friends.

Most of the time it was just me and him, so when he died, a part of me died too. When I got my diagnosis at his age, I thought it was some sort of sign from the universe. We weren't meant to be apart long. I'll never forget the looks on my parents' faces when they got the news, watching their hearts remember what it felt like to bury a son was excruciating. And now they would eventually bury another.

I felt guilty for wanting to see him again, wishing my diagnosis would send me to the same place he was. But that would leave Lily alone. Both brothers dead in a matter of a few years. I wasn't sure if I could do that to her. She would be left behind with whatever remained of our parents.

I was caught between wanting to see him again and refusing to leave her behind.

Those thoughts came to a screeching halt when I met her. I love Lily and wanted to survive for her, but Harriet made me want to live.

I stood at his grave, remembering when he took the fall for me with our parents. I accidentally broke their favorite vase from our great-grandmother. Or when he bought me my first playboy magazine. I was way too young to understand, but I figured it out a couple years after he died. His dark hair and light green eyes flashed through my mind, but it was his laugh that flooded me. How I wish I could hear it one more time. What I would do for that luxury.

Eventually, I dropped to the ground and sobbed. His laugh echoing behind my eyes as I clutched my face between my knees. My chest was aching with the pain of losing him all over again. It felt like my mind was splitting. His body being lowered into the spot I'm laying on. The casket we all fought over, what he would like, what he wouldn't. *Are you comfortable? What do your bones look like now, Sam?*

At twelve, I didn't know what it meant to be drunk behind a wheel. I knew beer made your mind go fuzzy, but I had no idea how detrimental it can be when operating a vehicle. Growing up meant understanding adult hardships, this was a hardship I never wanted to learn.

Sam was at a football rally the night of the crash. The night ended with a bonfire in the middle of the woods by our house. He had been drinking, but didn't drive. Our parents drove him and were supposed to pick him up, but plans changed. Cops busted the bonfire party and everyone scattered. He got in the car with a sober friend, Bobby Viera. They were on Highway 411 when another football player crashed into them.

When the cops showed up, *everyone* panicked, including the student that shouldn't have been driving. Duncan Rivers hopped in his truck, inevitably taking my brother's life. Sam was killed instantly when Duncan's front bumper slammed into the passenger side. The police report was gruesome, Sam's head was bashed in, a part of his skull completely missing.

They came to the conclusion that Sam must've been bending down to tie his shoe lace when Duncan made contact. I guess that meant his head took the brunt of the force. They would never know for sure, but the police wanted to be as thorough as possible for my parents. Bobby survived the crash but has been in a coma for the last eight years. Duncan Rivers was serving fifteen years in prison on a DUI manslaughter charge.

An immature and irresponsible decision made by one idiot, and countless lives were altered forever. Bobby's family, friends. Sam's friends, our family, me. Duncan's own family, his own friends.

The thought of that memory made me want to vomit. Instead, I settled for unleashing my pent up anger at the world. I let out a buried scream and collapsed back down on the ground. The ache in my chest growing by the tear.

I thought I was going to pass out from hyperventilating. This was not the place nor the time. It was after midnight and I was alone in Sam's cemetery. At least I thought I was.

I could feel someone's presence. I couldn't put my finger on the feeling, but it felt like someone was there, reaching out to me. *Sam?* I wasn't sure if I believed in the afterlife or anything religious, but the sky looks different when someone you love is in it.

Faith feels different when you bury your best friend.

I looked to the sky, letting out another scream. "Sam!"

Drawing a broken breath, I called for the part of me that died. "Sam...please..." I cried, begging to be woken up from a nightmare I couldn't dare call my reality.

I almost killed someone myself with these feelings. Cory. He didn't deserve it. Regardless of the look he gave me, it had nothing to do with him. I was grateful for Banks pulling me off him, and I was grateful for him dropping the charges. Yet again, another immature and irresponsible decision made by one idiot to ruin the life of another.

I opened my mouth to speak, but all that came out were sobs and mumbled words. I tried again, telling Sam about our parents, Lily, and my newfound drug, a simply complex woman by the name of Harriet Quinn.

"I think you'd really like her, bro. She's funny. She's thoughtful. She's amazing. She's blonde, so thank god she isn't your type." I laughed through my tears. "But you could probably steal her from me anyway. Then we'd really have to brawl."

"I'm about your height now. I put on a little muscle but it's deteriorating. Even so, I could probably make a good attempt to kick your ass." I ran my fingers over the crack in his headstone.

"Life isn't the same without you. Nothing is the same without you, but I'll see you sooner than we thought. I love you, brother."

As I turned to walk away, I walked over a patch of flattened grass. Someone must have come to visit Molly Wheeler earlier tonight.

I replayed our favorite memories as I walked back to Banks's car. As soon as I turned over the car, I closed my eyes and tilted my head back.

Three...two...one...

My feelings toward Sam disappeared and my thoughts of Harriet swallowed me whole.

CHAPTER

36

Harriet

We drove home in utter silence.

We sat in a row on the couch in utter silence.

No one moved. No one blinked. I'm not sure if we even breathed.

We sat there for over an hour before Kim broke the silence. "I don't think I've ever heard a sound like that."

"Me neither."

"Same."

"Uh huh." We were all blankly staring at the wall. "It feels like we committed a crime." I muttered under my breath.

"That felt illegal, for sure." Mia admitted. Her face was a shade of pale I hadn't seen before.

That sound, that *scream* he made was going to replay in our heads for days. I had no idea how much pain he had been holding in. How much pain his family holds in their eyes. In their hearts.

That's the thing about pain, it's a master in hiding. But once you're alone, mercy is foreign.

It starts off slow. A momentary lapse in the bathroom. A quick spark down your fingertips before you have to blink it away and carry on. There are people counting on your happiness, do your best to show them.

But when you go to bed, you flood. Your body relives everything. The memories. The emotions. Momentary pictures with the sole purpose of furthering your agony.

The spark that once ran through your fingertips now electrified every nerve in your body, demanding to be seen.

Only in the dark can you bend it to your will. Using it as a blanket to cover you in numbness because the alternative is nothing but reminding pain.

Even then, the darkness can entrap. Convince you that you're okay, telling your body you need it to survive so you won't try to kill it.

It made me realize why Maximus likes it so much when I sleep with him. He can lock out his feelings when he's buried in me. I'm still unsure as to why it was me he slept with, but regardless, he was using me as cover.

And I was going to let him.

I reached for my phone, even if he didn't know why, I wanted to be with him tonight. I wasn't sure if he screamed like that every time he visited his brother's grave, but I knew for sure he wasn't going to have to deal with the aftermath of tonight by himself.

HQ: Hey. You awake?

I would've waited an hour before I'd convince myself to sleep, but it wasn't even thirty seconds.

MW: I am. Why you up?

Good question. It was two-fifteen in the morning. It was Sunday, and I had class tomorrow, but not until four p.m. I could sleep until at least one p.m. before needing to get ready for class. Latest two p.m. We could've gone to the cemetery as soon as it was dark, but we figured people wouldn't be visiting much later than ten o'clock. We were so wrong.

HQ: Can't sleep. You?

He didn't bother to give me the truth. He thought I didn't know. If I was a normal chick, with normal roommates, he'd be right. Unfortunately for him, we're a pack of criminals.

MW: Thinking about that pretty pink puss between your legs ;)

Of course he would make this sexual. That was all we were. *We're just fucking. We are nothing. He is nothing.* Well, if he wanted to get his emotions out via fucking me, I'd allow it. Actually, I'd welcome it. I had some emotions I could get out too. So a rough fuck didn't sound so bad.

HQ: She's thinking about you too. Want some company?

I smiled, sending the text. My mind had completely shifted from sympathy to lust.

MW: Come over right now.

I took a deep breath. **Yes, sir.**

⋅⊰⊱⋅

When I walked up to the steps of his old rickety house, I saw Maximus through the window in his bedroom. He was gaming, simultaneously checking his phone every other minute. He could wait a few more.

I perched myself on the railing surrounding the porch. For a second I thought I was going to fall through it, but it held. I set my black backpack on the boards by my feet and crossed my arms. If he turned on his chair, he would see my shadow, but I was past caring about that. I just leaned there, watching him.

Wondering how a person could hold the death of a loved one so silently.

His fingers were moving a mile a minute over his keys. His headphones were set on his messy hair. One ear open, ready to listen for me. He looked so content. Even from behind. You would have never known he just spent an hour at his brother's grave, screaming in agony.

His hair was the blank definition of bed head. His shoulders were shaking from the laughter his online friends brought him. He was wearing plaid pajama pants with a hole down the side of his thigh. As usual, he was shirtless. I could still see the lines my nails made from the last time he was inside me. *I want them to scar.*

His back muscles were prominent, moving and rolling with every laugh. The forearm I could see was strong, filled with veins. The same forearm that caused my stomach to heat, my toes to curl, and my heart to flutter. He was just a lump of skin and organs, but to me, he was becoming something that I would now *miss* if it were to ever vanish.

It'd been ten minutes before he reached for his phone and called me. I answered.

"Hey, where are you?"

I paused for a few seconds, needing to collect my thoughts. "I'm right here."

He cocked his head, taking off his headphones and lightly jogging to his front door. I didn't leave my spot on the railing as the door flung open and he barged through it, looking for me.

"Hey, what are you doing out here? Come in." His voice was hoarse. He coughed and swallowed, noticing the same thing. I just kept looking at him, searching for the truth behind his eyes. He cocked his head again, not needing to repeat himself. "Hare?"

"Hi, sexy." I kept my voice down. I had to remind myself he didn't know I knew. *They don't know that we know they know we know.*

"Hi, beautiful. Come inside, it's cold out—"

I lunged for him, interrupting his kind words with a hug. I wrapped my arms around his neck and stood on my toes, pecking his cheek before burying my head in his neck.

My ear tingled with his breath. "You okay?"

"Yeah, of course. Just wanted some fresh air before you took it all." I knew it was cheesy, but it got a smile from him anyway. I felt his lips curl in my hair. He picked me up, wrapping my legs around his bare waist.

"You're getting soft on me, Hare. Might have to fuck that out of you."

There it was again. The snap. The mask. All my feelings but lust left. "I'm going to fight you."

"Oh, we're fight-fucking tonight? I hope you know what you're in for." His voice dripped with deviance and he gave me a hard smack on my ass.

I'd welcome his bruises if it meant we got our anger out at the world.

"Do your worst, Maximus." I smiled, remembering the consequences of such a simple sentence.

CHAPTER

37

Harriet

I bit his neck and he dropped me in the hallway with a groan. I didn't unclench as he pinched the back of my neck with one hand and slammed me into the wall with the other. His pinch ached through to my jaw and I released my teeth. The bite mark was littered with dots of blood. The taste of iron spread across my lips. The curiosity took over, I licked them clean and gave him a vile smirk.

He exhaled, watching my tongue run over my lips. I felt his body stiffen as he rolled his head on his shoulders. Loud cracks filled my ears.

"How do I taste?" He growled in my face, his eyes filled with erotic fire.

"Like more."

I stumbled as he dragged me to his room, catching myself on the wall and the couch. "Take off your clothes and get on the bed, ass up." *Yes, sir.*

I did as I was told. I could feel the cold air against my pussy. *Thank god I shaved.*

He fumbled around under his bed and pulled out a black bag. I peered over the edge of the bed for a peek. He pushed my shoulders back and I resumed my position. "Do as you're told." *Goodie bag?*

He came behind me, nudging my knees apart. "Maximus?"

I pressed my lips into a hardline, carefully walking the dangerous side of him I unleashed when I drew blood from his neck. "Remember your safe word." *Uh oh.*

I felt a cold drag along my back and over my ass. It came up and under my chin, tilting my head. It was a whip. A black leather whip with three tassels on the end of it. *Goodie bag, indeed.*

He made sure I knew what it was before blindfolding me. "No restraints this time?" It was a genuine question. I was looking forward to submitting my will to his anger. *Whip!*

Everything in me winced. My muscles clenched and my bones shook. I let out a pained gasp.

He slid his fingers in me. "Oh," he breathed. "You have no idea how much I needed this tonight."

I was dripping in excited arousal. His dick dipped into my pussy and with a loud moan, he pumped. I groaned at him stretching me. There was no easing into this one. One hand clutched the whip with white knuckles, and the other fisted my hair.

He gasped, "You're so wet for me." He pumped profusely into me, offering me gasping moans and hard whips across my ass. His whipping arm was getting stronger and harder. I winced at the anticipation, but my arousal was growing with every swing.

I couldn't tell which pain felt better, the constant hitting of my cervix, or the snaps across my ass. My pussy was dripping down my thighs, his skin hitting the streams with every thrust.

"Tell me why you couldn't sleep." He grunted between thrusts. No answer. *Whip!* He repeated himself.

"No." I gritted through my teeth. *Whip!*

"Tell me why you couldn't sleep."

"No!" I raised my voice.

Whip!

I couldn't. I couldn't tell him what I saw, what I *heard,* at Sam's grave. This was going so well. He felt so good. I didn't want him to stop. My orgasm was building in my stomach. *Ask me something else. Anything...please...*

"Tell me what you were thinking about." He leaned forward across my back, pulling on my hair so hard I felt my neck crack.

"Maximus...I'm—" I moaned. He pulled out. Immediately sending my orgasm into limbo.

"Not until you tell me why."

Whip!

"Maximus, don't..." Tears were beginning to brim my eyes. I needed to come. My stomach was rolling, my inner thighs were slipping, my lower back was arching. Everything in my groin was on fire, begging to be released. I was losing it.

Whip!

"Tell..." *Slam.*

"Me..." *Pump.*

"Why..." *Thrust.* I could feel himself swelling inside me, preparing to come, yet he wouldn't let me until I told him what he wanted to hear.

Whip!

I lost it.

"ENOUGH!" I whipped the blindfold off. Before he could register what was happening, I spun around on my knees and pushed him on his back, pinning his arms beside his head, growling in aroused anger. His teeth were bared as he fought against my wrists. I was far too angry to let up.

He wanted to give me *permission* to release the pleasure *he* gave?

I don't fucking think so.

"There she is." He lifted his head, staring in my eyes with a venomous grin. "Let me see the girl you've been hiding," he dared me in a mocking tone, staring at my lips before biting the air between us and whispering, "I can set you free."

I slid my hand between us, guiding his hard cock inside me. Slowly, I lowered onto him, receiving a low grunt from the back of his throat.

I wasn't hiding anyone. I didn't know this part of me existed. I closed my eyes, focusing on letting go of my morals, values, and beliefs, letting my mind wander to an unfamiliar place that seemed too welcoming. I chased that dark feeling.

There was a snap. I opened them.

"Oh, you want to play?" I taunted him, slowly. He shifted under my weight. "Bite me, bitch." His laugh was evil. I lifted and lowered my body, rolling over his cock, forcing moans as he threw his head back in pleasure.

I leaned down to his ear, dragging it through my teeth. "I'll do you one better."

My palm connected with his cheek with a loud smack. I didn't hold back. His face turned red as he thrashed under me. I hesitated in my next move, pondering if I had gone too far.

I, in fact, went just far enough.

He bucked me off him, spinning me on my back and collapsing on top of me, simultaneously pinning my arms above my head. "That was one hell of a move, my girl. Scare yourself?" He chuckled, licking my face all around, avoiding my lips in silent punishment. I replied with a grin.

"If you don't come around my dick within the next—"

"Finally." The attitude in my tone was paramount. I've needed to come for so long, my muscles were aching.

His palm stunned me and my entire body flushed with heat. I let out a surprised laugh and felt my pussy slick even more. My legs were starting to quiver. This was so fucking hot.

I needed him inside me now, but I had gotten ahead of myself. He wants control. One side of me wanted to give it to him because I knew it would make him happy.

Another side of me wanted to test his anger because it might make me happy.

Again, a silent war. Teetering on the sexually acceptable and morally frightening.

My cheek started to burn as he pried my jaw open. He spat in my mouth. "Interrupt up me again and I will end you."

I nodded eagerly. "Yes, sir." The burn on my cheek was almost as hot as the burns on my ass, but not nearly as the sweet spot between my thighs.

He continued, "...within the next thirty seconds, I'm going to shove my cock so far up your ass, you're going to choke on it."

I swallowed his saliva and wrapped my arms around his neck, kissing him like my life depended on it.

He slid into me with ease, distracting me from my thoughts. "And here I thought you couldn't get any wetter. God, you're killing me, baby." He moaned, his mask slipping for only a moment as he landed on my lips.

I giggled against his mouth. He kissed me hard, biting my ears and kissing down my neck. He lapped his tongue over my nipples before he bit down on my piercing so hard I felt a rush of hot liquid trailing my stomach. I let out a groan of pain, arching my back at the agony. I felt a rush of heat between my legs.

He leaned and licked the trail until he got to my nipple. Sucking the blood out of me and down his throat. "Fuck."

The sight of him over me with my blood on his lips made my body shake. I needed to know what that tasted like.

"You bleed beautifully for me." Every word dripped with venom as he overwhelmed my body, my mind. I wrapped my hands in his hair and pulled him forward. "Fight me." I huffed, feeling my muscles reach the brim.

His smile was sinister as he pummeled into me, hitting that spot curved inwards. He spat on my face again before slapping it, finishing me off with a choke so hard my world was going black.

His eyes darkened. I knew the mask took over, but I was unsure as to who I was fucking. *How far can he go?*

I felt his cock flex in me from my struggle to breathe. My own orgasm brimming from how I felt, closer than ever before.

"Maximus..." I choked. My thighs were shaking around him. I could feel my pussy clench around his cock as our orgasms reached their peak. "Please," I held back the best I could, but he felt too fucking good.

"Now, Harriet." He spoke deeply, pausing to allow me my moment. He released my throat, sending a rush to my head as my body seized.

Stars flashed in my vision, and my pussy pulsated around him. Filling my canal with warm fluid that rounded him, I spilled as his name left my lips. In all this time, this was the first orgasm with Maximus's name on my lips. Giving in, admitting that he was the one who got me here.

I couldn't help it, my body took over, knowing he deserved to hear it.

"Open." He spoke, pulling his soaked cock from my body. He put both his hands on the wall above my head and forced himself into my mouth.

He named his orgasm after me as he filled my throat. Taking him in two gulps as he throbbed over my tongue.

He was panting heavily while leaning down to my forehead. "That's my girl."

As much as I would've enjoyed feeling him fill my ass, the desire to come was imperative.

He got off me, immediately making me feel bare and ashamed. "Wh-where are you going?" My voice cracked against my will. *Are you leaving me like this?*

My eyes started to water again, this time with a different meaning. Everything that just happened came forward. He licked my blood. I swallowed his. I was whipped. I took control. *For like, two minutes.* I hit him. He hit me. My eyes were darting around the room, hand in my hair, trying to figure out what to do next. *Do I leave? It's like three thirty in the morning.*

He brought me back, the mask gone. "Hey, hey, woah, Harriet. Hey," he sat down beside me. I sunk into his bed and under his sheets. "I'm not leaving you." He chuckled, sending my embarrassment further. "I'll be right back, I just need to deal with some things before I climb in there with you." He smiled gently, running a gentle hand through my hair. His eyes twinkled and my chest relaxed. His mask was completely gone.

"Okay..." I pulled the sheets up to my face to cover my mouth. The mouth that still tasted like him. His blood. His come. His spit.

He tasted like every dark thought I've ever had.

<hr/>

He came back with an array of items. The best one, steaming hot earl grey tea. He set the same breakfast tray down in front of me, grabbing my face and kissing my lips before he took his seat opposite of me.

"You bought me chocolates?"

He smiled. I told him before Christmas break that milk chocolate was my favorite. "Just drink your tea and eat your chocolate." He said, gulping down ice water for himself. Next to the bowl of ice cream was a Minnie Mouse Band-Aid. He pulled off the two plastic pieces and placed it firmly on the nipple he tore open. It wasn't doing much since my nipple was still hard with arousal, but I smiled and thanked him anyway. "Who's the bowl of ice cream for?"

"Would you just shut up and let me take care of you?" He let out a low laugh, shaking his head hard enough his hair fell over his eyes. I was asking too many questions. "Okay, okay, sorry." I laughed in return, holding my hands up in surrender. "It's vanilla." He smirked. *Vanilla. Of course it was.*

"Turn over," he said. I turned on my stomach, flattening my legs out as I shoved chocolate in my mouth. He pulled down his sheets to uncover his handiwork. He scooped a small amount of ice cream on a spoon and smoothed it over my reddened ass, I hissed at the feeling.

He spread it with the round of the spoon, soothing all the whips. He bent down and licked it up. The coldness felt surreal against my burning flesh.

The two opposite ends of the spectrum meeting in one intense fuck.

It was startling and calming all in one. I let out an exhale, signaling how good it was feeling. I twitched under the cold metal.

"That feels good. Thank you," I closed my eyes, bowing my head. "Thank you," I repeated. He gave each cheek a light kiss and a gentle swat. I winced, hissing through my teeth.

"Too soon?" He giggled, covering his mouth. *The man actually giggled.*

We drank, we ate, and we laughed until our stomachs hurt. Reviewing and questioning everything that had just gone down within the last hour of my visit.

"Was that what they call CNC?" I'd read about consensual-non-consensual in one of my dark romances. Where subs will *act* like they don't want to be fucked to come off as *fighting* the dom for pleasure.

He shook his head. "No, that was just fight-fucking. We were beefing, but we were fucking while we did it." He smiled again.

Oh god, don't look at me like that! "Why are you looking at me like that?"

"You're really good at it." Simple and short, but he meant it. He tried to hold back a smile even if I could see the corner of his lips twitching. *That felt way too good for me.* "Well, you're a really good teacher." I smiled.

I was still reminiscing. "You're a great fuck, you know that?" I tilted my head at him while I shoved a spoonful of vanilla ice cream in my mouth. "Oh really? Is that all I'm good for?" He stole the spoon right from my mouth, taking his own scoop. No doubt soothing that hoarse voice of his that I know nothing about.

"Maybe." Was all he was going to get from me. I wasn't supposed to get attached. *We're just fucking. We are nothing. He is nothing.*

"No, no. Is that really all I'm good for?" His tone lowered. Oh... I felt bad now.

"Not at all. Your tongue is just as good as your dick."

He rolled his eyes, trying to hide the fact that wasn't what he was looking for. I moved the tray out of the way and pulled his hands into my lap. His eyes were inches from mine. Staring at me full of lust, but mainly questions. "Hey, I was just kidding. If you want the truth, y-you're..." I stuttered.

But he was eager. "I'm what?" His eyes widened, he turned our hands over, running his thumb over the back of mine.

"You're...like everything and nothing. You're in between and all of the above. You exist in this perfect pocket between dimensions where nothing but everything matters."

He tried to hide his smile. He certainly wasn't anything less. And wasn't anything more. *Was he?*

"What?" I asked, trying to understand his face.

"Understood. We're definitely not *friends...*" He was dancing around his words, trying not to show how he was really feeling. "Friends don't know how each other taste." He laughed. He started to back off me but I tightened my hold on our hands to keep him in place.

"I know, I know. You're not a *friend,* I don't know what you are. All I do know is you're becoming important." I offered him a soft smile. I was starting to panic. I did not want to have this conversation. I didn't want to confront the thing.

His shoulders relaxed and he fell in my lap, curling up on my legs.

"Say something, please." I rested my chin in his hair. He nuzzled his face in my bare chest.

We sat in silence for a few moments, my fingers tapping the side of my thigh, impatiently waiting for him to say something. Anything.

He drew a long breath, wrapped his arms around my middle and tightened.

"You're already important."

CHAPTER

38

Maximus

You're becoming important.

Fuck. This was getting too far, she was starting to get attached. When I heard *nothing* leave her lips, I wanted to smack my head against a brick wall. I hated hearing that at first. But after I thought about her words, she was right. We were *everything* and *nothing*. We existed in a perfect pocket between dimensions where nothing but everything matters.

It was better than nothing, definitely better than boyfriend and girlfriend.

The thing is…I was already attached.

I wanted to stay away from her, I really did. I thought about not seeing her after I "ghosted" her on New Year's. I would've just let her play out her feelings and eventually, she would move on. But then she sent me that damn photo and brought me crawling back to her, salivating on my knees. There was a chance I was attached right from the beginning.

I don't think I can stay away from her anymore. No matter how much pain it brings us, I had convinced myself the pain was worth it. If—*when*—she finds out, I will die with a smile, knowing I had her in my arms. She'll hate me, but that's probably for the best. It's easier to hate the dead. Hating me meant she couldn't love me. Eventually she would forget.

But not if I'm becoming important to her. *What am I supposed to do? I'm attached. I'm being selfish. This wasn't just my life anymore.*

We talked for hours about the way we fucked, life, school. But never each other. She was so intrigued with this type of sex, I thought I might just kidnap her right there.

I couldn't leave her. Not when she fucks like that. Not when she's willing to try literally everything under the sun and moon.

Who knew this petite woman could have such an appetite for sinfully delicious things? I made it my mission to figure out what else she liked. Perhaps she didn't even know. Perhaps she needed her teacher to show her. She knows her safe word, she'll use it.

My dominance a mask, her submission a shadow. Masks shield me from the outside world, armor to protect my most vital, self-destructing organ. Her shadow follows her around, always in the back of her mind, not appearing until the moon does. It hides behind her in the light, coming out to play in the dark. I should've known since winter is her favorite season. That's what she was drawn to. Dark and cold meant safety to her.

I've seen the way she watches the snow fall in the moonlight outside my window. She's captivated by it. The softness of it falling, the natural brutality when it hits the ground.

There was a push and pull aspect to it. What she was drawn to, she pulls in, what positively scares her, she pushes for like the moon against the sun, eventually creating a current yet to be explored.

She's never had the opportunity but when I pushed her to the point of fighting back...I saw it. She has both mask and shadow. Neither of which she knows she has. It's just a silent echo through her veins.

We slept peacefully until her alarm woke me up at two-thirty in the afternoon. I turned it off with an angry smack. We watched the sunrise from my window so I figured she needed the sleep. When it went off again at three p.m., I lightly shook her. "Hare, it's three o'clock. Get up."

She rustled in my sheets, retightening her grip. Her head was tucked under my chin and her arms were around my middle. Even after last night, she still smelled like heaven. Mixed with a little bit of sweat and a whole lot of sex. If anyone walked in my room right now, they would probably have to plug their nose. I'd need to air out my room and wash my sheets.

I shook her again. She mumbled something about needing five more minutes, so I gave it to her. Except I fell asleep again. When I finally woke up again, it was four thirty. *Uh oh. Didn't she have class?*

I shook her harder this time. She would freak out if she missed her class. I snuck a look at her schedule at the library, she had Cosmetology today at four. *Make-up? On dead people? Eeeeeks.*

"Hey, wake up, it's four thirty!" I spoke in her ear. She shot her head up. "What the fuck are you yelling at me for, bitch?" Her voice was husky and still full of sleep.

"Jesus, you're a morning person. It's four thirty."

She spun her head around. "What! Noooooo!" she gasped. She scrambled to get out of bed but was hit with a wall of light-headedness. She fell back, running her hand through her hair.

Rubbing the sleep out of her eyes, she sent a side glance. She took one look at my bed head and her morning anger disappeared with a howl.

"Good morning, Sunshine!" She didn't stop laughing at my hair. I tried to fix it but it was no use. The further I pushed it down the higher it stood up on my head. I gave up, I needed a shower.

I leaned down to her face, resting my forehead against hers. "Good morning, Moonshine."

———— ✣ ————

I watched her pull her car out of my driveway and speed off to catch the last hour of her lecture. I had no classes on Monday, so I planned to stay home all day, thinking.

I closed the door and slid to the ground. Wiping the remaining sleep from my eyes. My body felt off today. Perhaps it knew my sleep schedule was about to get fucked up, but she was worth fucking it up for. Last night was crazy. I couldn't stop thinking about it. *She swallowed my spit. Her slap.*

Her blood.

She obeyed without complaints. And when she did, it pushed me to a new discovery.

I liked when she fought back. I hadn't had that before. Granted, I didn't do these things with other girls, I never felt the desire, but when she made that move...

We were growing with each other. Exploring different parts of ourselves we didn't know we harboured. I already knew I could go far, I have nothing *but* ideas. I just never found the person I wanted to unleash myself on.

Until November fourth.

I pondered why she wouldn't tell me what was keeping her up before she came over. And it pissed me off. *Why couldn't she just tell me she was thinking about me?*

Or maybe she was studying, wanting the whip more than telling me her truth.

Chase, Dylan, and Banks came down the steps at the same time. All serving me glances as they walked by me to kitchen. They looked tired today too. A hint of grumpy in their eyes. "Guys..." I strained. I stood up from the floor to follow them.

"Guys?" I repeated. I leaned against the doorframe of the kitchen.

They turned to me, their pajamas hanging off their bodies, and moving swiftly with their movements. "We are so glad you don't sleep upstairs, bro."

"Legit. How many times you gotta whip that girl? Was she that misbehaved?" Chase grabbed his favorite coffee mug and sat at the table with a groan.

I smirked. "Y'all heard that, eh?" I crossed my arms over my chest and bowed my head to hide my smile.

"Heard it? I thought I might be in it." Banks's room was right above mine, thank god. He was just as fucked up as I was when he brought girls home. I'd heard him on countless occasions, so I didn't really feel that bad.

Something that felt that good can't be that bad.

"Y'all out here fucking bitches and I'm swooning over Amy like a lost puppy. How does pussy come so easily to you fuckers?" Dylan scowled. His jealousy was not his best look.

"For starters, we're not five—"

I leaned forward to swat Banks in the arm. "Leave the little man be!" We bent over laughing. Poor dude was the shortest in the house. In reality, he wasn't actually that short. But against my six-foot-four, Banks's six-foot-two, and Chase's six-foot, his five-ten was sad.

Dylan shot Banks a glare, Banks pressed his lips into a hard line to stop himself from laughing. My stomach was grumbling but I couldn't shake the weird feeling coursing through my body. My head felt too light, my limbs were sore and my chest felt heavy. I could only get one cough and one grunt out before Banks snapped his neck toward me.

"Max." It was stern, and I knew what it meant. The guys looked at us in question, but didn't push. They shrugged it off. Dylan joined Chase at the pong table with his espresso and they ate plain toast with peanut butter.

My eyes darkened into thin slits, I knew what he was going to say. "No," I snapped at him.

"Yes." He snapped back. The boys were sitting on their phones at the table, no doubt stalking Amy and the pages of hot girls from our school. I grabbed an apple from the basket beside the fridge and made for my room. Of course he fucking followed me, leaving Dylan and Chase to their pity party of one.

He closed the door behind me and stood with his arms crossed. "Max."

"No, Banks. Leave it alone." I sat at my desk in my chair and put my headset over *both* my ears. I wasn't listening to this. I had a fantastic night, and I wanted her to come back to someone who looked and acted alive, not some vegetable who can barely get up to fucking piss for himself. Banks just stood there. Waiting.

"I'm not going to die today, buddy, so go eat your breakfast or lunch or whatever. I'm fine."

"You're not *fine*," he huffed, pinching the bridge of his nose. "Not until you take—"

"You sound like my parents," I snapped.

"No, the fuck I do not. Your parents force them down your throat, I'm just going to stand here, annoying the shit out of you until you take them. Today. Right now."

I whipped my headphones off, resting them on my shoulders. "Look, I'm not taking them today. We had such a good night and if she comes back, I can't be..." I slumped back in my chair and made an impression of a person in hospice.

Her pussy danced across my vision, making me shift in my seat. *I can't believe I'm trying to justify myself to him.* He just stood there, not absorbing anything I was saying. *In one ear, out the other, right?*

"Oh ya? And if she comes back to find you cold and in stage of rigor mortis? You think she'll thank you for not taking them?" He angled his head, he was being sassy, I couldn't help but feel the heat build in my cheeks. He was starting to piss me off.

"Banks…" I began. "Stop."

He started scrambling through my black backpack on the floor. "What the?" He pulled out a baby blue iPad, a green pencil case, and a black lace thong. I gasped. *She has my bag.*

I started laughing at the irony. It never dawned on me that we have the same backpack so in her rush to get out of here, she accidentally swiped mine.

I shook my head, my hair falling over my eyes. "Guess I'm in luck."

"Until she opens the bag and finds your pill bottles. Maybe she'll be the one who can convince you to fight for your own fucking life." He slammed the door behind him and I heard the usual stairs creak under his feet.

Shit.

MW: Hey. Hope you got there before class ended. You swiped my bag when you left.

I started pacing around my room. *What if she finds the pills? What do I say then?*

CHAPTER

39

Harriet

I applied make-up to a cadaver. A real cadaver. I held someone's loved one in my hands. Dotting foundation, concealer, lip gloss, even eyeliner to imitate the image we were given. Learning about the postmortem effects that happens to skin, how applying cosmetics properly can make it last longer so it stays for the funeral service.

After that, it really doesn't matter. Respectfully. Although, many religions believe our body are just vessels and it's our souls that fly away at the point of death.

A few of my classmates fainted, vomited, or just out right left the lab. It reeked of chemicals, even I needed an adjustment period. I felt lightheaded but if this was going to be my career, I'd have to get my system used to formaldehyde sooner rather than later.

Fortunately, by the end of the lab, the room just smelled like oxygen.

I may have enjoyed myself a little too much. I was humming over my cadaver while getting disapproving looks from my classmates. However, our prof gave stunning remarks about my accuracy and attention to detail. The comparison between the photo of the deceased while she was alive versus when she was dead on my table was almost one hundred percent.

I tuned out everyone's looks and bumbling comments. I was proud of my handiwork. I was respectful, clean, and delicate. After all, she was someone's person once upon a time. In the real world, I wasn't sure if we would get their life stories before we embalmed and took care of them. We definitely didn't in school, no charts, no history. So I made up my own.

I approached my lady, trying to slow my excited feet along the way. Someone was bound to call me Morticia Addams any time now. It made my chest heavy to see she was no older than forty. By the looks of her skin, she was only dead for about a week. Or extremely well preserved. I assumed I'd be eventually learning about that in my theories and procedures class.

I gave her the name Dayna. Mom of two boys. Ages three and five. The younger one likes to color Disney characters, and the other is in a hockey phase. Her husband sits at home every night, flipping through their wedding album. They got married at twenty and lived happily ever after until she got hit by a car. Then she ended up on my slab. Boom. End of story.

After we had lecture, more like after I got there in time for the last thirty minutes, we were led into the lab connecting to the hall. Twenty bodies were laying on cold metal slabs, respectfully covered. The smell in the air hit my lungs like a brick wall. My remaining classmates were woozy before they even got to their stations. I was practically trying not to rub my hands together and jump up and down.

I was okay with the name calling, the looks, the sounds, but that didn't mean I was going to go out of my way to give them ammunition. So what if I loved this stuff? Would you rather someone who didn't care to prepare your loved ones? I thought it was a compliment to death. To the inevitable. A silent thank you for allowing us to experience the earth before it came and took us away. It was the one thing that humans knew nothing about. What was after, what was before. They say our life flashes behind our eyes in seven minutes. Does anyone know if that's actually true? Has anyone lived to tell the tale?

Once you're dead, you're dead. It's why the best sayings and quotes are rooted in death.

"You can sleep when you're dead." — Warren Zevon
"You only live twice: once when you're born and once when you look death in the face." — Ian Fleming
"The meaning of life is that it stops." — Franz Kafka
"Our dead are never dead to us until we have forgotten them." — George Elliot
"Death smiles at us all, all a man can do is smile back." — Marcus Aurelius
"What is dead, may never die." — George R.R. Martin

My family tried to hide their cringes when I informed them of what I would be going to school for, but once I explained my view on the proper treatment of someone transitioning from this life to the next, they thought less about me being creepy, and more sentimental. Roxy had the gall to ask me if I played with dead animals as a child. I smacked her annoying ass upside the head that day. We laugh about it now, seeing as I went through with my education. She takes me more seriously, though I keep the details of my studies to myself.

With the way my program works, families donate their loved ones' bodies to our institute to allow us to practice on them at a discounted rate. Funeral costs were ridiculous, everyone knew that, so the school started a program that allowed us to practice on real bodies and the ones who were adequately *completed* were allowed to go back to funeral home.

The ones who weren't had real morticians redo the procedure, which happened to be our prof. Aileen Anderson was a practicing substitute mortician for the funeral home connected to our university, so she would tend to our cadavers if a student royally fucked up. Which wasn't very often because she was a fantastic, hands-on professor who knew the trade inside and out.

"Harriet!" Ms. Anderson called after me as I was washing my hands for postmortem lab protocol. Gloves off. Masks off. Gowns off. Garbage. Garbage. Garbage. I turned my head over the sink in the back of the lab. "Hello!" I was cheery, maybe too cheery since she noticed. She jumped, her eyes doing a little squint at the octave of my voice.

"Sorry. I just, I had—"

"You had fun today." It wasn't a question. "I did, yes, ma'am." She wasn't particularly old per se, but my mom taught me manners when speaking to authority figures. This woman could fail me if she wanted to.

"What can I do for you?" I wiped my hands on the paper towel and carefully threw it in the can beside the washing station. I took off my lab coat and hung it up on the wall.

"Actually, it's what I can do for you. I know today was your first day with a cadaver, but even so, I was amazed with your work. Like I said earlier, your attention to detail, the gentleness you put into your cadaver, it was quite impressive." She clasped her hands in front of her.

I gleamed with excitement. I was never a huge scholar in high school, so this kind of praise over something I enjoyed was blowing me out of the water. "Thank you! This class is a great opportunity. And it helps the Greenlake community."

"Yes, of course. As you know, I'm a practicing mortician at the Greenlake Funeral Home. I was wondering if you have looked into placements yet?"

"Uh—no, ma'am. This is only my second semester of my first year. I didn't think placements were needed until until third year. Why?" I pulled on my hoodie from the cubby system on the wall and slung my bag over my shoulder, listening intently.

"I was thinking maybe you would like to join me? I don't usually take students under my wing, but I think you would make a great mentee." She was smiling, the lines in her face angling upward as she peered at me over her round glasses.

She reminded me of a modern hippie. Her long wavy graying black hair complimented the frame of her glasses, and her flowing romper-dress with random designs. She had a brown tote bag slung over her shoulder and a pair of clogs with a leaf and a coffin pinned to them.

I thought I could hug her. "That sounds amazing. Thank you so much!"

She gathered her own belongings and walked out with me. She asked me why I chose this program, how I dealt with the backlash that came from other people, and ended with letting me know she would contact me in August before the next school year starts.

I leaped and skipped to my car. Throwing open the door, outstretching my arms and cheering at the sky. The moment I sat in my seat and closed the door, I smelled the chemicals on me. *Shit. I need to shower. Bad.*

I unlocked my phone. A message from Maximus. Probably about his bag. I accidentally swiped it rushing out the door.

HQ: Hey, sorry about that. I had to take notes in your notebook because you have my iPad. Can I give it back to you tonight?

I drove home without waiting for his response. His response time when he gamed was astronomically poor. If he needed it right away, I would go back.

MW: No problem. See you later.

————⟡————

"You smell like death." Was the first comment I got from Mia as I walked through our front door. Kim was splayed out over our table studying, Jane was high out of her mind catching up on *The Office* and Mia was making dinner. "Holy shit, is it almost seven?" Kim rubbed her eyes and yawned. "This accounting test is going to be the death of me."

I walked over to her, skimming the papers spread over the yellow wood. "Don't worry, I'll make you look pretty in your coffin." I laughed.

"Oh god, you really do smell like death." She plugged her nose and made a gag face.

"I know, I know. I'm going to take a shower right now, I promise."

Jane giggled to herself on the couch with her box of Cheez Its and a blanket stuffed up her chin. "You good over there, Jane?" I yelled across the room, over the television. She didn't stop laughing, "Oh ya. I'm good. But don't you dare come over here, Mother Death."

I rolled my eyes with a smile and headed up to my room. I stripped naked and turned the water to hot. I climbed in it, feeling all the tight muscles up my back and down my neck. Leaning over a cadaver for an hour was new to my body, and I was feeling it. So I sat down. I let the water run over my shoulders, between my breasts, and down to my *pretty pink puss* as he would say. I hadn't thought about him all day until I looked at my phone in the parking lot.

But once I had a single thought, the rest came flooding. Before I knew it, my hands were between my thighs, making small tight circles over my clit. I imagined it was his hand as his teeth were bared behind my eyelids. His carved muscles, his tattoo, the lightness of his touch. And then as I was about to explode, his roughness, his bites, his grip in my hair.

The pace I gave myself was the momentum of us last night. Remembering the way he licked my blood from my body before sucking it right out of me.

"You bleed beautifully for me."

His words echoed in my skull as I reached my climax. Covering my mouth with my palm so my roommates wouldn't hear the sex we're having.

Crying his name as I came with him inside me was one thing, it was another to moan his name when I was by myself. I refused to give him that much power.

My orgasm washed away with the rest of the dirt and the chemicals. Like nothing ever happened. I continued on with my shower, thinking of him often. How he would hold me from behind to whisper something dirty about my soapy titties or bending me over. His light kisses on my forehead as the water washes over us. But mostly us being in one the place no one else could go.

A shower is just a thing to do for most people, a hygienic necessity. But for me, it was one of my favorite places. A place I could find peace. A place I could be alone, with no interruptions.

It was a safe space for me.

During the difficult years as a teenager, this is where I would hide. I spent a lot of my time in the water, feeling it wash away the parts of me I loathed. Letting it run down my legs, my face, my arms. Letting it blanket me in a protective film. From them. From myself. It helped me pretend I didn't exist and where I didn't exist was peace.

In the worst years, I'd used it to wash away the blood dripping from my wrists. That's where the pleasurable pain really started, the echo of the drops against the ceramic tile.

Hearing the beauty of the pain I created.

That was the trigger point. In a sense, I think I outgrew cutting. I dug my own grave, but I was too tired, too numb to put myself in it.

I found other outlets. I found other ways to kill myself.

Smiling when I didn't mean it. Laughing when something wasn't funny. Forcing myself to eat. Alcohol. Weed. Those few weeks I tried ecstasy. Anything to stop the pain in my head. Anything to die, but then again, I died when I was fifteen.

Until three months ago when I felt the crack in my chest.

After growing up in household of lies and heartache, I made my heart cold enough not to break.

But even ice cracks.

CHAPTER

40

Harriet

After I got out of the shower, I pushed away the thoughts of my past. If I could outrun my scars, I would. But that's another thing about pain. No matter how much you've healed, it always leaves a mark.

It was eight o'clock now. I sat down with my legs crossed at my desk and pulled out extra lined papers and another pencil case. I would have to recopy my notes again onto my iPad when I got it back from Maximus.

I reached across my bed for his backpack, accidentally pulling the zipper, and everything fell out of it.

"Great." I exhaled. *Now I have to get up.* With a grunt, I undid my legs and spun on my chair, reaching the floor on my knees to pick up the remnants of his backpack. A gray pencil case, a green notebook, a pack of gum, an old condom—of course—and a gray zip up hoodie.

I picked them all up, but something fell out of the sweater, tumbling to the floor. "Ugh, what—*huh?*"

Again, I got to my knees and picked up the two neon orange bottles on the floor. I spun the first bottle in my hand. *Maximus White. Take two daily.* Then again, *Maximus White. Take two daily.* Bright blue stickers were added to the sides of the bottles: *Take with food.*

I looked over at my door. It was open. I rushed to close it, checking the hallway to see if anyone saw. All clear.

I sat back at my desk. The rest of his backpack's contents were spilled over the floor again. My focus tunneled on the bottles.

I titled them to the side to read the labels. Enalapril and furosemide. "What the hell?"*Pills? Prescription pills?*

I dug around the drawer of my desk for my old laptop. Since I had gotten my iPad last Christmas, I barely used my laptop, but I couldn't throw it away. I opened it up and clicked on Google.

"Shitty old laptop." I scowled at the screen as it took forever to connect to the internet. My fingers were pumping with adrenaline. My mind was racing a mile a minute. I couldn't make anything of this. The page finally loaded and I let my hands hover over the keyboard.

I paused. "I shouldn't be doing this. This is an invasion of privacy. *Again,*" I muttered to myself. I shook my head and rubbed my forehead. After a quick five, maybe two, seconds, I said, "Fuck it."

I typed in Enalapril and what it was used for, the cursor hovering over the search button but didn't click it. *Stop.* "This is quite literally none of your business, Harriet."

I pushed away from my desk to stand. Only I started pacing my room. I walked back and forth, juggling the pill bottles from hand to hand. I paced for several long minutes before my phone chimed.

I jumped. "Ah! Shit!" I was thankful for it bringing me back to reality. I grabbed my phone off my desk and unlocked it. The text was from Maximus.

MW: Hey, you coming over still?

I threw my phone on the bed with all my might. "Ugh!"

Kim came through our bathroom and stood in my side of the doorway. "You good?"

I hid the bottles behind my back, trying to hide my suspicion with a smile. "Yeah, just frustrated over a test I'm studying for. Needed a break." I chuckled, hoping it was convincing. "Yeah same. Okay, well, if you need anything, let me know." She walked back the way she came and closed her side of the bathroom.

The pill bottles rattled in my hands as I pulled them out from behind me to read them again. *You're not imagining this. This is real.*

I flopped on my bed, leaving the pill bottles upright on the edge of my desk. I unlocked my phone and touched my finger to our chat. I began typing.

I found your pill bottles.

Delete.

Why do you have pills in your backpack?

Delete.

WHAT ARE YOU HIIIIDDDDIIIINNNGGG???!!!!

DELETE.

I bowed my head on my bed, exhaling a sigh of pent up frustration and disbelief. *If he wanted me to know, I would know.* I needed to convince myself more.

"If he wanted me to know, I would know. If I needed to know, he would tell me. This is none of my business. I am not his girlfriend, nor am I his mother. I did not see these." My voice echoed between my arms and my bed. I wasn't convinced. Had to try harder.

So finally, I closed my eyes and said the words out loud.

"We are just fucking. We are nothing. He is nothing." I repeated that sentence four times over before my phone rang this time. I picked it up. "Hello?" I tried to keep my voice from shaking.

"Are you still coming over?" No hello. No hi. His voice was antsy on the end of the line. He really wants me to come over.

Or does he really want the backpack back? He doesn't want me to know.

"Hello?" he repeated. "Hi, yeah, sorry. I'll come bring your bag right now. Just finishing up my notes."

"Okay, see you soon." And he hung up the phone. I rolled over on my bed and hid my face behind my hands. I grabbed a pillow and screamed into it. Kim yelled from her room. "I feel that too!" *You have no idea, Kim.*

Slowly, I got up from my bed and packed his bag. Throwing everything in it, wrapping the pill bottles in the sweater so evidence of my snooping wasn't obvious. *If he wanted me to know, I would know.*

I hesitated over the bag for a minute. Before I could stop myself, I pulled out the pill bottles and a notebook and grabbed my phone.

CHAPTER

41

Maximus

She knocked on the front door, and I practically ran into it trying to open it. She stood there, in a oversized tee and pajama shorts. In the middle of winter.

Her face twitched. She wasn't smiling. She looked at me with wide eyes. *Uh oh. Here it comes.*

"Here you go," she spoke, handing me my bag. "Sorry about that."

Phew.

"Not a problem at all. I'll go get yours. Come in." She stepped just inside the door. Her snowy boots dampening our welcome mat.

I quickly walked down the hall and around the corner where I left her bag. I zipped it back up and handed it to her. "You good?" I pried.

She slung her backpack over her shoulder. She snapped out of it. "Yeah, I'm good! Just not happy about missing most of my class today. Now I have to wait for the lecture to be uploaded and blah, blah, blah. So I'm bugged." She sighed.

"Hey, wait." I stepped out into the snow with my bare feet. Ice ran up my ankles and spread through both my legs. She walked back, wonder across her face.

"Stay?"

"I have to start studying for a quiz in one of my other classes, so maybe later? I'll text you to see if you're awake." She got up on her tippy toes, grabbing the back of my neck to bring me down to her level. She planted a light kiss on my lips. "See ya!"

She sped off and by the time I turned to close the door, Banks was leaning at the end of the hallway with his arms across his chest, again.

"She didn't say anything," he muttered as I walked past him.

"Because she doesn't know." I smiled proudly. Pausing at his back, I gave him a pat on the shoulder as I headed for my room. He followed me. Again.

"Come on, man. Let it go." I sighed, spinning on my heels to face him. I threw my bag on the floor.

"You got your backpack now. Take them." He reach for my backpack and whipped it open, digging around for the two pill bottles that awaited me in my sweater. He popped the caps and handed me the pills.

"She's coming back tonight," I tried to be as nonchalant as I could. "She's coming back." I pushed away his hand.

My chest panged. "Agh," I breathed, resting a hand on my chest and falling back on my bed.

"Come on, Max. You know they help the pain!" He wasn't yelling, but he wasn't speaking lightly either. "Take the fucking pills."

"No," I glared at him. "Not tonight."

His gaze hardened as he crossed his arms over his chest. "I'm not leaving until you take them."

I was beginning to get mad now. "You're pushing it." I stared at him through my brows. "Maybe I'm not pushing it enough, Max." His voice was stern, he was feeling far too confident. I told him again I was not taking the pills tonight, not with the possibility of Harriet coming back.

"Ask me if I care." He challenged, stepping closer. He needed to get out of my room. Instead he moved around to lean on my desk.

"Banks..." I started. I rolled my neck on my shoulders before I continued. I did not want to fight with him. He's my best friend. "I appreciate your..."

He leaned forward and grabbed the collar of my shirt, his eyes were glossy. "I have watched you *struggle*. I have watched you hold your chest *begging* it to let you *breathe*. I have watched your eyes *sink*. I have watched you *calculate* the remainder of your *life* when someone talks about the future. I have seen the *toll* this is taking. So tell me, why the hell you won't take them? One girl can't possibly be the reason you're so willing to die!" He was yelling now.

I slammed my hands down and pushed up to get out of his grip and in his face. "Enough!"

He angled his head at me, waiting for me to finish, but in all honesty I had no idea what I was going to say. Neither of us were scared of each other. We both knew it would be a continuous fair fight. Not that it would ever come to that.

My head felt light. I had to admit, the pain was really bad today. My eyes swelled. I didn't say anything.

"Fine." He threw his hands in the air. He turned to leave, hesitating at the door, but I interrupted his pace.

"She makes me feel alive, Banks." My voice cracked. He let out a breath, evidently giving up. "Banks, I—"

He turned around. "Then take them for her," *Fuck you.*

"Please." *Fuck you.*

I ripped the pills from his hands, swallowing them dry. My head pressurized, my chest lightened.

I hate when you work so perfectly.

"Happy?" I scoffed.

CHAPTER

42

Maximus

An hour later, probably after he paced his room and stewed on our altercation, Banks came back down to my room, opening my door with a hard knock.

He walked into my room and sat on my bed, making a face like maybe that wasn't the best spot to sit down. He stood up. I managed a laugh, he gave me a smirk in return.

"I sit on your bed," I reminded him. "True." He sat back down. "Now, you're going to tell me what happened on New Year's and what the situation is with Nicole."

I joined him on my bed, in silence at first, but he never left my side. My mind was fuzzy, my body heavy. I didn't want to do anything, let alone talk. The side effects of these pills really sucked.

My voice was still hoarse from the cemetery, and now my mind was foggy as fuck. The words formed, but it was exhausting.

"I collapsed on New Year's. I was rushed to the hospital and... and the doctors did a fuck ton of tests on me, everything you can think of. Nicole was a student nurse there. She wasn't working my case, but she kept me company by my bed. We talked, she flirted, I rambled about Harriet. They wouldn't let me have my phone so

Harriet was in the dark. Then Harriet confronted me about it...
and..." I paused. I didn't want to finish.

"And?" *Ugh.*

"She thinks I ditched her to fuck Nicole, but I told her my
grandfather was in the hospital."

"So you lied?"

"Yes, I lied. And I would do it again."

He sighed, shaking his head, his blonde hair swaying. "Did
you?" He arched a cautious eyebrow at me. His ice blue eyes were
piercing. I had no idea what he meant. "Did I what?"

His expression dropped and then he asked me, "Did you fuck
Nicole?"

I stood from my bed as fast as I could, which from the outside
probably wasn't very fast—or stable—but it felt dramatic enough
for me. "What? Hell no!" He pulled my arm and my ass was back
on the bed. I had no energy to fight tonight. *Thanks to him.*

He tossed his hands up in the air in surrender. "I was just
asking! Needed to prove my point."

I turned my head away from him, he was starting to annoy
me. How could he think I would want to fuck anyone else? My
lips curved in a vile smile and my pants started to tighten at the
thought of her before registering what Banks had said.

"Wait, prove what point?" Banks could be sneaky when he
wanted to, and often insightful at the worst of times. I had a
feeling this was going to be one of them. I rolled my eyes. "Prove
what point?" I repeated.

"You're addicted to her, the way she feels, and it's going to kill
you," was all he said before marching out of my room and up to his.

CHAPTER

43

Maximus

"Am not!" I yelled after him. *He can't just say shit like that and run away.* I reached him before he hit the top of the stairs.

"Oh yeah? You had to come tell me that? Who are you trying to convince? Me? Or you?" *Damn you.* "The Max I knew last year would've fucked Nicole. Probably on his hospital bed, IV tubes and all. But now—"

"I'm not addicted to her." I huffed, running had become more difficult since my last collapse over the break.

He clicked his teeth. "Okay. Then let her go."

My stomach hurt. "What?" I started to sweat. Never speak to her again? *Let her go?*

"Break off whatever this is and let her go. You're not taking your meds, which is just going to make you feel worse, and then what?"

I interrupted him again. "It hurts when I take them and it hurts when I don't. I'm going to die anyway so what's the fucking point?!"

He paid no attention. "You've been saying that for months now, right? Why drag her down with you?" He turned his head, nudging his chin forward expecting an answer from me.

I opened my mouth to speak, but no words came out.

"Mhmmm." He hummed, keeping his mouth in a thin line. He wasn't angry, he was just trying to get his point across. Rendering me speechless was certainly doing the job. *Damn it.*

I wasn't angry at him and he knew that. He has always given it to me straight, no bullshit, no sugar coating. Just straight up truth. I respected him for that. In my world of eggshells and carefully chosen words, I appreciated a friendship where brutal honesty was the foundation.

"You're worse than my parents!" I joked, yelling at his back as he walked into his room. He turned around to stick his tongue out at me, and both middle fingers. I returned the gesture and went back to my room.

I tried so hard to focus on biochemistry. I should've been caring about the functions of living organisms, but it was proving difficult when my phone was glued to my face, waiting for Harriet to text me. Especially when my brain was fuzzy from the side effects of the enalapril and furosemide. *God, this is pathetic. I'm not addicted to her.*

She did make me feel alive, though.

Like I was born to live.

I felt no pain when I was around her. The doctor would just tell me the excessive amounts of dopamine or serotonin or some shit was blocking out my pain, but I wouldn't care. *How can something this good be bad?*

I had no heart problems, no family problems, no dead brother, no stress, no reminder of death. Everything melted away with her. Faded into a black background. *Maybe because I'm living the same lie she is?*

Maybe she was only a distraction from my problems because she didn't know what my problems were. *Her ignorance is my bliss.*

I could live in her truth. A deceitful truth where I was the king.

I shrugged to myself, why would I pop my own bubble? It was comfy in here. Warm. Deliciously soft. I shook my head with a smirk, my hair falling in my eyes.

"Argh." My dick was hard, sticking straight up out of my pajama pants. I wasn't wearing boxers so there was nothing securing it down. I tried to slip it into my waistband, but the moment it was in my hand, it was her hand.

I closed my eyes, leaning back on my chair, her pretty little face was in my mind. Smiling at me with her blue eyes and scattered freckles.

I stroked myself under the desk. The closer I got to my release the more vile the images became. Her bouncing tits. The way her pussy folds around me. Her cheeks red with arousal, the way her mouth forms when she moans my name. How warm she feels when I'm inside her. How her come runs down the veins in my dick, creating small pools in my groin...

"Oh... Harriet..." I threw my head back against my chair as I moaned her name, spilling into my hand.

Immediately, my face reddened with shame. *Fuck, maybe I am in trouble.*

I cleaned myself up. Maybe Banks was right, maybe I needed to distance myself from her.

HQ: Can't study anymore. You still awake?

Never mind!

MW: Yes! Come over!

Bite me, Banks.

CHAPTER

44

Maximus

I left the door unlocked for her, I was already in bed by midnight. She walked in wearing black sweatpants and a white tube top under her black sweater. "Hi, Sunshine." She set her bag down and tried crawling in beside me.

"Hi, Moonshine." I held down the blankets so she couldn't get in.

"Let me in!" she whined, holding out her bottom lip. I clicked pause on *Gilmore Girls* and sat up on my elbows with a sly grin. "New rule. If you want in my bed, you have to be naked, or else you will be punished."

"What if I want to be punished?" she teased. *Well shit, bend over then.* My naked dick was heating up under my sheets.

I shook my head, pushing my hair out of my eyes. *I need a haircut.* "I'd be more than happy to give such punishment, but you'll regret it." I winked.

She cocked her hip and crossed her arms over her chest. Well, if she wanted to play, I was game.

"Alright then, bend over." I smirked. I got up on my knees to get off the bed. She stepped up to me, my dick poking her in the stomach. We still weren't the same height. She put a hand on my chest, wrapping the other around my dick. Looking slightly up at me, "Would it be weird if we didn't fuck?" She asked softly, I angled my head at her. *You're literally touching my dick, woman.*

"What do you mean 'weird'?" I air quoted her. If she didn't want to have sex tonight, she needed to unclench the hand around my cock. *Now.*

"I know that's what we use each other for, and I can go if you want, but I kind of just want to chill and watch"—she finally glanced at the TV—"oh my god, you're watching *Gilmore Girls*?!" she shrieked. Her mood completely changed. She immediately started undressing herself and climbed in next to me.

She wasn't paying any attention to me, only searching for the remote as she nuzzled into my chest, wrapping her legs around mine. I pulled her in close and hit play on the remote. I twirled her hair in my fingers and leaned my head against the side of hers. "I know we have this insanely awesome, fantabulous fuck buddy system going on, but you do remember that you're worth more to me than that *delicious* puss, right? That I actually like you?"

She turned her head up to me. She thought about that for a minute, like she'd forgotten I told her I think she's pretty cool. Emphasis on the pretty, and emphasis on the cool.

She never responded. She kissed my chest and lightly pulled my skin between her teeth. She whispered something, but I couldn't hear her over Dean yelling at Rory about cheating on Lindsay.

Harriet didn't say another word for three episodes. I've never seen her this quiet before.

I nudged her head with my shoulder. "Are you okay?" I pulled her in tighter in case she needed it. No response. "Hey." I nudged her again.

She angled her head up at me again, resting her chin on my chest. "Yeah." She turned back toward the tv.

"Why don't I believe you?"

"Because talking ain't our thing, fucking is." She chuckled. I told her a lot about me. What did she mean? "We talk, I mean you know a lot about me—"

She spun on her elbows, looking me dead in the eye. "You had a brother."

Okay...that is not what I thought she was going to say.

I sat up shocked, she scooted off me. "Harriet. Be very careful choosing your next words." *How did she find out?*

"Why didn't you tell me?" Her voice shook and her eyes softened.

"Is it any of your business?!" I snapped, closing my eyes immediately after. I knew that was the wrong thing to say. I ran my hands through my hair. I could feel the back of my throat closing. I did not want to have this conversation. I did not want to talk about Sam.

I could tell by her face she wasn't expecting that snap either. She pushed off the bed, getting redressed. "You can't leave." I started moving toward her to pull her back. "I'm sorry I snapped. I wasn't expecting that. You caught me off guard, I'm sorry."

She paused, her shirt in her hands. This was not a conversation I wanted to be having, especially with her tits hanging out with hard nipples.

"I don't talk about it. I don't even know how you found out."

"Ryan. Mia is sleeping with him." She sat back down, I gave her a look, and she took off her pants with an eye roll. "Cory's roommate, Ryan." She was trying to jog my memory but I knew exactly who she was talking about. The dude at breakfast. The roommate of the guy I almost beat to death.

"Harriet... I—" I stuttered. I don't know where to go from here. "Yeah, I had a brother. I don't talk about it."

"I'm nobody, remember? Talk about it with me." *Nobody.* I laughed in my head. *Nobody.* She cuddled up beside me. "Tell me about him."

I pushed off her, backing into the corner wall of my bed. "I'm sorry, I'm sorry." I was panicking. She put her hands in the air and moved away from me. I cringed. I didn't want her to do that. I didn't want to push her away.

This just...I...

"Harriet...I..." I began. I couldn't form words. I stuttered beyond belief.

"I'm sorry, I'll go." She started dressing again.

"No, wait." I reached forward and pulled her back. "Other than my family, the only person who knows about Sam is Banks." I took a breath. "You caught me off guard." I offered her a nervous laugh. I was in shock. If I wasn't counting her knowledge of me fucking up Cory, this was the first real-world problem she'd known about. All of a sudden my bubble felt a little smaller.

She was looking at me with sad eyes, tracing the muscles in my arms and chest. *Fuck, she pities me. Fuck!*

I sighed, taking well-needed breath. Ironically thanking the pills in my system for keeping me relatively calm. I told her about Sam. The good things, the bad things, our relationship. She smiled, and offered me soft laughs. She was listening intently, laying on her stomach with her hands under her chin and her feet in the air. Like she wanted to hear about my dead brother.

And then I told her how he died. Her face softened, and she sat up in front of me, I was still leaning in the corner. For whatever reason, the pressure against my back and shoulders offered me comfort. She reached for my hands and I didn't back away this time. I let her take them and kiss my knuckles. She knew not to push me, but still wanted to tell me she was there. She was listening.

"Maximus, I am so sorry for your loss. I could never imagine the pain that brought—brings your family," she whispered. There were tears in our eyes. My chin quivered, but I clenched my jaw to keep it at bay. I was not about to cry in front of this—my... whoever she is.

"He was my best friend," I managed, unable to make eye contact with her. When I didn't look up, I felt her forehead press against mine. Giving it a light headbutt as a way of saying *I'm here.*

I appreciated the little touches. The small notions of her presence. Once I started talking about him, the words flowed. Like releasing a dam. It was easy. *I'm getting way too comfortable here.* I never talk about him, so retelling his stories, replaying my memories made him feel alive again.

Like he never died on me.

I lifted my head and kissed her forehead, embracing her in a koala hug. I collapsed in her arms, wrapping all my limbs around her little body. I tried my hardest to fight them, but tears were brimming my eyes. She felt the tension and cupped the back of my head.

Memories of Sam raced through my mind in circles. Once they started, I couldn't stop. I set a time and place for these emotions, the cemetery, but she cracked me wide open without knowing it. I couldn't tell if I was thankful to her for getting me to talk about him or if I was going to ghost her in the morning. There was a fifty-fifty chance for either option.

"I'm right here," she murmured in my hair. "I got you." She tightened her hold on me. *This is fucking embarrassing now.*

After a few minutes, I pulled back. She brought her hands to my face and held it. In an attempt to cheer me up, she licked my lips. Smiling and humming, *mmmmm!*

It wrenched a laugh from the depths of my chest and I embraced her again. "Thank you, Moonshine."

"I promise I won't bring him up again, but I would love to hear more stories whenever you're ready. He sounds really cool."

Sounds. Present tense.

In one simple sentence, she got me to open up about my brother, bring him back to life, reassure me this didn't scare her off, and got me to think about him on a day that wasn't Sunday.

Yeah, I'm in trouble.

I would never be able to repay her for the kindness she showed me that night. I've never felt that way about anyone before. Never trusted anyone so deeply, other than Sam and Lily. But then again, she is no one. *Nobody.*

I nodded in agreement. I would tell her more stories in the future. But for now, that was enough. I laughed outward and she questioned me. "Nothing, I'm just thinking." I mumbled as I moved down.

I laid flat on my bed and opened my arms in invitation. *Please, Hare.* She obeyed, curling herself into me.

She drifted off to sleep, tracing my tattoo with her nails. When her hand went limp, I felt like I could breathe again. I closed my eyes, leaning my head against the wall while she slept peacefully on my chest. I let out a breath.

"Sometimes I wish I met you earlier. Sometimes I wish I never met you at all. I'm torn between making you mine and letting you go. I hold so much pain, it's not fair to you. Pain I have the ability to prevent, but too selfish to do so. I'm not sure I will ever be able to tell you the truth. The truth that I will never be forced to live in a world where you don't exist. But…" I whispered, my voice cracking as I took another breath.

"The ground is slipping. I can feel us falling." The back of my throat started to close. I gave her a squeeze and bowed my head to hers.

"I'm so sorry, Moon." Accidentally letting a sob escape, I clamped my free hand over my mouth.

"Loving me is going to cause you so much pain." I cried into my hand. I kissed the top of her head and closed my eyes.

I begged God not to let me wake up.

CHAPTER

45

Harriet

Days passed and we hadn't spoken. I caught up on my lectures, studied for upcoming midterms and hung out with my roommates. By the third day of no contact, my anxiety had gone down and my heart calmed. For the first time in a while, I remembered how good it felt to be alone. I even left the photos I took of his medication alone.

Being with Maximus was awakening, he was teaching me new parts of myself but my feelings for him were developing into something terrifying. I needed those days to clear my head. Gather myself, renew my perspective. Remind Harriet that she's okay alone.

I had self-care nights, treating my skin, my hair, my nails. I even dyed my hair lighter, closer to ash white. I had no doubt that Maximus was feeling the same way. After spending so much time together, it started to feel like we were getting lost in it, like the addiction was growing. It became clear we needed space. Our feelings were beginning to scare us. Our feelings were starting to become real. Like the dimension was slowly splitting open.

When I confronted him about his brother, everything became true. He was no longer my fuck toy. No longer someone who offered escape in the eye of euphoria. He was a real person. A person with real problems I couldn't fix.

I settled into my bed that night thinking about what to do. If there was even anything I could do. *Has the light turned yellow? Am I past the point of return?*

I knew I couldn't teach him how to swim, but I could hold him above water.

"Have you heard from him yet?" Mia mumbled as she stuffed Corn Pops in her mouth. I shook my head, not looking up from my notes.

Disease, Death, and Body was one of my most intense classes, learning about the top twenty diseases that take us out. Our prof already told us we will most likely need to use the whole three hours so to study thoroughly. *Great.* I spent half my day working the twenty and the other half scouring rarities just in case.

I took my glasses off, rubbing my eyes. "I haven't thought about him. This class is taking up all the space in my head." I grumbled into my hands.

"You know what tomorrow is, so maybe you should text him." Kim said from the other side of the table. "Besides, he still hasn't told me where he got those donuts. And he's missed movie night. Twice."

Tuesdays and Thursdays were our movie nights. Taking turns deciding what we watched. Last week, Mia chose *How to Lose a Guy in 10 Days*, and Kim chose *Transformers*. It was my turn tonight, and Jane's on Thursday. I was in the mood for something funny, something to get my mind off the ridiculous amounts of school work I had, and the fact that I wasn't sure where Maximus and I stood. *Jumanji.*

"I have a plan for tomorrow. I think I'm going to keep it a surprise. I want another night to myself. Free of thought." I took a breath as I leaned back in my chair. Jane came from the balcony, filling my nose with this week's weed strain, the joint was still lit. "Give me that." I reached for it, taking a puff.

My head filled with...smoke. Nothing. I immediately relaxed. I started to hand it back to her, but thought twice before putting it back between her fingers. She was staring at my notes.

"There are pictures of dead people in your textbook." She shuddered and walked back to couch, putting the joint back in its holder.

"Harriet, what movie are we watching?" She shouted from the couch.

"*Jumanji!*" I shouted back. Kim cheered and Mia did a little dance. We were all in the mood for a little comedic relief. "Let's get it then," Kim said as she slammed her finance textbook closed and headed to her spot on the couch. "I'm tired of studying!" To the real world, it was only nine p.m. on a Tuesday, but we've been up studying since eight. It felt like midnight in our den of doom.

---·◈·---

Jumanji was well over, we fell asleep on the couch. I woke up at three in the morning, forcing myself to crawl up the stairs to my bed. I tried to drag Kim along with me, but she just grunted and swatted at me, so I left her there.

When I woke up again, it was almost noon. I had slept almost twelve hours. Twelve hours of studying, twelve hours of sleep. *Sounds about right.* I felt as rested as I ever have. I got dressed in black pants and black body suit with a black zip up hoodie. *Colorful.* I smiled. I felt good.

"Look good, feel good." I quoted myself in the mirror. I thought I was so smart for coming up with that I almost wrote it on the mirror in lipstick like a bad nineties movie. I did my make-up, basic eyeliner and mascara. Leaving my skin to breathe and flaunt my freckles. Eyeing my curling wand, I opted for beach waves. I haven't curled my hair since Christmas, I hope this goes well.

I burned myself twice. Once was a tap, the other started to blister before I was even finished. I topped my outfit off with a half-up half-down hairdo, clipping it with a black satin bow.

"Perfectly colorful." I looked hot. I felt hot. It was going to be a good day.

"You look like you're going to a funeral."

I jumped, not seeing Kim standing in her doorway. "Well… when the suit fits." I winked.

"God, you're morbid." She rolled her eyes and laughed her way back into her room. She came back into the bathroom with white jeans, and a burgundy tank top. I angled my head at her.

"Two types of people." She laughed, giving us a glance over in the mirror. I was blonde, pale as shit, blue eyes, drenched in all black. Her dark brunette hair and honey skin complimented her brown eyes and colorful outfit. "And they're best friends." I finished. Opposites attract and all that bullshit. She brushed her teeth but kept staring at me.

"What?" I asked.

"How do you think tonight's gonna go?" Over her toothbrush. I could barely make out what she was saying, but I could guess.

"Not a single clue. He could see it as me being thoughtful and kind, or he could see it as a total invasion of privacy." I turned my head to the drawer where I printed out the photos of his prescription.

"Cross your fingers." She spat, crossing her fingers, legs, arms, and ankles. I appreciated the dedication to the superstition. Mia shouted something from the bottom of the stairs. We looked at each other before making our way to the kitchen.

Ryan and his roommate were standing at the bottom of the stairs. Kim and I's steps slowed half way through the staircase.

"Hello." I knew I sounded wary, but it was warranted here. You'd have no idea that Cory was beaten to a pulp a year ago. His nose was perfectly set, his jaw was strong, his eye was back to normal—oh, he has a scar. A slight white line going into his right eyebrow. His brown curly hair covered it mostly. Kim smiled and cocked her head, noticing how attractive he was. *Two for two.*

"Hello!" She sauntered down the stairs and stepped past the guys, into the kitchen. Cory stuttered, "H-hi." He didn't take his eyes off Kim as I smirked, following her lead and headed to the fridge for water.

Mia was fumbling in her purse on the kitchen counter. "We're going out for lunch. I know you have plans today, Harriet, but Kim, do you want to come with us?"

Kim's eyes lit up, she was trying to cover her excitement, but we knew she wanted to go. She coughed, "Yeah I'd love to." She ran up the stairs to grab her purse.

"So you have plans, Harriet? What you got going on today?" *Damn, you're so nice. I'm so sorry you got your ass beat.* I know he was just making conversation, but what the hell was I supposed to say? *Going to hang out with the guy who beat you half to death?*

So I came up with a half-truth. "I have lots of studying to catch up on. Midterms are coming up." I gave him a shrug, telling him maybe next time I would join them. *Definitely not.*

"Do you know where Jane is?" I turned back to Mia. "Yeah, she left this note." She handed me a small piece of paper with Jane's chicken scratch on it.

Hi bitches ♥

Had to go home early this morning, forgot I had a doctors appointment. Going to see my mom for the day afterward, see you tomorrow night for movies!

XOXO Gossip JANE

They headed to lunch, and I contemplated dancing naked around the kitchen. I had the whole house to myself for a while, thought I might make use of it.

CHAPTER

46

Harriet

The clock struck ten p.m. while I packed my car with all my supplies for the evening.

I planned a perhaps very morbid picnic. It was Sam's birthday. He would've been twenty-six today, by my calculations. So I got a small cake with a two and a six candles, some snacks, wine and other essentials. Much needed wine. I wasn't sure how this was going to go. His reaction was going to make or break this crazy idea. If he was home.

I drove in complete silence, debating if I'd lost my mind in the last few days. I wished the drive was longer so I could continue convincing myself to turn around. Or crawl under a rock and die.

But instead, my tires crunched on his gravel driveway. I carefully pulled my backpack from the back seat, not wanting to squish the baby cake inside. I took a breath and opened the door with shaking fingers. I walked up to his window and there he was, sitting at his desk.

But he wasn't playing games. He was just sitting there. I could only see the back of him so I wasn't sure if he was awake or not. I tapped on the window. He spun on his chair, his face was hollow. He didn't so much as give me a grin before he made his way to the front door.

He opened it, but didn't move to let me inside.

Without a word, I threw my arms around him. He buried his face in my neck and slid his hands underneath my backpack, pulling me in close. His shoulders shook, and I thought he was crying. When I tried to pull back, he squeezed me harder. Not allowing me an inch.

I muttered in his hair instead. "Let's go. I have something for you." I was soft, but I tried to keep my cool. Careful not to show the nervousness boiling in my chest. He pulled back, resting his forehead on mine but still not looking at me. He shook his head on me.

"I promise it'll be okay. I think." I convinced myself, giving him an uncomfortable laugh. He had no reaction, he just stared absentmindedly at our feet.

My hands were on his cheeks, they were wet. He let out a sigh and finally nodded on me. *Shit*. Part of me wished he would say no and force me to go home, not needing to ever find out his reaction to my absurd plan.

He looked me up and down, noticing I was wearing proper winter attire this time. He turned to grab his coat and a beanie, still no eye contact. Still no words. Just slow movements like he was a ghost in his own life.

He hauled on his boots and locked the door behind him. His shoulders were sunken, his eyes were bloodshot. He hadn't been sleeping either, his under eyes were black. He looked dead. The mirror image of what he was probably feeling on the inside.

He climbed into my passenger seat and pulled his knees to his chest. I was learning he preferred the feeling of pressure when he was in a bad place. The walls of his bedroom when I blurted out I knew about his brother, and now the pressure of his knees and arms around himself. He closed his eyes and put his head down.

I was grateful he wasn't watching where we were going. But sooner or later, he was going to realize I did some serious cyberstalking. I knew what today was and where his brother was buried.

The major criminal invasion of privacy my roommates and I committed not so long ago.

I didn't play any music on the way to the cemetery. I rested my hand on his knee and he squeezed my hand so hard I thought he was going to break my fingers. I pulled into the parking lot, rolling the car to a stop. He didn't look up until I pulled my hand away to put it in park.

He took one look at where we were, immediately recognizing it. His face went white and shot me a quick glance. His eyes narrowed, darkening by the second. They were glossy, red, but I could still see the blue through the moonlight.

His entire world changed in one night, and now here I was, some random girl, cyberstalking his family and finding out where his brother was buried so we could celebrate—or mourn—his birthday together.

He scrambled out of the car and started speed walking for the road. I grabbed my backpack, not caring if the cake gets smooshed. I ran after him, the gravel crunching under my black boots. I grabbed his arm, and he spun on his heels, grabbing my throat as I tumbled backward.

His teeth were bared, his hand squeezing tighter. He grunted at me. In an instant, the sadness in his eyes was overcome with rage. *Shit.* His eyes went black as his nails dug into me. They were empty. No one was there. I stayed as stiff as I could, holding my ground. I never broke our gaze. Never made an expression. I wasn't going to let him break me over this.

The need for oxygen was right at the tip of my tongue. I could feel my face going red, soon to be blue, if he didn't let go. I was going to pass out. I had to grab his hand and dig my nails into his muscles, but he didn't budge. I didn't think he could see me.

He was blinded by red, a darker synonym to the mask he was teaching me.

Even if I wanted to, I couldn't speak. He blinked a couple times and finally let go. Both of us collapsed to the ground, gasping for air. He curled up in a ball in the middle of the gravel road and leaned on his heels, clutching his head between his hands.

The gasp I took was so harsh I thought I was going to suck the trees in and operate photosynthesis myself. My eyes started to water. *He just choked me. Out of rage. Not lust.*

He couldn't see me.

After a few—very—deep breaths, I shook it off, grabbing him under the arms and pulling him to his feet. He just looked at me as tears flooded him, the agony behind them was back. The blue returned.

He knew if he spoke he'd have to acknowledge what he just did. So he stayed stone-cold silent. No whimpers. No sobs. Just tears as I led him to where his brother lay in the ground.

Once we got to his row, Maximus stopped, never letting go of my hand. He pulled me back, and I stumbled in front of him. His anger was back, but it wasn't the rage. His eyebrows were pinched together and his lips were in a hard line. I wiped a tear. "I'm right here," was all I could manage, fighting my own tears. I couldn't tell if it was the fact I've never seen Maximus this *raw* before, or because I could feel his pain.

Or simply because the man almost killed me approximately three and a half minutes ago.

Either way, I made a promise.

He took the lead, trailing us to his brother's grave. He stood over it, letting go of my hand to rub his engraved name.

Here goes nothing.

CHAPTER

47

Harriet

I knew this was horrible timing, maybe horrible in general, but I couldn't help it. Even in pain, he was angelic. His face was glistening, his cheeks were pink with the cold, the shadows of snowflakes were falling down his skin. We stood there, in the middle of the cemetery, being lightly blanketed by snow as we held hands in front of his brother.

I quietly set down my backpack to begin pulling things out of it. Maximus just silently stared at Sam's name. I laid down an old quilt over the snow and set up the wine and the glasses. At last, I pulled out the half-smooshed cake. It was vanilla. An inside joke between us that I hoped he'd appreciate. Also because I didn't like chocolate cake.

I sat down and unpackaged the candles. It wasn't until I sparked the lighter did he turn around. His eyes widened and his lips parted. His shoulders sagged and he tilted his head at me, sitting on the old quilt I brought to school with me. He slowly lowered himself, staring into the centers of my eyes. I was starting to think maybe this wasn't a good idea.

The pressure under his gaze was overbearing. "D-Do you want to sing?" I stuttered. It was a stupid question, and I shamefully laughed as soon as it came out of my mouth. But thankfully, it pulled a saddened laugh from him too.

"He would've been twenty-six today. I thought maybe we'd celebrate," I coughed—celebrate is total wrong word here, but I couldn't think of anything else under his gaze—"or at least just eat some cake with him."

He looked at me with such longing I felt my heart skip. He set the cake to the side of the blanket and grabbed my face. He kissed me hard at first, before pulling away and kissing me again softly.

"It was you that night." His voice was raw against my lips. I cocked my head at him, I had no idea what he was talking about.

"Molly Wheeler." He spoke softly. I instantly cringed, I probably looked crazy to him right now.

"That was the only night I didn't feel deafeningly alone, oddly enough, I thought it was Sam. But it was you." He whispered against my forehead.

"We—I didn't follow you, I swear. I just needed proof with my own eyes. I stalked your mom's Facebook. I'm sorry." I blurted out. It felt like I was yelling in an exam. I immediately lowered my voice, repeating my apology profusely. He pretended not to notice the "we" portion, knowing exactly who came with me.

He offered me the first smile all evening. He kissed my cheek and my knuckles before tackling me to the ground and kissing me everywhere.

"Every time I think I have you figured out, you surprise once more." He laughed above me. I scrunched my face and blushed, assuming these *surprises* were a good thing.

We leaned up and sat cross legged, facing Sam with our knees touching. "I don't think he's going to blow out the candles, so..." I laughed.

Maximus looked stunned by my joke but could tell he quickly remembered the career I was about to have. He laughed hard, accidentally blowing out the candles. Which called for more laughter between us, until he spoke again.

"Happy Birthday, Sam." He sniffed, unscrewing the cap on the wine.

"Happy Birthday, Sam," I repeated. "My name is Harriet, by the way. I'm kind of…" I turned to Maximus as I spoke. "…fucking your brother…" My voice lingered. He snorted. *We are nothing.*

"According to your mom's Facebook, you were a real gentleman. I guess I missed out! Maximus here seems to be the hectic one." I gave a sarcastic sigh and rolled my eyes. Maximus smirked while playfully punching me in the arm, but kept intently listening to me talk to his brother.

I told him about my parents, about my dog, about my degree—Maximus had a good laugh at that one. I told him about my roommates and how they thought he was hot. Maximus just sat there, never breaking his stare, even to blink. His cheeks pinking as time went on. His eyes were still filled with longing, making me blush every time I glanced in his direction.

He told me stories, he told me jokes, he told me about his favorite memories. We talked about Sam for almost an hour before remembering the cake wasn't going to eat itself.

Maximus took the candles out of the cake and screwed them into the snow in front of Sam's headstone. I tore through my bag for the cutlery I packed, but Maximus had other ideas.

He dug his fingers into the cake and as I turned my head to look at him, he covered my face in cake. "Oh! You son of a"—another handful to the face—"bitch!" I finished. My words were muffled by cake and frosting. I dug my hands into the cake and smeared it all over his face and neck. Immediately regretting my decision. *Ugh, not the place, Harriet.*

It was the cream cheese all over again. I thought about all the things we could do with cake as I started to throb in my pants. His jugular moved with every laugh, making my stomach knot.

I've never heard his laugh like this, it wasn't a laugh of humor, it sounded like a laugh of relief?

Maybe for the first time in a while, Maximus felt free.

As I clenched my thighs together, he caught me staring at the side of his neck. His wholesome smile softened, and he moved inches from my face.

"Do it." He whispered at me.

I nodded, unable to speak with the sight of his veins pulsating at me. I leaned forward and licked the hollow of his throat from bottom to top, catching his lips on mine at the end. He breathed in my mouth and returned the favor.

He licked the cake off me, letting go smalls laughs as he did so.

This needed to stop. My thoughts were already fogging my judgment. I wiped the rest of the cake off our faces with my quilt. "We are absolutely *not* doing this on top of your brother." I pulled back from him, but he pushed me on my back and got on top of me.

"I don't care where we are, I need you." He purred. As soon as he said that, he realized his judgment was clouded too. I gave him a look. He laughed and nodded. "Yeah, okay. We should definitely go, I'm about to rip your clothes off."

I needed him too, but this is what not I wanted. I wanted to show him I care, that I'm here for him. As anyone. I wasn't sure why I wanted to show him this side of me, but I felt the need to. Maybe I could be more than just his toy. I had to push my thoughts away before that got too far too. I had to bring us back to reality.

"Sunshine, look at me." I grabbed his face. "I'm here for you. As much as I would love to jump your bones right now, this"—I angled to our set up—"isn't for that part of you," I splayed my hands toward Sam. "I'm here for this. The part of you missing."

He leaned in to kiss me. I let him, then lightly rested my hands on his chest. "Maximus."

"I don't know how else to thank you," he mumbled quietly, lowering his eyes. I tilted his head up with the hook of my finger, giving him a questionable look. My heart was hammering.

He leaned his head against my shoulder, taking a deep breath before answering my look. "This might be one of the best nights of my life on one of the worst days of the year. I don't know how to thank you for this. How to thank you for being who you are to me. How..."

He choked once more, shaking off his thoughts as he looked at the trees surrounding us. "I don't know how to tell you."

I understood completely. *You're already important.*

I said nothing, letting his words sink in before having to come up with an answer. I came up short. Letting them flow through one ear and out the other kept him at a distance. A distance where I could still separate the man from my...

"Love and miss you, Sam, but I have something I need to do. Let's go, Moonshine." Maximus rose from the ground with a smile that reflected in the snow.

Without a care in the world, I shoved everything into my backpack and quickly zipped it up. I'll clean out my backpack another day.

I giggled. "I'm sorry, Sam. We'll come back soon." I whispered-shouted at his headstone as Maximus held out his hand for me to take.

We walked back to my car hand in hand, staring up at the snow falling down on us. He paused to stare at the sky. "Get in the car, I'll be there in a second."

He disappeared behind the trees.

CHAPTER

48

Maximus

As soon as I was out of her sight, I found the nearest tree and leaned against it. I needed multiple deep breaths or my chest was going to give out. I could feel it coming. The overwhelming weakness, the need, the fear. My bones were collapsing.

I almost said a thing. A *big* thing. A *confusing* thing. A thing that might be *true. I can't be this crazy about her.*

I leaned my head against the tree, bashing it softly a couple times before opening my eyes to the starry night. "Thank you, Sam." Emptying the breath in my lungs.

"Thank you for sending her to me."

———⋅❧⋅———

She played soft music on our way back, never letting go of my hand. Even putting the car in drive with the opposite. Attempting not to show the struggle, but I knew she didn't want to let go, I didn't want her to either.

When we got back to my house, I took her jacket and sweater off, letting them fall to the floor. I hooked my fingers in the straps of her backpack then slowly set it down in the foyer. I took one look at her and I knew. She wasn't looking at me like I was going to break; she was looking at me like I was strong. Her smile lit up her face as her eyes shined. "What?" she spoke softly. I knew right then it was tonight.

Towering over her, I brushed my fingers against her jaw and softly held the back of her neck. She angled her head to give me passage to her lips, but I swayed my nose back and forth over hers. I softly kissed her forehead, then her cheeks, then her neck. I kept my pace slow.

I wanted her to feel this. I wanted her to feel me. This way. The only way I could tell her.

I held both of her hands and walked her to my room, never breaking her stare. Her eyebrows pinched and her lips opened to speak but nothing came out. Her eyes were wide and the corners of her mouth were twitching. She wasn't sure where this was going either. She was waiting for me to fuck her.

But I wasn't going to fuck her tonight.

She stood at the edge of my bed, beginning to take her clothes off. I rested my hands on hers and she paused, staring up at me with questioning eyes. I've never fully undressed her before. I toyed with the hem of her pants, pulling them down to her ankles. Our eyes met, and I kissed her inner thighs. Holding them, I unsnapped her bodysuit with my teeth.

Kissing my way up, one strap, two straps. Until her breasts were bared. I trailed kisses over her entire body, flicking her nipples gently with my tongue as I looped her panties in my fingers, letting the damp fabric fall to the floor. Her hands rested on my shoulders as I put my mouth on her. She was hot to the touch. Allowing small purrs to escape her perfect lips above me. I didn't know it possible, but she tasted even better tonight.

I moaned against her, sliding my tongue up and down her clit. I couldn't get enough of her. The feeling of her skin. Her sweet scent.

The way her fingertips had the power to bring me to my knees.

I lowered my body, bending down to kiss the tops of her feet. I licked from her ankles to the bottom of her neck, gently holding her throat under my palm. Her eyes were wide, her breaths were short and shallow, desperately awaiting my next move.

I kissed her slow and deep, moving my hands behind her head, careful not to fist her hair too tightly. I straddled her around my waist and laid her flat down on her back. When I began taking my shirt off, she curled up, trying to take it off for me. I stopped her again. She cocked her head at me, eyes still wide and lips parted.

I knew she wanted to give, but tonight's focus was on her. It was a need I'd never felt before.

Careful not to spook her, I slowly leaned us back. Planting one hand beside her head and the other on the side of her jaw, running my thumb over her bottom lip. Her eyes had a sparkle in them, a sparkle I hadn't seen before. I was slow at first, teasing what she's used to.

I felt no need for speed. I just wanted to fall into her, her embrace, her warmth. She was all I needed right here in this pocket of time. Our little dimension. Nothing else mattered. Not the pain in my chest, not the missing person in my life, not the troubles in my head. Nothing. All I could feel was her. Our veins intertwined, tongues molded.

Her heartbeat gave mine strength.

I could look at her like this forever. Raw, vulnerable, *certain*. Her lips were the most addictive part. She put her hands in my hair and pulled me closer, wrapping her legs around me and locking me into place. I hesitated between her legs, knowing everything was about to change the moment I felt her around me.

Gently, I guided into her, slicking myself with her arousal. She was dripping on my sheets, pooling beneath the slit of her thighs. The deeper I went, the more hungry I got. My usual instinct was to pound into her, make her scream my name, call me God, but all I wanted—all I *needed*—was to feel her.

I pushed slowly, running my fingertips over her arms in my hair, and back down to lace them in hers. Her eyes were filled with questions I didn't have the answers to. Hopefully, this moment would show her everything she needed to know. She pushed her head up to nibble on my ear, I smiled.

I kissed her lips, making gentler bites on her bottom lip than she's used to. I trailed kisses all over her neck, her ear, and finally her fingers in my hand. With every kiss, every breath, every beat, I fell more and more.

I could feel our climaxes, the slow burning ones. The ones that appear out of nowhere, flood your mind, send stars behind your eyes and euphoria through your veins. She arched her back to gain access to all of me, and the heat in my stomach ignited, the knot slowly undoing. Her lips parted again, allowing soft moans to escape. Her breath kept hitching, and I felt her muscles convulse around me. She felt so beautiful when she came around me, filling the pool beneath us. I flexed and spilled into her. Not caring about the consequences. It felt too good—she felt too good. I needed her.

I needed her forever.

I offered her a gentle smile when she ran her fingers through my hair. Her eyes softened, knowing exactly what had just happened, but she didn't dare ruin the moment.

I pulled out, hearing the sounds of us releasing. I kissed all the way down and licked the remaining liquid pooling out of her.

For the first time, I got a taste of what we would be like together.

She was still swollen with need, so I forced another orgasm from her as I palmed her breasts gently and watched her face reach her breaking point. She deserved it. She deserved every last drop of it.

She pulled me by my jaw from between her legs, us still dripping from my lips. For the first time, she tasted us too.

Like setting a bone, it snapped into place.

All that remained was the sun, the moon, and the stars we made.

CHAPTER

49

Maximus

Whatever happens the moment we wake up, I knew we would be okay. I felt the tether knot.

But for now, I was happy in our dimension. The first time in eight years I was happy on February the fifth. And the first time waking up on February sixth not feeling like a bag of dicks.

I woke first, determined not to disrupt her sleep until I had a cup of earl grey tea and blueberries in my hands. I carefully slid from under her, but even in her sleep, she tightened her hold on me.

I gave her a squeeze until forcing myself out anyway. The world outside my sheets was cold, I shivered and my dick shrunk to everyone else's size. I threw on my favorite sweatpants and the black zip up hoodie she was wearing last night.

Last night.

She planned this incredibly thoughtful date for me, and I hadn't talked to her for almost a week. Frankly, I discovered I needed some alone time to readjust, but I don't want to be alone anymore. All I want is her. I knew she absolutely cyberstalked my family to find out the details I refused to tell her, but the moment I turned around and saw her face light up with those ridiculously ugly candles, everything melted away again.

I was caught between emotions when I figured out it was her the night in the cemetery, I really wanted it to be Sam. I really wanted to think he was coming to talk, to hold me, to sham me into thinking he never died.

By the end of that date, I knew it was Sam. No one else could have sent someone so perfect. No one else could've seen her coming. Only the dead who lie beyond. She was perfect. Perfect for me, perfect for my family, perfect for my friends.

Everything about her made me forget everything about me.

As I was making her tea, my chest started burning. I hadn't taken my meds since we switched backpacks. I'd been avoiding Banks like the plague. It hasn't been causing me any trouble, but I can't have it acting up after the night she gave me, and the morning I gave her.

I went back to my room at the perfect time. She was just waking up. "Good morning, Sunshine." She said sweetly, sleep still lingering in her voice as she rolled over in my sheets. She looked so beautiful in the morning, even with the mess on the back of her head. The corners of my mouth curled as I set down the tea beside her. She immediately reached for it, blowing on it.

"Good morning, Moonshine. You're in a good mood." It was nine thirty, prime time for feral Harriet. She chuckled, knowing she's cussed me out on multiple early occasions over the last few months. Don't poke the sleeping bear, I had to tell myself.

"How do you feel this morning?" Her question caught me off guard. *How do I feel? How do you feel?*

"Like I don't deserve you. Or that morbid date."

"Date?!" She yelped. "You thought that was—yeah... okay...I guess." She succumbed. She knew it and I knew it. She took me out first.

In the state I was in last night, I didn't think I'd look at it that way. I was livid when I realized where we were at first. So much so

I choked her out without realizing what I was doing. The memories in my hands started to sting. *I put my hands on her.*

In among all the thoughts and feelings, I had forgotten. She saw the look in my eye, her hand found her throat, softly massaging the half-moon shapes in the side of her neck. Avoiding her eyes, I shook my hair in my face.

"Hare..."

"Don't," she interrupted me. "Don't ruin this. I'm fine. I crossed a line you didn't know needed crossed." She opened the blankets, offering me to slide in. I had a lot of apologizing to do, and a lot of making up.

I climbed in and hugged her. I held her for a few long minutes before she whispered in my ear, "But if you ever do that again, I'll kill you."

She said it with a smile, but I knew she meant it. I nodded, taking her words seriously. *I* crossed a line. I couldn't see her through my rage. All I saw was Sam's exploited body and my family's pain uncovered. It was none of her business; she knew that, but she was only trying to show she cares about my pain. Asking me to let her carry part of it.

If only she knew how heavy it was.

"I'm sorry," I whispered. There I go again making stupid, immature decisions. Her blue eyes were on mine and I couldn't look away. I wouldn't. She needed to know how sorry I was, how that will never happen again. Ever. Thinking about it makes my heart hurt. I waited for her to break our stare but it didn't happen, not even when she swayed her nose back and forth against mine.

It wasn't until Banks called from the living room that she turned away, covering herself in case he walked in my room. Which he did. He knocked and then opened the door immediately. *What's the point of knocking if you're just going to come in anyway?*

"Max. Come on. It's Thursday. We got class in thirty minutes." He threw my backpack at me, as if that would get me up. I groaned and buried my head in Harriet. "Hi, Harriet."

She smiled shyly against my hair. "Hi, Banks."

CHAPTER

50

Harriet

"Stay here for me?" he asked, holding down the blankets so Banks wouldn't see how obviously naked I was. I seriously contemplated it, I could. But I won't.

"I need to shower and get some things in order for my midterms next week. My diseases and procedures classes are kicking my butt." It was the truth, I needed to go home and study. Being in his house was far too distracting, even if he wasn't here. I knew myself. He probably did too. I was going to snoop around his room, maybe even his entire house. It was hard to resist. It felt like there was still so much I didn't know about him.

"I'll see you at yours then? Movie night with the girls?" He flopped his hand over and puffed out his chest, raising his voice as if that's actually how girls act or sound. I rolled my eyes, "Eight p.m."

"Deal." He smirked, the pit in my stomach reaching high temperatures. I smirked back, seeing Banks roll his eyes behind Maximus and saunter out of the room.

"You guys are gross."

"You're just jealous!" Maximus yelled back as the door slammed. He kissed me and got dressed. I laid back down to tell my roommates I was coming home, and he was coming for movie night.

⸻⬦⬦⸻

It was love. I felt it. I know he felt it, he acted it. There was no mask, no pleasurable pain, no fun little toys. For the first time, I felt him.

Everything has changed. It's gone unspoken, but the feeling has been there. Maximus was starting to love me, and my "date" did him in. I had to admit, I didn't think he'd appreciate the night *that* much.

I felt it in the parking lot. Watching him walk himself back from the red rage to keep himself from killing me. From making me another Cory. I imagined him over Cory's unconscious body, beating him bloody. He pulled back for me. Granted, he shouldn't have done that in the first place. But he came back, feeling worse than before.

And then I felt it again when he was watching me talk to Sam's headstone. He didn't hear a single word. He appreciated the effort, even if it was only one-sided.

I did it for Maximus. I know Sam is watching him constantly, which means he's watching me too. So I wasn't too worried about what I was saying, Sam already knows everything. More than any living human being. If the afterlife exists.

I blinked my eyes a few times to stop myself from zoning out again. Slapping my books closed. I walked to the counter to switch the kettle on. More tea. Always more tea.

My hair was up in a bun to hide the mess on the back of my head and I was wearing granny panties under my basketball shorts with a t-shirt that wasn't mine. *Sorry, Maximus.*

"Dude! What happened to your neck?!" Kim came from behind me, Cory on her heels. *Shit.*

I did the only thing I could think of. Besides, it was literally true last week. I cocked my eyebrow and bit my bottom lip, giving her a naughty smirk. "Oh? Y'all kinky like that?" She tilted her head to get a better look at the half-circles dug into my sides of my neck.

"Trust me, it was hot." I half-lied. *Maximus almost killed me, but it was hot.* "I couldn't even feel it until the deed was done." I smiled and she just laughed in shock, turning to Cory. Giving him a look that they were never going to try such a thing.

"Cory's going to stay for movie night tonight, that cool with you?" She asked me, right in front of him.

"Did you look at the group chat?" I replied quickly. Was putting Maximus and Cory in the same room a good idea?

"No, I haven't. Why?"

She pulled her phone out of her sweater pocket and scrolled through the chat. "Oh shit, he's coming."

"Who?" Cory was standing rigid as hell in the corner of our kitchen, not sure how to act. He was clearly shy, which I appreciated in the sea of crazies our house harbors.

I turned to walk back to my study set up. *Kim can deal with that one. I'll deal with Maximus.* She spun on her heels to face him, quietly whispering something about Maximus, I'm sure. His eyes widened and his face went red. "Uh…" *Uh oh.*

"It was a long time ago, right? Would you be okay?" She put a hand on his arm, trying to comfort him the best way she knew how. "Yeah, yeah. It'll be alright. We've talked, doesn't mean I'm gonna cuddle the guy, but he's forgiven."

I sighed in relief. I didn't mean to eavesdrop, but I thought I should tell Maximus too.

HQ: Soo… Cory and Kim have kind of become a thing. He's coming to movie night tonight.

I waited for his response. It was four thirty, his class must be over by then. Unless he had another one. The corners of my eyes tightened, realizing I didn't know Maximus's school schedule, and I didn't think he knew mine.

MW: Orgy?

I laughed out loud. Kim spun her head at me. I covered my mouth, sorry I brought them out of their moment.

HQ: Cuck!

I laughed again, thinking my response was funny. Kim now cocking her hip at me and raising her eyebrows.

MW: Maybe one day, Moonshine. ;)

Slowly putting my phone down, I made it obvious I wasn't going to bother them anymore. I needed a shower anyway. I went the long way around them, around the wall, careful not to disturb whatever they were shivering about. The stairs creaked beneath the balls of my feet as I skipped two at a time.

The head on my razor was thinning, so I was shuffling through all my drawers. Finally finding a moisturizing razor head in the desk, underneath the photos of his medication. My fingers hovered over them, careful not to touch them. If so much as a graze, I'd google them.

He will tell you. Eventually.

"Why am I torturing myself? What if he just has anxiety?" I lied to myself. I've never known anyone with anxiety to take furosemide or enalapril. *Just do it...*

I did it. I reached for my iPad, eagerly whipping it open. I typed in the search bar. Not hesitating to click.

Furosemide: used for eliminating excess liquid build up. Side effects include nausea, vomiting, dizziness.

Enalapril: used for helping the body pump blood. Side effects include fainting, chest pain, weakness.

I slammed my iPad case shut; the guilt starting to eat me alive. My thoughts weren't aligning, all my blood rushing to my head I thought I might pass out.

Enough, Harriet.

If I thought someone was hiding something from me, my brain immediately thought the worst. This surely couldn't be that case. I was simply getting in my head again. He didn't want to burden me with whatever it was. If I tried really hard, I could convince myself they weren't his, that he was secretly a drug dealer. I think I could handle that.

Obviously he didn't think the same.

Even before all that, he had no obligation to me. Technically speaking, we are still nothing. He still has a choice not to tell me parts about himself. I had no right to know. I had no right invading his privacy, sneaking into his property, and taking pictures of something so personal.

He has no obligation. I have no right.

CHAPTER

51

Harriet

"Jane! What are we watching?!" Mia shouted from the bottom of the stairs, Jane was putting her pajamas on.

"Something violent!" she screamed back at the top of her lungs. We needed walkie talkies. It was hit or miss if we ever heard ourselves with the high ceilings and muffling carpets.

I cheered from the fridge, sifting through drink options. I wasn't particularly in the mood for anything romantic, especially since Maximus was supposed to be joining us this evening. I had enough romance issues going on in my head, I didn't need to watch Rachel McAdams and Ryan Gosling swoon over each other.

The front door swung open and Maximus stepped inside, locking it behind him. "Honey! I'm home!" he yelled sarcastically like an old movie. I rounded the fridge and saw him walking toward me in a black sweatsuit. He looked so hot.

"Hi, honey! How was your day at work? Here's your scotch on the rocks!" I handed him my water, completing the generational joke. He tried to take a sip. His eyebrows raised as I turned to walk over to my spot on the couch with my water in my hand, and a smile on my face.

He brought a backpack full of yummy things. Miss Vickie's salt and vinegar for me, donuts for my roommates. He refused to tell them where he got them, keeping the hole in the wall a secret.

He wouldn't even tell me. They groaned in protest when he denied them once more. Pulling out a giant jug of cranberry juice, he took a swig. His throat bobbing as he swallowed.

"Get up," he demanded. Giving him a questionable look, I slowly got up from the couch, glancing around at our audience. One thing about Maximus, he was unpredictable. There was a fifty-fifty chance he was either going to take my spot, or bend me over this couch. Either way, I enjoyed the thrill.

He took my seat. "Not a chance, mister, this is my—"

"Would you relax?" There was attitude behind that smile. He positioned himself before opening his legs and patting the space between them. "Sit." *Ah.*

I happily scrunched my face and planted my ass between his thighs, right in front of his groin. I tried to curl my legs to sit criss cross but he smacked them down.

"Would you give up control for one fucking minute?" He snapped jokingly, reaching for my legs. I shot him a look. *As if I don't do that constantly, Mister Dom.*

"Stop struggling, woman. I have a vision." I rolled my eyes and made my body limp. He ended up crossing my legs when his *first* vision didn't work, then crossing his long legs on top of mine, pinning me to the couch and to his chest. He put the couch blanket over us and pushed my head back, resting his chin on the crown of my head.

"Daddy long legs," I spoke under my breath.

I felt his chest rumble. "Damn straight, Moonshine."

I snuggled in, noticeably relaxing. "See. You *love* giving up control," he whispered in my ear. *Shut up.* Even if he couldn't see, I rolled my eyes. His chest rumbled again.

Jane and Mia made smooching noises and cuddled close, wrapping that couches blanket around themselves. Finally, Kim and Cory came down the stairs to take the longer couch opposite us.

Maximus and Cory made eye contact immediately and Cory nodded. "Hey."

Maximus's hold on me tightened. "Hey, Cory."

The four of us exchanged looks, sensing the tension between them. Jane's eyes widened as she hit play on *The Purge*, a satisfying grin taking over her face. They sat down, curling close to each other like Maximus and I did on his first movie night. I giggled to myself. Kim was sitting up right with a head on his shoulder. Cory had his arm wrapped around her shoulders and his hand fidgeting on his thigh.

Maximus and I didn't know how to sit together either on our first movie night. We ended up casually cuddling, similar to Kim and Cory.

Okay...maybe a little closer.

Now, him and I were a bag of limbs, all entwined. Yet, I always manage to be the one who gets pinned down. I shifted my ass against him and nuzzled into his chest again. He brought his arms around me under the blanket and slid his hand up my shirt.

To his pleasant surprise, I wasn't wearing a bra. He cupped me, giving me a really hard squeeze. My breath caught at the pain as he flicked my nipple. "Mmmm..." he hummed in my ear.

Silently, I nudged him in the ribs. "Sh." Short and sharp. *Sh.*

"Make me." He hardened against the small of my back, moving down the couch to get himself closer to my ass. As quickly as the thought came, so did the action.

I shoved my dirty sock in his mouth, not bothering to look if anyone saw. *That'll shut him up.* His grip on my tit tightened, and I fought a groan of pain. I rested my hand over my shorts, it was damp.

He spat out my sock and it landed in my lap. He pulled the blanket up higher so only my face was showing. It was warm and smelled like morning air. I curled it around my fists and held on tight. Fearing—wanting—his retribution.

His hand wrapped around the front of my throat, carefully under the blanket. "Don't make a sound." He took the blanket from under my chin and stuffed my mouth with it. *The Purge* alarm wasn't the only alarm going off.

Both of his hands slid down my stomach and into my shorts. He felt what I felt. I could feel his chest rising and falling quickly. I rolled my eyes, squeezing them shut to avoid further humiliation.

His heartbeat was pounding against my head, increasing as his fingers found their way to my clit. One hand pinched my clit while the other slid in and out, careful not to disturb the only blanket of privacy we had.

On instinct, my hips bucked. He hissed in my ear and I tried to relax. His pace quickened, I was fighting with all my might not to moan. The ache in my stomach was beginning to unfold, coursing through my entire body like fire and ice.

His fingers twirled ever so slightly, while his other remained its pace. He was going to send me over the edge. I was going to pool on this couch and everyone would know what he was doing to me. He was driving me crazy. Crazy enough to flip myself over and straddle him. Crazy enough to fuck him right here on this couch.

My breath quickened and I pushed my head farther into his chest. Grabbing my jaw, "Watch the movie," he whispered.

My muscles clenched, leaving me on the brink of pleasure. Fighting not to show any reaction.

He pulled his fingers out. I turned my head to look at him. The question *why* all over my face.

"That's how you make me feel."

Crazy.

Immediately, he switched. Hugging my middle and kissing my shoulder. He let out a satisfied breath, he was happy with himself. He edged me. Drove me crazy and then abandoned me. *Prick.*

I arched my lower back hard enough to send a small jolt of pain into his crotch. He winced, flopping his head on my shoulder.

Like I said. Prick.

CHAPTER

52

Maximus

"If *The Purge* existed, I think I would rob a bank and flee the country." Mia said after the rolling credits.

"I would go shopping." Kim said. Jane nodded eagerly. "I'd steal a plane." Cory said, they were full-blown cuddling now. "Do you even know how to fly a plane?"

"No, I would just kidnap a pilot." Everyone laughed, including me. Harriet turned to me, "What would you do?"

Steal a heart, kidnap a surgeon, ransack the painkiller carts.

"Probably rob the liquor stores. Oh, and kill everyone in the government." I shrugged. Everyone stared at me, stunned. "I'm kidding!"

They all chuckled and relaxed.

"I wouldn't rob a liquor store."

They burst out laughing. Hearing Cory laugh with me in the vicinity brought me relief. I never thought he'd get past what I did to him, but he was a good person, clearly. I, on the other hand, would not forgive so easily.

Harriet yawned beside me. Seeing my opportune moment, I shoved my finger in her mouth, making her gag. She swatted my hand away, angry that her yawn was incomplete. One of the annoyances of being human. Finishing a cough sequence, yawning until your chest pops, and three consecutive sneezes were all mandatory for satisfaction. I smirked at the little bit of misery I brought her.

Cory kissed Kim on the cheek before claiming he had to go. They bantered for a bit about why he couldn't stay the night, but he ended up leaving a few minutes later anyway. Harriet got up too, heading for the staircase. "One second."

I was too tired to move, I slouched back into the couch and watched Jane scroll through Netflix again.

"Are you ever going to tell her?" Jane never took her eyes off the screen on the wall. "No." I had no idea what she was talking about, but considering her tone, the best answer was no.

"You should." Mia said.

"And why's that, Miss Mia?" I sat up, resting my arms on the back of the couch. I tilted my head, waiting for her response. I still had no idea what they were talking about, but I enjoyed a little guessing game. "We know."

I raised a brow. "You sure as hell don't."

"Oh, please." Mia scoffed. "We have eyes too, you know, and they're not blinded by..."

They shot each other a glance and simultaneously looked back at me with crossed arms.

"I don't."

"But you really do though. Maybe you don't see how you treat her but we can." Mia pointed between themselves and Jane nodded in agreement. Jane chuckled and threw her hands up. "It's none of our business, but you should tell her. We think she loves you too."

We think she loves you too. Fuck.

That panicked me. "I can't." They picked up on the change in my voice and shuffled closer to the end of their couch. They were beginning to annoy me. *I can't.*

"All you gotta say is, 'Sweet baby Harriet, I looooove you,'" Jane made kissing noises and Mia wrapped her arms around herself, mimicking a make-out session.

"I can't love her, alright?!" I practically shouted as I raised from the couch. They were taken aback and gave each other odd looks before giving me one.

I know how this must seem. I wasn't blind. I know how I act. I know how I feel. I know everything. That's the fucking problem. I know too much.

I know I can't love her and I know I do anyway. *Loving me will only bring her pain.*

Living in our own little bubble was one thing, but people on the outside of the bubble shouldn't be allowed to comment on shit. It was none of their business.

"We're sorry, Max. We know it's easier said than done." They said together. I nodded in agreement. This conversation needed to end, so I told them the one thing that would alter the course.

"Mandy's Art Gallery." They had no idea what I was talking about. You wouldn't think donuts would come from an art gallery. The owner liked to bake, so she added her own pastry shop just inside the entrance of the gallery.

"The donuts."

They gasped and cheered before leaping into my arms like I just told them they won the lottery. They thanked me profusely and said they were grateful for my existence. I knew the donuts were good, but I didn't think they were this good.

"You're welcome." I smiled, resting my arms on their shoulders.

———⊰⊱———

"Hare?" Her door creaked open slowly. She was curled up in her blankets, her face covered with pillows. She didn't say anything, I wasn't sure if she was awake or not.

"I'm trying to sleep." The tone dismissive.

"Why didn't you come back downstairs?"

"I'm tired." Again, dismissive. Something between downstairs and upstairs upset her.

"You okay?"

Nothing. I inched closer to the end of her bed.

Not bothering to look at me, she muttered under the pillows, "I think you should go home. I need to get up and focus tomorrow, I have a midterm at noon."

CHAPTER

53

Maximus

Harriet blew me off for weeks, claiming midterms were kicking her ass and couldn't afford any distractions until they were over on February twenty-eighth. *Only three more days to go.*

My own midterms were surprisingly going smoothly. Genetics, physics, and biology were my easiest classes. It was the biochemistry and statistics I struggled with. I used my alone time wisely, catching up on lectures and reviewing my notes. Redoing the practice questions over and over until it stuck in my head like glue. By midnight, I considered myself a statistic expert. Even gave myself a congratulatory pat on the back.

I exited all the academic tabs on my desktop and messaged my online friends if they wanted to play a game or twelve. I wanted to relax. Thinking about the chilled beers in my fridge, I spun on my chair and cracked open a beer with my teeth, the cap making a hissing noise.

The first beer went down swimmingly. So did the third. And the fifth. By the end of our third game—third defeat—I said bye to Cole and logged off. Finally hearing the loud music and voices outside my door when I removed my headphones. There was a knock at my door and instantly my stomach dropped.

"Yeah." Responding to the knock. It slowly opened. My longing for Harriet shot from my stomach to my pounding head. "Yo, come hang out. You've been in here for days, man." Dylan was standing shirtless in my doorway, in shorts and a beer in his hand. "We misssss you," he slurred jokingly.

"White! Get your ass out here, bro!" Chase yelled from the couch.

"White! White! White!" Banks chanted. Everyone joined in until the thoughts of Harriet disappeared and a smile formed on my face. Dylan was right. I have been in here for days, yearning on about the missing girl from my dreams. I could use some more guy time.

"Alright, alright. I'm coming." I laughed. I had no idea what I was about to walk into. Xbox games, drinking games, a blow up sex doll, who knew.

But I can tell you one thing for sure: I was not expecting to see Cade sitting in my fucking spot. *That was about to change.*

I leaned against my doorframe, staring at him and his friends spread out around the room. My plaid pajama pants were hanging low on my waist, emphasizing the V leading down. I crossed my arms and my muscles flexed.

"Hello, Max." He taunted at me, both of us remembering our encounters thus far.

"Cade." The tension in the room was thick as thieves as the guys shared glances. Chase handed me another beer and I chugged it, not taking my eyes off him. Then I looked to my friends, now why the fuck did they bring him here?

I needed more time to process before forcing his ass out of my seat, so I went into the kitchen to grab an apple. I couldn't remember the last time I ate. Banks followed me, his expression worried. He leaned against the fridge while I chomped down on the apple. "I didn't know Luke was friends with him, so when he asked if he could bring a few of his friends, I said yes."

"It's alright. She's not my girlfriend, remember? She's fair game, I think is what you said." I said, biting down into the Granny Smith again.

He cocked his head and gave me a *really?* look. "I know, cheap shot. Sorry. He just gets under my skin and she's been blowing me off."

"Because you think what? That he has a chance? No way, Max." He slapped me on the back to reassure me. He was right. Cade stood no chance. *She's mine.* But if her actions of late were to prove anything, she could be unpredictable.

His dark features and muscles could've been a swaying factor. He was tall too. I'm no idiot, it's clear he's a good looking dude. Banks snapped his fingers in my face. If he wasn't my best friend with good intentions, I'd break his fingers for that. "Yoohoo! Come back."

I shook my head out of the trance and gave him a nod, my lips in a line. "Yeah, I'm here. Let's go." The buzz in my head wasn't going to help Cade if he dared to try me tonight.

"God's Plan" by Drake was blasting through our speakers on the floor while some guys played beer pong in the hallway, and the others were playing FIFA on the couch. Unfortunately—not for me—Cade was still in my spot. I stood between him and the tv, blocking his view.

"You're in my spot."

"So?" He leaned back, throwing an arm over the back of the couch and crossing his foot over his knee.

I wasn't dignifying that with an answer. If I say I have a spot, I have a spot. *How about you just move before I break your nose?*

"You can't just sit over there?" He motioned to the open spot beside Dylan. *No.* This was my seat. It was close to the bathroom, a quick walk to my room, and the right angle for the tv. It was calculated, not whimsical.

I bent down, putting my hands on my knees. "My house. My spot."

"Max," Chase warned. "Just move, Cade. It's one of his things." He teased. I looked at Chase. *Thank you for that, dickhead.*

"*Things,*" he emphasized. "Tell me…is Harriet still one of your *things?*"

That was it. I hauled his ass up by the collar of his shirt. "You keep her name out of your fucking mouth." His smile was slimy. If the next thing out of his mouth was anything vile against her, I was going to throw him in the street.

"You think you're the only one she wants? I saw the way she looked at me. I could have her too," he sneered.

My fist connected with the side of his jaw, sending him flying back into the couch. He lunged for me, trying to take me down by the middle. To no avail. I landed punches over his back, in his face, on his stomach. I had to admit, his throws were powerful. My jaw ached and I could feel hot liquid running down my chin. But not enough to overpower me. Or my soon-to-be-dead body. Anger fueled me. *Thank fuck.*

"Enough!" Banks tore me off Cade. "Enough."

Cade just stood stiff, acting tougher now that I was pinned by Banks and Chase. Dylan stood between us, but we were only looking at each other.

"How about we just take a second and drink some more beers?" *Of course that's Dylan's solution to this.*

The next words out of Cade's mouth boiled my blood enough for me to see red.

"The next time I see Harriet, I'm fucking her."

I ripped myself from Banks and Chase's grip and lunged for him. Before my punch could land, a voice from behind us spoke up.

"I dare you." Her voice was cold. She was leaning against the hallway wall with her arms and feet crossed. The pong game came to a stop. Her hair was curled, a black oversized hoodie with black jeans and black socks. *The usual.*

"Harriet...I—" Cade turned to her.

"Save it." She walked right past him, not sparing him another second, and came to stand right in front of me. "You good, Sunshine?" She asked me in a playful tone. Cade snorted. She wasn't mad?

"Always. You?" I was panting, blood slowly dripping down my chin.

She turned to Dylan who was still placed between me and Cade, and now Harriet. "I'd be better if I had a beer in my hand." She winked and offered him a kind smirk.

"Coming right up, milady." Dylan handed her an opened beer bottle. Making sure not to stray too far from the center of the room. Just in case.

Cade took a step into the middle, stretching out his hand. Assuming he was going to try to talk to her, my teeth gritted and my body went cold.

"Think again." My voice was ice, I refused to blink. He stopped in his tracks. He looked down at his feet and shook his head with laughter. Harriet turned to everyone, ignoring what just happened. She threw her arms up in the air and smiled.

"Now, shall we get fucked up or do you idiots want another go at each other?" She cheered. Just like that, music resumed, the games commenced. Everyone was back to their typical Friday night.

"Have I ever told you I love you?" Chase said from behind me, the question obviously directed toward Harriet.

"Nice to see you too, Chase." She smiled, taking a bow like the lady she was. I sat in my spot and patted my lap. She paid no attention and dragged Cade—and his loser friends—out the front door by the ear. I heard it slam, but she didn't come back for several minutes. I wondered what was happening, I wanted to go out there.

Be the bite to her bark.

Finally, she came back in and marched right past us into the kitchen. She returned with a warm wet paper towel and some Advil she found in the cupboard by the toaster. And another beer. Seems she can keep up with the rest of us.

I winced when she put the towel on my nose and my lip. Her hands were gentle and she was looking between my mouth and my eyes. "Guys are stupid," she said jokingly. I couldn't help the vile things going through my mind as I saw her fingertips covered in my blood.

"I was thinking something else, but stupid works too." Chase said.

"Hey, he tried to warn him, he didn't listen." Banks reminded Chase.

"I'm sorry, man," Banks continued. "I didn't think the chip on his shoulder was actually the size of Harriet." He rolled his eyes and slouched back into the couch. I know he felt partially responsible, but I didn't care, I wanted any reason to deck the fucker.

He was lucky tonight. If it ever came down to me and him in the street, there's no way of knowing what I would do. Or if I would stop. She means everything to me, and I will not allow anyone to speak such vile things. Regardless of where I end up.

She licked my blood off her fingertips like it was nothing and it made me sweat. Banks's eyebrows raised and he slowly turned his head away from us.

Sex was the last thing that was supposed to be on my mind right now, but something had to keep me from dragging Cade by his neck. She took a deep breath after popping her lips, "All Cade had to do was ask," she mumbled softly.

Everyone froze. She looked up from my face and noticed everyone staring at her with wide eyes. *Ask what?*

"So I could've said no! Jesus!" All four of us literally sighed. We buckled in laughter, Harriet pleasantly joining us after rolling her eyes.

She spoke directly to me this time. "He didn't know he doesn't stand a chance."

I gave her a bloody smile.

"We're friends. That's it…" she trailed off, shrugging. I knew what she meant. She didn't know he thought that way about her. She thought he actually wanted to be her friend. *Wrong.*

"That's naive."

"Excuse me?" *Oh shit.* The room tensed and the guys backed up, making themselves small enough not to be noticed.

"I'm just saying that a guy—"

"What? I can't be friends with guys because they all want to fuck me?" Her voice was raising.

"Well, yeah. When a guy wants to be 'friends' with someone who looks like you, they want—"

"*Looks like me?* Oh, you pompous asshole." She stood up, throwing the bloody paper towel in my lap. She turned to my friends, "So which one of you wants to fuck me then? Since you're my *friends* too, right?"

Chase slowly started to raise his arm, but Banks smacked it down. I couldn't help but laugh. She shut me up with a glare. It wasn't funny, but fuck, that was great.

"That's different. They're *my* friends." Shit. That sounded a lot worse than I intended. They were her friends too, I just meant my roommates know their place.

She scoffed. "Bye, guys."

"Harriet, wait… that's not what I—"

"Fuck right off, Maximus!" She slammed the door behind her. *Well shit.* I put my head in my hands and leaned forward on the couch with a groan. All I meant was I knew Cade didn't want to be her *friend* before she did and I clearly didn't communicate that right.

"Looks like her?" Banks quoted me. "Dude…"

"Ah, shut up. I know. She just drives me crazy. And adding Cade into the mix makes me—"

"Feral," Dylan finished. I nodded in agreement. *Something like that.*

"You know girls and guys can be friends, right? Platonically." Banks reminded me. I shot him a look and stuck my middle finger up at him.

"I know that, dumbass. I'm not stupid, it just came out wrong. She has no idea how beautiful she is, so when I saw him…"

Chase laughed, smacking Banks beside him in the process. "Bro, you called her *naive*. She's not going to just forget that."

CHAPTER

54

Harriet

"Oh, you *pompous*, *idiotic*, *ridiculously beautiful* human being." I was pacing in their driveway, speaking to myself as I kicked rocks.

"There I was, trying to persuade Cade that Maximus meant no harm, that he's just drunk or some shit like that, he didn't mean it, I'm sorry, blah, blah, blah. God, what an idiot I am."

After he apologized for speaking about me that way, I made sure Cade knew he didn't have a shot. He really didn't. Maximus is a handful. There was no time to entertain anyone else, even if I wanted to. But damn, can he be absolutely idiotic and stupid. *Think you know everything, huh?*

"Oooooooooh." My blood was boiling as I squeezed my fists so tight my knuckles turned white. I didn't care it was freezing and I was in just a hoodie. I was so hot with anger I could furnace a stadium.

"Fuck this." I couldn't be here anymore. I got in my car and sped out of their driveway, listening to my thoughts the whole way home.

<hr>

I walked through the front door. "Men are idiots!" I yelled loud enough down the foyer that it echoed through the house. All my roommates' heads turned. Jane and Mia were on the couch, Kim was still where I left her at the kitchen counter. I did plan on coming back to study some more after I went to talk to Maximus. I wanted to talk to him about what I overheard.

It ate me alive for a week. At first, I didn't want to speak to him. I was stunned by that proclamation. He couldn't love me? I wanted to know why.

I talked to Mia and Jane about it but they had nothing. They also had no idea why he said that, and apparently it's the complete opposite of how he acts. I didn't believe them at first. But after a week of alone time, I started to think about all the things he does. *My tea. The ice cream incident. The graveyard. The standoff with Cade at the party. The donuts for my friends. The soft touches. The looks. The stares.*

Not to mention the fucking sex we had last time.

The motherfucker loves me and when I went to confront him about it, I got a mouthful of disrespect instead. *Assface.*

"What happened?" Kim was eager for a reason to stop studying. We sat there from nine a.m. to now. She was practically one with the chair, and I with the table.

I replayed the scene for them, careful not to over exaggerate or miss any details. Still, they scoffed.

"Guys and girls can definitely be friends." Mia and Jane made their way to the table from the couch when they heard the beginning of the story.

"Thank you!" I threw my hands up in the air. "Not every guy I meet wants to fuck me, Jesus!"

"Cade might, though." Kim scrunched her lips and moved them. I cringed, yeah… I might've known that. I had a weird feeling since the night we met when he threw me over his shoulders. Plus the whole balcony moment. And then the party. Neither of us spoke about it, so I assumed it was just a drunk thing we'd move on from. *Guess not.*

"But hey, if you don't want him, I'll gladly take him." Jane raised her hand like a kid in school. I laughed. She most definitely could.

"He's all yours, chiquita." I nodded.

"I love you guys." I smiled. "Thanks for this." It was nice to hear people have the same opinions as I did. *Guys and girls can be friends.* Cade did apologize, but he still said it. And even worse, he said it to provoke Maximus.

We had a very girly moment, telling each other we love one another and they even forced me into a group hug. I didn't mind it this time. It felt needed.

"Soooooo... should we smoke a joint and watch a movie?" Jane jumped up and down. Mia agreed, and after the long day of studying, Kim did too. I couldn't. I had a midterm in the afternoon.

———◈◈◈———

"What midterm do you have?" Jane asked as she lit the joint on our balcony.

"Death, Diseases, and Body." I rolled my eyes, sniffing the smoke. "I'll be home around five. It's three hours."

"Saturday exams should be illegal." Kim coughed, smoke coming from her throat.

"Amen," we said in unison. University was hard, we knew that, but what we didn't know was how much high school did *not* prepare us. The only thing they were right about was your professors won't care if you show up or not, so it's up to you. That part didn't worry me, I didn't skip classes very often after first year. I got too afraid of what I was missing, or if there was ever bonus credit given out.

I wanted to be top five in my graduating class when the time came and skipping classes was not going to get me there.

"We should throw a party tomorrow. Tomorrow is the last day of midterms and then reading week starts Monday." Kim suggested. Her eyes were bloodshot and her grin was wide.

We all nodded. We could use a party after all the studying we've done. Hard work pays off, but hard work must also be celebrated.

"It's a done deal then. Let's text everyone. And let downstairs know too." Jane whipped out her phone and started texting her friends.

Tori, Lori and Cade would definitely need to know ahead of time if we were having a party. Without a doubt, they can hear our footsteps. Plus, they'd probably want to come. We have a group chat with them so Mia shot them a text. Quickly, they responded. Sending confetti emojis and agreeing we need to let off some steam after exams. Even Cade responded with a "Fuck yeah!"

CHAPTER

55

Harriet

I woke up bright and early to squeeze in some last minute studying. Not that my brain would absorb any of it, I was too nervous already. But it was the effort that counted.

I usually liked to look good, feel good, but not today. Not when I would much rather use my spare time to cram in more definitions and diagrams. I opted for a cream sweater and black sweatpants that were four times too big for me. I had to tie them at the waist. I put a tube top underneath in case I get the nervous sweats in the gymnasium.

I brushed my teeth and threw my hair up in a messy bun with no make-up. I found my Uggs and fuzzy socks and tossed my backpack over my shoulder.

"I'm gone! See you later!" I shouted, closing the front door behind me. I ran directly into Cade's chest with an *oouf*. "Sorry, hey." He didn't seem the least bit concerned.

"Hi. Where are you going?" he asked. He was literally wearing the exact same thing I was. Cream hoodie with black sweatpants and black Uggs—the men's version. We gave each other a look down with wide eyes and an awkward giggle. "I got a midterm. You?"

"I'm coming to see if I could convince you guys to have a theme party." He smiled. He seemed completely fine, totally over last night. Was that suspicious or mature? Couldn't tell.

"You have my vote. They're inside, let me know. See ya!" I stormed down the steps and into my car. He wished me luck and waved as I pulled out of the driveway.

———◈◈◈———

"You got this, Harriet. It's just an exam. It's literally slices of trees with some fancy ink on it," I tried to play it down. It didn't work. My legs were shaking and my throat was dry. I had to guzzle my water before I got into my exam position.

Always, and I mean *always,* cross your legs on the chairs for ultimate comfort. The more comfortable you are, the more relaxed you are, the more answers you'll remember.

My pencil case, my student ID, and my extra pencils were all directly parallel from one another in the top right-hand side of my desk. I chose the tenth row, in the middle. Feeling surrounded by students made me feel less alone, yet more invisible. I could never sit at the front, or against the wall, and definitely not all the way in the back. The gym was huge, probably twenty rows of forty-five filled with old high school desks and extremely uncomfortable chairs.

The teaching assistants passed around the exam. When the clock was about to strike two, the profs spoke to their respective classes. "You cannot flip your papers over until exactly two p.m. You will have three hours to complete all the questions and put your answers on the Scantron. You may use the bathroom after one hour, and any electronics are absolutely prohibited."

We all nodded, seeing the other classes doing the same. The clock chimed two, and one by one we began. I pulled my legs under me and grabbed my favorite pencil.

There were fifty multiple choice and fifty true or false questions, with one bonus question. The bonus question would have to wait. My priority was the first one thousand bajillion questions before it. One by one, I answered them. Leaving a few blank to go back to after I had finished the ones I knew. Process of elimination would have to be my best bet for the ones I got stuck on.

I could confidently say I knew well over half the questions. Answers for tuberculosis, scarlet fever, sepsis, heart disease, measles, malaria, diabetes, Alzheimer's, cerebrovascular diseases. My studying was paying off. For the questions I knew anyway.

By the time I got to the last question after circling back, it was four- fifteen. I had forty-five minutes to attempt the bonus question. Might as well, it couldn't hurt. When I saw it was worth fifteen marks by itself, I knew it was going to be a hard one.

After taking a deep breath, I took a drink and replaced my pencil, adjusting my glasses and my sitting position. Finally, whispering the question out loud to myself:

Cadaver X was born with stenosis. X participated in years
of alcohol, drug, and physical exertion. X developed chest
pain, weakness, nausea, and poor blood circulation from
extenuating circumstances. Before Cadaver X died, they had
fainting spells, vomit, confusion, and weight loss. After they
died, you noticed they had excess fluid buildup in their limbs.
What is your diagnosis for Cadaver X?
What procedure would prolong their lifespan?
What medication would Cadaver X have been prescribed? Why?

I worked through the problem, dozens of diagrams and graphs flipping through my head like a preprogrammed textbook. *Stenosis. Chest pain. Vomiting.*

Okay, so it was a heart problem because of the stenosis and the chest pain. I flipped through the pages of the multiple-choice questions, hoping I could find a clue in another question. One of the questions talking about a weight loss patient buckling over in pain, weakness.

Clutching their chest. Sunken eye sockets.

Chest pain can lead to high blood pressure, which would force the body to take long deep breaths...

I skipped the first question. Maybe figuring out the prescriptions would help. First off, excess fluid build-up would require a diuretic like ethacrynic acid or indapamide.

Or furosemide...

If Cadaver X struggles with pumping blood through their body, that means they would need a vasodilator to open up the blood vessels. Such as fosinopril, ramipril, or vasotec.

Or enalapril...

So Cadaver X was born with stenosis but developed something after years of drug, alcohol, and bodily abuse or extenuating circumstances. They had bad blood circulation, nausea, shortness of breath, chest pain...

"Oh my god."

My heart started ramming against my ribs. Was I reading this right?

"Oh my god." I said louder. A couple students shushed me. I couldn't believe what I was reading. There was no way. Except that I knew the answers to this question. It was right in front of me the whole time. *He was right in front of me the whole time.*

I scribbled down my answers. Furosemide. Enalapril. A transplant would prolong his life. *Class two congestive heart failure.*

I flung my papers onto the desk at the front, not bothering to see if they landed in the finished pile, and ran as fast as I could out the gym doors. The hallway was closing in on me. The silence was deafening.

I was finding it hard to breathe. I needed to get outside. My heart was seconds away from coming up my throat. *This can't be. This isn't—no...*

I couldn't see. I stumbled out the building's doors to my car, hyperventilating, while fumbling the keys into the ignition. I chugged my water and held my head between my knees. My hands were shaking and my stomach was in knots.

I opened my car door and puked out the side. Students walking past gave me a gross look and continued walking.

I drove home blinded by the memories of the last four months. Everything was coming into view. Holding his chest, the deep breaths, the pills, losing his balance. He wasn't having a panic attack that day, he was just trying to stay alive.

This can't be happening. This can't—

———◆◆◆———

The door slammed, the sounds of my feet breaking down the stairs.

"Harriet?"

I whipped off my backpack, tripping over my feet as I took off my shoes in my room. Without thinking, I ran right into my desk, fumbling around my drawers for my diseases textbook.

"Where is it? Come on...Where is it?!"

Page 457. I read it aloud.

Aortic stenosis is a valve disease where the valves between the lower heart chamber and aorta do not function properly, which doesn't allow proper blood flow. Without a healthy lifestyle, stenosis can develop into more serious conditions.

I had to pause, but I couldn't take my eyes off the page. I wasn't sure I was breathing.

Drugs, alcohol, strenuous activity, or severe distress are heavy factors on such developments. In extreme cases of prolonged abuse or detrimental stress, Class 2 Congestive Heart Failure. Medication and lifestyle changes are recommended. In such extreme cases, implantable cardiac defibrillators or heart transplants can prolong a patient's life.

I gasped. The death of his brother. The lump under the tattoo, it must be a scar.

The sides of my eyes were growing black. I had to shake my head. I couldn't believe what I was reading.

I flipped the page. I knew what was coming, and I didn't want to face it, but I couldn't stop. I needed to know.

Prognosis: 35% of patients only survive 10 years after Class 2 CHF diagnosis.

I threw my head back to try and stop myself from crying. But it was no use.

He wasn't going to live past thirty.

CHAPTER

56

Maximus

"We'll take the bill, thank you." Dylan waved down the waitress. After our midterms were finished this afternoon, we took ourselves out for a cheap dinner at Bobby's. Another secret hole in the wall only my roommates and I go to. They serve half price beer after four p.m. and all day breakfast. Nothing like pancakes and a cold brew for dinner.

The jerseys and tv screens displayed across the dark paneled walls smelled like musky men and beer. Bar stools and booths littered the sticky floor. Technically speaking, it was gross. But it was comfortable.

Later we planned on going to Harriet's party. Banks got the invite from Luke, who got it from Cade, who got it from Jane. The social conga line. It was black and white theme, basic as shit but whatever. I could scrounge up something to wear. I knew exactly which color Harriet was going to be in.

"What time did Banks say his exam was over?" Chase asked, taking a big bite out of his wings. "Six, I think. He should be back at the house by now." Dylan replied.

"I'm assuming we're all going together?" They nodded while chewing. The syrup was delicious here, totally fake but still tasted so good.

I was almost finished my beer when the waitress came back with our bills. She passed around the debit machine, but I had cash left over from Christmas. "Keep the change." I gave her a thin smile, a bright one in exchange.

"Are you guys going to that party tonight?" she asked, eyeing me once over.

I nudged my head toward the guys. "That's the plan."

"But you are going, yeah?" She cocked her hip and bit her bottom lip. *Once upon a time, sure. Now? Not happening.*

"Not with you." I sipped my beer and smirked at Dylan. He smirked back. She rolled her eyes and sulked away.

"Down bad." Dylan chuckled, nudging Chase in the ribs across the booth.

"Sorry, what was that? I couldn't hear you over Amy's tit in your mouth." I scoffed, smiling over the rim of my beer. I took the last bit down in a gulp and slammed it on the table. Dylan made a face, eventually nodding in defeat.

"Shall we?" Chase said, wiping the last of the barbecue sauce off his chin. I chuckled. His eyebrows pinched. "What?"

"Nothing."

──────⋅⟨⊰⊱⟩⋅──────

"Banks?! You here?" I yelled as we stepped through the door. Our shoes clunking on the floor, all spread out over the foyer. Dylan and Chase went upstairs to change, and I made my way down the hallway.

I rounded the corner to see Banks leaning on the back of the first couch with his head down and his arms crossed. "Hey. You okay?"

He nodded, giving me a pat on the back. For a moment, I thought he was going to hug me. "What's wrong?"

"Max..." He looked toward my bedroom door. It was closed, just like I left it.

"What?" I asked.

No answer. I shook his shoulders, "Banks, what?!"

Still no answer. He moved out of my way and I barged into my room.

There she was, drenched head to toe in black, sitting on the edge of my bed. Not a party outfit, a black hoodie with paint splatters, and black sweatpants with our university's logo on them. Her leftover curls were thrown into a messy bun atop her head and her hands were trembling in her lap.

There were papers and textbooks splayed out over my entire room. I picked up one of the papers on my desk.

My body went cold.

Signs and symptoms of congestive heart failure. Another, *life expectancy of a young adult with CHF.* Another, *experimental treatments.*

All the air in my lungs depleted, making my veins feel like sandpaper. My heart was hammering. I was going to vomit.

Every thought I've ever had replayed over and over again. All the opportunities. All the moments. Every chance I had.

Painfully, I looked over at her, frozen in my spot. The treatment paper crunched in my fist. She finally looked up at me from the paper in her hands and turned the laptop screen toward me.

The look on her face made me regret my own existence.

Her eyes were red and puffy, confusion written all over her face, and her voice was cold.

"You're sick."

ACKNOWLEDGMENTS

I would just like to thank the following people who have helped me achieve a dream I didn't even know I had.

My publishing consultant from Milton & Hugo, Sandra Gonzalez, for all her hard work. This would not have happened if it weren't for her. She was nothing but pleasant and was always willing to lend a helping hand for whenever I got stuck... or needed to figure out a title (LOL).

For my marketing consultant from NewLink Media, Jay Cabrera for his undeniable effort in getting my book in bookstores across the globe and for reaching out to production companies. I can't thank you enough.

For my fulfillment officer from Milton & Hugo, Marie Parker for sticking with me when I changed my title and cover page three million times. You're a champ, thank you so much!

For my editor, Jennifer Herrington, thank you so much for taking my project and helping me turn it into a masterpiece, making sure my thoughts made sense and that the public would love it just as much as we do.

My friends and family, for not pushing me to tell them what I was doing. I was terrified about putting myself out in the public like this, so I felt like I had to keep it a secret until I could figure out how to own up to this part of me. I'd like to take a minute to thank my best friend, Julia K. I know you figured it out way before this was published, so thank you for never bringing it up and basically always playing dumb. You rock. Thank you, everyone, for your patience, love, and undeniable support. I love you guys. I hope I make you proud.

To my bunny, Zibil, thank you for sitting with me during the hard chapters little one! You never failed to cheer me up!

And finally...

Thank you to Maximus and Harriet. I have no idea where I would be without this story, the characters, the emotions, especially the playfulness. The growth you have shown, the development within my story, I can't fathom how important this was to me. Without you guys, I wouldn't be who I am today. Your lives gave me a path. Thank you. I love you.

Maybe I should thank myself? For finally not giving up on something and going through with it? What do you think?

Nah...maybe my next book.

Stay tuned…

Love always, love forever,

CB

www.ingramcontent.com/pod-product-compliance
Lightning Source LLC
Chambersburg PA
CBHW030911090426
42737CB00007B/163